THE
RECKONING

THE RECKONING

DEBT, DEMOCRACY, AND
THE FUTURE OF AMERICAN POWER

MICHAEL MORAN

Foreword by Dr. Nouriel Roubini

palgrave
macmillan

THE RECKONING
Copyright © Michael Moran, 2012.

All rights reserved.

First published in hardcover in 2012
by PALGRAVE MACMILLAN®
in the United States—a division of St. Martin's Press LLC,
175 Fifth Avenue, New York, NY 10010.

Where this book is distributed in the UK, Europe and the rest of the world,
this is by Palgrave Macmillan, a division of Macmillan Publishers Limited,
registered in England, company number 785998, of Houndmills,
Basingstoke, Hampshire RG21 6XS.

Palgrave Macmillan is the global academic imprint of the above companies
and has companies and representatives throughout the world.

Palgrave® and Macmillan® are registered trademarks in the United States,
the United Kingdom, Europe and other countries.

ISBN 978–1–137–27833–3

The Library of Congress has catalogued the hardcover as follows:

Moran, Michael, 1962–
    The reckoning : debt, democracy, and the future of American power /
    Michael Moran ; [foreword by] Nouriel Roubini.
        p. cm.
    Includes index.
    ISBN 978–0–230–33993–4
        1. United States—Economic policy—2009– 2. United States—
    Economic conditions—2009– 3. United States—Foreign economic
    relations. I. Title.
HC106.84.M67 2012
330.973—dc23   2011044895

A catalogue record of the book is available from the British Library.

Design by Newgen Imaging Systems, Ltd., Chennai, India

First PALGRAVE MACMILLAN paperback edition: June 2013

10 9 8 7 6 5 4 3 2 1

Printed in the United States of America.

For Caitlin, Griffin and Hannah Marie

CONTENTS

FOREWORD

Dr. Nouriel Roubini

In the autumn of 2011, global markets endured yet another phase of a European sovereign debt crisis. It started in tiny Greece and was allowed to spread, like a communicable disease, up the food chain of euro zone economies until the threat landed at the door of Italy and France, the eighth and sixth largest economies in the world, respectively. As in European crises of times past, when local leadership failed and the crisis threatened to spread beyond Europe's borders, the call went out for someone, anyone, to save the day. Yet, contrary to the crises of the past century, beginning with World War I, the target of these urgent appeals was not the United States. Instead, emissaries from Italy, Greece, Ireland, and other distressed euro zone countries reached out to China, even if the willingness of China to bail out distressed euro zone members was more wishful thinking than reality.

Not long ago, the idea of a Group of Seven (G7) stalwart like Italy turning to the chief proponent of authoritarian state capitalism for economic help would have set off alarm bells in the United States. America would have intervened to engineer a rescue, as it did in Mexico in 1994, South Korea in 1998, Brazil in 1999, and in many other countries with emerging market crises, and as it had in both of the twentieth century's great global conflicts. But the past three years have delivered a stark reality check to the superpower. Offering financial help to even its closest allies these days would be an exercise in keeping up appearances. America—and Japan, Britain, France, and, yes, even Germany—has its own problems.

As Michael Moran argues in the forthcoming chapters of this book, *The Reckoning: Debt, Democracy, and the Future of American Power*, the world that emerged out of the cauldron of the American Century is in crisis. Much has been written about the relative decline of US economic and political influence, of the rise of the BRICS—Brazil, Russia, India, China, South Africa, and other emerging powers—and of the policy mistakes and demographic and debt problems that beset the old "West" and its Asian protégé, Japan. But few have considered the practical consequences for the United States and its allies as the economic and political status quo that American power has sustained in various regions all over the planet begin to show strain and fray and even break apart.

Just as the uncontrolled bankruptcy of Lehman Brothers nearly caused the global financial system to collapse in 2008, and just as the threat of the default of a relatively small sovereign player like Greece—or other euro zone sovereigns—could destroy the European common currency, an uncontrolled unraveling of US power would be a disaster of global proportions. As Moran writes, "as with Britain's long retreat from global dominance in the early twentieth century, the pullback of American power in our time will expose, for the first time in decades, parts of the geopolitical shoreline that American might, political will, and diplomatic influence have heretofore sheltered."

THE CRISIS OF THE DEVELOPED WORLD

Perhaps we should not be surprised that Italy's desperate plea failed to set off alarm bells. After all, its appeal to China for massive purchases of Italian government debt followed the effective near insolvencies of three European states—Greece, Ireland, and Portugal—met feebly by European Union politicians with half measures, parochialism, and denial. Meanwhile, 2011 also witnessed the battering of Japan's economy by a combination of natural, man-made, and policy-induced disasters—a combination that has Japan well into a third consecutive "lost decade" of debt and near depression. And, of course, there was the spectacle of a near default by the United States and the downgrade of its long-term credit rating by Standard & Poor's (S&P).

How could this happen? As Moran persuasively argues, a good part of the problem is that, in Italy as in America and other advanced economies, the economic conversation today is driven by politicians and investment professionals—fund managers, traders, stock pickers. The former are crippled by a lack of knowledge, partisan self-interest, and short-term electoral cycles; the latter are internally wired to maximize short-term profits even at the expense of long-term economic stability and to take positions—exacerbated by high-frequency trading—that fuel the volatility that underpins their returns. And all of this is amplified by the echo chamber of the financial media and blogosphere where the 24/7 news cycle of instant information is amplified by instant and often noisy commentary.

But today, more than three years after the collapse of Lehman Brothers shed light on the rot and misconceptions that underpinned capitalism in the early years of the twenty-first century, the world finds that it cannot pull back from the brink. Indeed, like a ship chugging with all its power against the pull of a mighty waterfall, the global economy is being starved of fuel by governments applying excessively front-loaded fiscal austerity, insisting on treating aggressively the long-term problem—too much private and public debt requiring deleveraging—even as the short-term weakness and crisis threaten to throw us all into the abyss.

A swift (if thankless) reaction by central banks and economic policy makers in the wake of Lehman Brothers' collapse in 2008 prevented a second great depression. This time, however, if wrong-headed policy measures push the world back into recession, it will be far more difficult to prevent the slide from ending in a full-blown depression and a financial crisis as bad as, if not worse than, the one in 2008–2009. The developed world is too indebted to save the day; the United States, economically and politically, has simply run out of policy bullets. Meanwhile, the emerging world lacks the institutional sophistication, political leadership, or the raw economic power required to pull the global economy away from the brink.

BULLETS AND BAILOUTS

Until the middle of 2010, policy makers could always produce a new rabbit from their hat to fuel a modest economic recovery in the developed world. Government fiscal stimulus; near-zero interest rates from central bankers; two rounds of quantitative easing, or QE—essentially, printing money—from the US Federal Reserve; the ring-fencing of bad debt; and trillions of dollars in bailouts and liquidity provision for banks and financial institutions: officials tried them all. Now they have run out of rabbits.

Fiscal policy—the decision almost everywhere to radically cut spending and focus on the size of national debt rather than on the crisis at hand—is currently a tremendous drag on economic growth in both the euro zone and the United Kingdom. Even in the United States, and even if President Obama's proposed $447 billion jobs bill were somehow to have to become law, state and local governments, and now the federal government, will still cut expenditures. Soon enough, they will be raising taxes to make up the shortfall between the demand for services and government revenues.

Another round of bank bailouts is politically unacceptable and economically unfeasible: most governments, especially in Europe, are so distressed that bailouts are unaffordable; indeed, their sovereign risk is actually fueling concern about the health of Europe's banks, which hold most of the increasingly shaky government paper.

Nor could monetary policy help very much. Quantitative easing is constrained by above-target inflation in the euro zone and United Kingdom; it will occur, but it will be too little, too late. The Fed seems poised at this writing to launch a third round of quantitative easing (QE3), but it will also be too little, too late. Last year's $600 billion QE2 and $1 trillion in tax cuts and transfers delivered growth of barely 3 percent for exactly one quarter before growth slumped to below 1 percent in the first half of 2011. QE3 will be much smaller and will do much less to reflate asset prices and restore growth. And more than traditional quantitative easing, central banks should engage in credit easing to ensure that the creation of credit, especially to small and medium-sized enterprises and to fragile households, is restored.

Currency depreciation is not a feasible option for all advanced economies: they all need a weaker currency and better trade balance to restore growth, but they all cannot have it at the same time. So relying on exchange rates to influence trade balances is a zero-sum game. Currency wars are thus on the horizon, with Japan and Switzerland engaging in early battles to weaken their exchange rates. Others, including the United States, will soon follow.

AVERTING THE FALL

Is there a way to avoid disaster—to give the global economy's engine room the burst of power it needs to pull away from the roaring falls? The right balance today requires creating jobs partly through additional fiscal stimulus aimed at productive infrastructure investment. It also requires more progressive taxation and more short-term fiscal stimulus with medium- and long-term fiscal discipline that begins, over time, to slow the mountain of debt most of the world's advanced economies have accumulated. This cannot be done quickly or easily: it will be, to quote Donald Rumsfeld, a long, hard slog.

In the financial sector, steps are needed to shore up lender-of-last-resort support by monetary authorities to prevent ruinous runs on banks and especially sovereigns; banks need to recognize that it is in their interest (in some cases, literally a question of self-preservation) to lessen the debt burden for insolvent households, businesses, and government entities; global financial officials need to impose stricter supervision and regulation of a financial system that is still running amok, including the breakup of "too big to fail" banks and oligopolistic trusts; and short-term forbearance of capital ratios is needed to restore credit growth.

Similarly, as the forthcoming pages will argue, America and its allies must begin to build the structures, relationships, and rules that will maintain stability in the Pacific Rim, South Asia, Europe, Africa, and Latin America before US power deteriorates much further. The hedging, as you shall see, is already well under way among some of America's closest allies. From Berlin to Ankara, Taipei to Tokyo, there is a growing realization that the American military—unsurpassed and dominant as it is—cannot remain so forever in the face of long-term economic stagnation, the march of disruptive technologies, and a growing ambition on the part of emerging regional powers to revisit some of the "givens" imposed upon their neighborhoods by Washington.

Over time, both the United States and other advanced economies it has provided security for over the course of the past 70 years will need to think about effecting a soft landing from the collective global dominance they engineered in the wake of World War II. This means investing less in satellite weaponry or hypersonic fighter aircraft—though these will still come in handy in an unpredictable world—and more in human capital, skills, and social safety nets to increase productivity and enable workers to compete, be flexible, and thrive in a globalized economy. The alternative is—as it was in the 1930s—unending stagnation, depression, currency and trade wars, capital controls, banking and financial crises, sovereign insolvencies, and massive social and political instability. In that scenario, no one—not China, not Russia, not America or Europe—wins. It is that scenario, above all, that *The Reckoning* seeks to avert.

DR. NOURIEL ROUBINI
New York, December 2011

INTRODUCTION

Fate dealt me a fair hand. The prime of my career—first as a reporter, then as an editor and analyst of international affairs for the BBC, the Council on Foreign Relations, and ultimately Roubini Global Economics—coincided neatly with the apex of American influence in the world. As Europe's communist regimes tumbled, I witnessed and chronicled these events firsthand for Radio Free Europe/Radio Liberty, the US-funded "surrogate" broadcaster then based in Munich. A journalist by training and a historian by temperament, I seized every opportunity to surf the wave of goodwill for the United States as it flowed into the forgotten corners of southeastern Europe. Suddenly, where an Iron Curtain so recently stood, the flash of an American passport opened all doors.

That American dream, however, has since become a hypnotic trance. Well before the 9/11 attacks, it was made clear to anyone paying close attention that the Cold War "victory" had imposed great burdens on the United States that would eventually threaten its place as the "sole remaining superpower." Even after terrorists killed thousands on that fateful summer day, the American political establishment continued to base domestic and foreign policy decisions on the assumption that the United States was destined to tower in perpetuity over all other nations. This myopia has afflicted great powers in the past. The French Army in 1940, regarded at the time as the finest military force in the world, crumbled before Hitler's blitzkrieg in a mere five weeks. "We suffered from an illness that is not peculiar to the French, the illness of having been victorious [in World War I] and believing that we were very clever," said General Andre Beaufre, a member of the French high command. "Victory is a very dangerous opportunity."[1]

The miscalculations that led to war in Iraq and the reckless policies that nearly drove the entire global financial system over a cliff should have had a sobering effect. Yet some Americans feel that the United States is still entitled to a "first among equals" place in the twenty-first-century sun. Most of the rest of the world, not surprisingly, given recent history, is not so eager to linger much longer in its shade.

This is not a book bent on predicting America's decline—the variables entailed in such predictions encourage wildly dark scenarios that current facts do not support. Nor is this a book written solely for Americans. Whether by fate or necessity, and oftentimes unwittingly and even unwillingly, much of the world depends for its prosperity and stability on the economic performance of the huge American economy and the ability of the US military to make good on dozens of guarantees, spoken and unspoken, that sustain regional balances of power across the planet. America will remain powerful and relevant to global affairs for a generation or more, though its days as the world's unrivaled economic and military giant have ended. To my American readers, understand that I have no intention of providing a pep talk. Making Americans feel good about themselves or suggesting that some miraculous combination of ingenuity and divine favor will keep their country at the top of the heap until the end of time is the job description of a politician—an occupation that bends truths to fit short-term goals and employs flattery to engender support. If either is your desire, close the cover now. But if reality appeals to you, this is the book to read. *The Reckoning* is just what the title suggests—an attempt to get a dead-eyed, unemotional fix on American power and to posit the implications for the prosperity, security, and external guarantees that flow from it. Whether you are a citizen of the great republic, an ally dependent upon its security guarantees, or a trading partner benefiting from the global economic system that American power sustains, understanding your exposure to these shifting dynamics is essential as America descends from the superpower stratosphere back to earth.

All but the most detached ideologues now comprehend that new economic and geopolitical realities will require the United States to rethink the open-ended commitments made during happier, healthier times to its own people and to its friends and allies across the planet. Over the next few years—probably during the term of whoever wins the 2012 election—the extent of the slippage in America's global power and influence will become more and more apparent. Its government will either get its fiscal and foreign policy priorities in order during this period, or it will begin a much more rapid descent than anyone in the mainstream currently believes, prodded onward by credit downgrades, financial turmoil, and, quite possibly, an emboldened foreign rival.

Such changes can arrive at daunting speed—easily within the span of a human life. My great uncle Tony Berry was born in England in the 1930s in an empire that still ruled nearly a quarter of the world's inhabitants, not to mention the waves. Tony spent much of his boyhood drawing pictures of the Royal Navy's great battleship fleet. As soon as he reached age 15, he joined up. While he missed World War II by a few years, he served in the Korean War. One day, years ago in his living room in Hamilton, Ontario, where he had retired after a long navy career, he related the shock that ran through the crew of his destroyer when their flotilla, led by a British aircraft carrier, finally rendezvoused with the huge American fleet off of Korea in the Sea of Japan.

"We looked like a bunch of broken-down target ships compared to the Yanks," he told me. The British quickly realized that their aircraft—worn-out, poorly maintained World War II designs—had neither the speed nor the range to fly with their American counterparts (let alone against their Soviet-equipped North Korean adversaries). The British fleet lacked stamina, too, Tony remembered, forcing constant retirements back to port for resupply as the Americans sustained their warships at sea.

"It was humiliating for a young sailor," he told me years later. "We still thought of ourselves as the best of the best. But the sun really had set on the Empire."[2]

For the United States, the script will unfold very differently. US economic, military, and intellectual power remains the envy of the world in spite of the hype over China and other emerging powers. Similarly, despite reckless behavior in the first decade of this century, the United States remains impressively capable of true self-awareness, something that cannot be said of the Soviet, British, or myriad other powers that have dominated the globe throughout history, where pointing out that the emperor had no clothes would be a poor career move at best, and possibly fatal. Of late, even hawkish American politicians have abandoned their embrace of unilateralism—the idea that America can do anything it likes in the world to perpetuate its dominant position. Left-leaning figures, peering into the abyss of American national debt, have reached similar conclusions, albeit with different motives. The debate over Libya in mid-2011 was instructive: in responding to Libya's rebellion against dictatorial Colonel Muammar Qaddafi, President Barack Obama forced European powers to take the lead in heading off the humanitarian disaster and refugee crisis brewing in their Mediterranean backyard. This was the right decision. Back in the United States, meanwhile, the debate in Congress not only focused on the "exit strategy" but, for once, also made much of the financial share the United States would bear in a mission projected to cost about $100 million a week. Senator Richard Lugar, the Republican former chairman of the Senate Foreign Relations Committee and a happy interventionist until recently, typified the new thinking in Congress. "We are debating seemingly every day the deficits, the debt ceiling situation coming up, the huge economic problems we have," he said, "but in the back room we are spending money on a military situation in Libya."[3] That the mission ultimately succeeded in removing a dictator that had murdered hundreds of Americans in terrorist attacks mattered little to those focused on counting beans or winning political points in the run-up to an election.

So have the days of the blank check in America's dealings with the world really ended? I believe the psychological hangover remains and that Americans will struggle to come to terms with the limitations that global changes will force upon them. It will take time, after all these years, to put "exceptionalism"—the idea that America is somehow divinely ordained to rule the world—in the same historical museum where "the white man's burden" and "separate but equal" now dwell. Based on the observations of the French writer Alexis de Toqueville that the America he visited in the 1820s was so focused on practical, commercial concerns that it formed an exception to the barbaric nationalism that plagued Europe, "American exceptionalism" has in some minds become a myth of infallibility that encourages irrational behavior.[4] At least in part, the decisions that ended in disaster in places as diverse as Vietnam, the NASDAQ index, Somalia, Lebanon, Iraq, and the local mortgage broker's office can be traced to this misconception. The United States *is* a unique, revolutionary, innovative, and often transformative force in the world, but none of those truths "except" it from the laws of physics or morality. Like any giant, America can stumble, will bleed when cut, and someday, will pass into history. Treating these facts like heresies can only hasten that day's arrival.

I find it ironic, after a career devoted to getting Americans to pay attention to the world, that I now find it necessary to help them untangle the country from it. This is not the same as turning one's back—the global economy makes isolationism impossible, just as it makes nonsense of old distinctions between economics and foreign policy. One has no meaning without the other. This has been true for decades, and yet still the silos of expertise within government, academia, and the financial industry have failed to adjust.

Two decades ago, as Germany reunified, I was a journalist based there for Radio Free Europe/Radio Liberty. Almost immediately, the grim calculus of nuclear throw weights, heavy-armored divisions, and other staples of the Central European order of battle became obsolete. Creating viable banking and consumer sectors—all while balancing the fragile nationalist reawakening in Eastern Europe and the humiliation of a collapsed empire in Moscow—proved to be a trickier proposition than just turning out armaments.

One decade ago, while based in New York City, I witnessed with many of my neighbors another historic turning point as airliners disappeared into the glass faces of the World Trade Center towers on September 11, 2001. In the days that followed, I learned that four people I knew were among the dead, including my aunt's brother—FDNY lieutenant Thomas O'Hagan—and an old friend from England, Graham Berkeley, who was on United Flight 175. That attack capped a period of inwardness in the United States, which had since 1989 declared victory and let down its guard. Unfortunately, rather than provide the occasion for introspection, 9/11 instead opened the door to reactionary policies that profoundly misjudged the ability of even the United States to remake the world according to its preferences. It saddled us with the wrong allies in Pakistan and Saudi Arabia, prompted the launch of a misguided war in Iraq, and ultimately squandered much of the admiration and goodwill that the peaceful end to the Cold War had garnered.

Largely as a result of these mistakes, compounded by a Darwinistic approach to the deregulation of its financial system that nearly wrecked global capitalism, the United States now faces a crisis as poignant as any since the Civil War—a crisis of capabilities and self-knowledge. This challenge will either see Americans tap the huge reservoir of resilience and creativity that has seen them through previous crises, or wallow in denial and enter an ever steeper dive toward bankruptcy and global irrelevance as global economics is dominated by newer, more virile competitors.

Blame for the failure to chart a sustainable path for the promises the country made to its own retirees, civil servants, wounded veterans, and working poor belongs to both parties, because both bought into the economic charlatanism that led to the Great Recession. But the GOP must accept the burden of having pulled the rug out from under America on the world stage, destroying goodwill and confidence in American leadership, which took the entire Cold War to establish, in the short space of seven years. The job now, whether a Democrat or a Republican occupies the White House, is mitigating the damage and preventing the kind of uncontrolled unraveling of American power that proved the undoing of prior empires led by shortsighted and self-interested men.

MICHAEL MORAN
Hoboken, New Jersey
December, 2011

CHAPTER 1

EXCESS BAGGAGE: THE WEST'S STRUGGLE WITH REALITY

Many people watching tonight can probably remember a time when finding a good job meant showing up at a nearby factory or a business downtown. You didn't always need a degree, and your competition was pretty much limited to your neighbors. If you worked hard, chances are you'd have a job for life, with a decent paycheck and good benefits and the occasional promotion. Maybe you'd even have the pride of seeing your kids work at the same company. That world has changed.

—President Barack Obama, State of the Union speech,
January 25, 2011[1]

The 2012 presidential election will go down as the moment when the rise in wealth, influence, and power of the rest of the world finally made an impression on the American voter. It will not be the result of some sudden surge of public interest in foreign policy, or even the two wars raging for the past decade. Rather, the United States has reached a point in its history where the spread between its growth trajectory and that of its rivals can no longer be hidden. The debt-fueled model is imploding. The gap between US government obligations and revenues cannot be bridged by simple cuts or even by a return to the steady growth of its gross domestic product (GDP). What's more, the even larger gap that lies between this economic reality and what passes for "truth" in the American political debate may prove an insurmountable obstacle as psychological and strategic adjustments accompany efforts to get control of national accounting. The blanket security guarantees the United States provides to other countries all over the planet, the poorly structured and even more poorly funded promises it has made to its poor and elderly, and most importantly its inflated self-regard and sense of global entitlement, all must be tackled simultaneously to arrest the slide in America's global power, influence, and relative wealth. The narrow gauge prescriptions of the current Washington debate—ranging from spending cuts targeting social welfare programs to huge infusions of stimulus funding—will fail to slow the arrival of America's day of reckoning if the larger context remains unchanged.

This book aims to broaden the current debate with its focus on spending cuts, marginal tax rates, and "shovel ready" infrastructure into a true look at the trajectory of American power in a radically changing world. This means facing the costs of overstretch abroad as well as at home and confronting the psychological implications, too. Once again, after a period of hyperactivity abroad and bubble-fueled growth at home, America has realized its power is finite. This time, however, for the first time in its history, that healthy realization is accompanied by evidence that America's binge years have damaged its future prospects. To borrow the language of economics, there will be no "V-shaped" recovery for US global influence. Yet an honest assessment of America's situation, followed by clear policies based on the country's actual realities rather than the hopeful bromides of its creation myth, can ensure the dominant power of the last century continues to shape its own destiny in this one.

Rethinking America's global role is an essential part of this formula. Ever since the United States entered World War II, the dollar costs of sustaining "global stability" and keeping the more dangerous elements of the outside world at bay have been, at best, secondary considerations for politicians on the campaign trail or Americans sitting around their dinner tables. Of course, debates did occur over the wisdom or morality of foreign entanglements, and the cost in the blood of the young Americans sent to war. But to question the actual dollar outlay was considered unseemly if not unpatriotic. "National security," the rubric under which the government lumps together defense spending, intelligence, wars, and diplomacy, existed in a world beyond accounting. With the exception of the recent wars in Iraq and the campaign in

Libya, the vast majority of Americans have shrugged off the financial aspects of foreign and defense policy over the past seven decades as the price of doing superpower business.

In the second decade of the twenty-first century, however, this approach no longer works. As the S&P downgrade of America's sovereign credit rating recently underscored, the United States faces a series of tough questions about the burdens it has imposed on its taxpayers, soldiers, citizens, and allies. The answers will determine the trajectory of the world's most important country for decades to come, as well as the fortunes of smaller economies all over the planet. This will pose a huge challenge to a public accustomed to a reassuring drone from its politicians about its manifest destiny and divine anointment as the last, best hope of the civilized world. At times in the past century, these words rang true enough: American power tilted the scales against authoritarian monarchs in World War I, genocidal fascists in World War II, and finally revolutionary communists during the Cold War. But America today has lost both the financial and moral standing to claim that its interests automatically coincide with the interests of the rest of the planet. America's interests are its interests alone—the rest, as they say, is coincidence.

No one is sure just how long the United States has to get its fiscal house in order, and of course, the domestic ideological divide, deepened constantly by runaway "gerrymandering" of electoral districts at all levels to suit fringe elements, will make the process harder. Most economists estimate that the US government must chart a convincing course that would slowly reverse the size of the national debt and show tangible results within a decade. Yet this "medium-term" reprieve only works if, much sooner than that, the United States convinces its largest foreign debt holders and the international bond markets (along with the credit agencies that stand guard on their behalf) that Washington has the political and financial will to act rationally—to neither ignore the debt peril, nor collapse in supplication to it and start gutting those parts of its government that support growth, innovation, education, and military excellence.

The recent behavior of American politicians—from the obstructionist nihilism of the Tea Party to the overly indulgent, cerebral aloofness of President Obama—was precisely the wrong way to instill confidence. The aforementioned grace period for American policy makers can only exist if the United States avoids a cataclysmic sell-off of US Treasury bonds, the vehicles through which the country borrows money abroad to fund its deficit spending.

In the next several years, as these politicized negotiations continue to produce theater of the absurd like the failed "Super Committee" debacle,[2] it will
not be hard to imagine another ratings agency downgrade or perhaps a major
creditor—China, Russia, Japan—deciding that America is not, after all, good
for the money it owes. That nightmare scenario is to be avoided at all costs.
Yet the current political behavior—particularly on the American right—is all
but inviting it. Congressional leaders—and perhaps the White House, too—
seem to think the United States is still in a position to control the outcome of
political brinksmanship on these issues.[3] The truth is, America lost its financial credibility when it drove the global economy toward oblivion in 2008; no
one, at least outside the Beltway, has forgotten that. The only thing preventing
America's creditors from dumping their Treasury bonds is a lack of alternatives.
Rest assured that economic policymakers and the investors who control the sovereign wealth funds of the emerging world are working furiously from Berlin to
Beijing, Rio to Riyadh, Moscow to Mumbai, to create those alternatives.

But let's say the center does hold and US creditors remain calm as fiscal
reform begins to brighten the long-term debt picture. That still leaves in
place new challenges that American policymakers had taken for granted for
decades. Increasingly, for instance, the health of the US economy depends
not on American political decisions but on the goodwill and investment
strategies of other nations. Some of its major creditors—the British, the
Canadians, the Japanese—would prefer to preserve a world in which the
dollar remains the global reserve currency and the United States the most
influential actor in political and military affairs. But other nations, especially
China, Saudi Arabia, the United Arab Emirates, and Russia, who together
have even more invested in US Treasury bonds than our allies, are less eager
to perpetuate America's influence, let alone underwrite a second "American
Century."

America stood for decades as the "indispensable nation," to quote former
secretary of state Madeleine Albright. That, too, has changed. The ground is
shifting away from American dominance, and the United States must either
adjust to that reality or lose control of its own fate.

Why has this moment of truth arrived today, in the twelfth year of the
twenty-first century? Four important trends have forced the tipping point.
These trends predict an era in which the United States will in many ways still
be the most powerful country on the planet but will no longer set the agenda
unilaterally:

- **A crushing national debt will force the United States to run a cost-benefit analysis on the enormous size of its global defense and foreign policy footprint, as well as the promises made to its next generation of retirees.** Abroad, the influence of the old G7 (Group of 7)—Canada, Britain, France, Germany, Italy, and Japan—will fade further, as the huge sums it spends on defense, intelligence, diplomacy, and policing world trade routes come into direct conflict with the sacred cows of US domestic politics: Social Security, Medicare, and Medicaid. The growing costs of social programs cannot be wished away. Unlike for the troubles of Greece or Ireland, both of which have recently collapsed into the arms of richer European Union (EU) partners when their debt burdens became unsustainable, there will be no "rescue" for America. A bankrupt American treasury goes far beyond "too big to fail"; it's "too huge to contemplate." A US default would precipitate the mother of all fire sales, as foreign money would rush in to snap up distressed US companies, properties, and other national treasures. As the Greeks, Irish, Portuguese, and now the Spanish and Italians, too, understand all too well, default means that monetary and fiscal policies are suddenly dictated from abroad. A sovereign default in America also would negatively affect dozens of countries that have based their own financial policies, investment strategies, and defense calculations on the stability upheld by the United States over the past several decades. No "advanced economy" would emerge unscathed; countless emerging nations would lose important customers and sources of foreign direct investment (FDI); and in many subsistence societies, where the United States is the largest aid donor and provider of implicit stability guarantees that hold fragile fault lines together, the risks of war, famine, and anarchy would rise.

- **Unprecedented information technologies will blunt America's global influence.** New technologies, including software-laden cell phones, peer-to-peer social networks, and widespread wireless Internet access, pose challenges not just for dictators but for all governments. While America's technological prowess has rendered its military unbeatable for the time being, this very reliance on technology represents a vulnerability. Indeed, open democracies are even more vulnerable to disruptive technology than their authoritarian rivals. Software, digital, and network innovations have placed power in the hands of

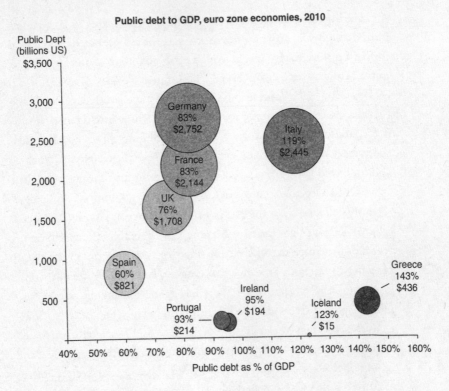

Figure 1.1
Source: European Financial Stability Fund

once-powerless people, giving them the ability to circumvent censorship, challenge taboos, and even bring down repressive regimes. SMS
text messages coordinated the actions of demonstrators in Tehran and
Tibet, Facebook "flash mobs" rose in Tunis and Cairo, and WikiLeaks
released thousands of classified pages of American diplomatic traffic
that shook the halls of the superpower. America's global influence since
the collapse of the Soviet Union has rested on the notion of "maintaining stability"—in effect, the status quo. Technology will short-circuit
this function, inevitably unseating some unsavory characters, including those propped up by United States over the years, and it also will
diminish Washington's ability to influence events.

• **Rising prosperity, ambitions, and confidence among emerging
nations will create a power vacuum that will encourage reckless
behavior and, if truly mishandled, a horrific war.** Nations as diverse
as India, China, Brazil, Turkey, Indonesia, South Africa, Iran, India,

and Venezuela now wield real influence on the world stage, and some will have serious influence on the future of the American economy. The diversity of interests among this group augurs ill for global stability. Neither the so-called Group of 2 (G2)—the United States and China—nor the old G7 or even the new G20 lacks the clout or internal consensus to coordinate global responses to megacrises. Moreover, many of these states, particularly in Asia, absolutely reject the concepts of multilateral diplomacy or collective security that kept the peace in Europe since World War II. As economist Nouriel Roubini and political analyst Ian Bremmer wrote recently, "We are now living in a G-Zero world"—a planet where "no single country or bloc of countries has the political and economic leverage—or the will—to drive a truly international agenda. The result will be intensified conflict on the international stage over vitally important issues."[4]

- **The cumulative damage of a lost decade of policy mistakes and misconduct in American economic and political life has discredited American leadership and lowered the US economy's long-term GDP "speed limit."** These lethal mistakes, based on messianic fallacies, have burdened the United States with a national debt nearing historic levels, GDP growth that has collapsed to near zero, and diminishing political and economic credibility. These errors have also destroyed a global consensus about the quality of American leadership and the resilience of the American financial system. The fallout of the disastrous Iraq War drove even close allies away from American initiatives. And quick on the heels of the Iraq fiasco, US-inspired economic policies that encouraged global capitalism to run riot brought the world to the brink of a second Great Depression. Bold but thankless action by Western governments and central bankers, including the Bush and Obama administrations, managed to forestall that fate. Yet this should be cold comfort for those concerned about America's international reputation—a bit like a drunk driver who causes a multicar wreck and then expects thanks for administering first aid to its victims. Sadly, the admiration Americans worked for decades to create—the reputation for economic dynamism and the triumph of a relatively bloodless victory in the Cold War—was squandered in a matter of five years between 2003 and 2008. The damage will haunt America for a generation.

A world in flux is hardly news. But can the United States weather these changes? No one should glibly assume the worst; after all, the United States has regularly defied predictions of decline in recent decades, from Sputnik to the aftermath of Watergate, through race riots and the oil-fueled inflation of the 1970s right up to the present. But today's particular thin ice threatens not only the United States but everyone who depends on the global systems, markets, alliances, and relative stability the United States fashioned after World War II.

The crisis is manageable if American politicians set aside outdated and discredited orthodoxies and properly plan for the wrenching decisions ahead. These choices will exacerbate existing political divisions among Americans over issues as varied as financial regulation, immigration policy, defense costs, scientific research, free-trade agreements, and education funding. Difficult as the journey may be, the tough decisions must be tackled while time remains. But the United States could permanently damage its standing in the world and accelerate its decline if the crisis is mishandled—for instance, if the White House and Congress continue to prove incapable of agreeing on both short-term and long-term plans to fire up GDP growth, make a dent in the appalling jobless figures, and limit deficit spending over the medium term. Such a failure would not merely delay a return to prosperity; it would hurt the living standards of its citizens, the security of its allies, and prompt the next generation of great powers—India, Turkey, Brazil, Indonesia, and others—to rethink the need for close, warm ties with a superpower whose star seems to be dimming. This is the fate Americans must avoid.

SIGNS OF INTELLIGENT LIFE?

Happily, some of the adjustments required to avert catastrophe have already begun: The Iraq War and the trillions of dollars spent there will soon be history. The deployment in Afghanistan, more rational than the Iraq misadventure from a strategic standpoint, is also slated for withdrawal. Economically, "green" technologies, the discovery of vast reserves of shale gas in the United States, rising labor and transportation costs globally, more temperate labor demands in the United States, and the continued excellence of pure research at the country's world-beating universities, the source of American innovation, have helped spur a small revival of US manufacturing in some industries. And, in a groundbreaking move, a Democratic president has conceded that changes to Social Security and Medicare, the most sacred of all Democratic cows, are both inevitable and necessary—though the party could still lose its nerve in the heat of a close election. Democratic concessions, however, have found no similar flexibility on the right with respect to the need for defense cuts or tax increases, or job-producing investments in desperately needed infrastructure projects. The ability of Congress to do something substantive before the 2012 election to produce short-term stimulus and a long-term deficit reduction plan—ideally split about evenly between tax cuts and government spending—will determine whether S&P's summer downgrade is truly the canary in a coal mine. The previously mentioned failure of the deficit super committee to even offer a few options bodes ill for the little bird.

This political breakdown—at precisely the moment when the rest of the planet is striving to undo the damage wrought by the 2008 "Made in America" financial disaster, has been infuriating. Yet non-Americans ignore all this at their own peril. It takes a very strong stomach to watch the sausage making in America's convoluted legislative branch. Love them or hate them, America's congressional nabobs can easily devastate growth prospects around the planet with a few wrong moves over the next several years and push America's economy to the brink of default or, alternatively, with spending cuts based on ideology rather than sound economics, throw the country into a recession even deeper than 2008–2009. In either scenario, the America that comes out the other end begins to resemble a twenty-first-century version of Louis XIV's France, the military juggernaut of its day, felled by venal, overcompensated elites, corrupt politics, bubble economics, and foolish foreign wars.

DEFAULT AND DENIAL

Can America avoid another, even worse financial catastrophe? My own answer is typically evasive: "Yes, but…" If history is any guide, US politicians in the 2012 season will bend over backwards to avoid any talk of decline (remember how well Jimmy Carter's speech on "malaise" went over back in 1979, the last time the US government's dysfunctions led to a technical default? In that instance, an accounting error caused the US Treasury to miss a $120 million interest payment. The result was a *permanent* increase in American borrowing costs of over a half percentage point—costing about $500 billion per decade since, according to economist Terry Zivney of Ball State University).[5] The jury is still out on the costs of the S&P downgrade brought on by the feck-less brinksmanship over the federal debt ceiling that consumed Washington for months in the summer of 2011. Global markets, by and large, held their nerve. But the uncertainty created by this dysfunction almost certainly contributed to decisions in corporate board rooms around the country to slow hiring and investment, bringing the US economy to a virtual halt by autumn. It also hastened the day when the US dollar would be knocked off its valuable throne as the "global reserve currency," a situation that confers enormous benefits on the United States that its citizens may only comprehend once they disappear.

The solution to all of this lies neither with the Democratic nor Republican leaders in Congress, nor with President Obama, and certainly not with those who embrace fiscal policy positions for purely ideological reasons. In the end, only American voters can punish the shortsightedness of the recent debate and force a reasoned conversation about the country's future. The world must hope they support candidates in both parties brave enough to off-load party orthodoxies that prevent Republicans from ever, under any circumstances, considering new taxes, or Democrats from dealing with the urgent need to reform the giant domestic entitlement programs. The 2010 primaries once again demonstrated a terrible flaw of US democracy in the past half century: a two-party system beholden to radical fringe elements who, unlike average, largely apathetic Americans, are motivated by a combination of zeal and unchecked campaign spending to turn out even in off-year elections. The rest of the country has only itself to blame for this situation. Reforms to the primary system, abolishing the archaic electoral college, fixing the redistricting process, and instituting more reliable balloting and vote counting procedures all make sense, as do changes in the way Congress apportions its power internally. But by not showing up at midterm elections, Americans deliver their franchise to whatever fringe happens to be most aggrieved in that particular cycle.

In an impassioned and insightful essay in the *Atlantic Monthly*, Mickey Edwards, a former congressman from Oklahoma, laid out a six-point plan to "turn Republicans and Democrats into Americans."[6] The recommendations focus on processes, mostly congressional, that, like US midterm elections, tend to give vocal minorities a veto on decision making. But no reform is big enough to overcome apathy, and the fact that a majority of Americans take their most important right for granted cripples American democracy and throws open the door to activist factions.

THE GLOBAL STAKES

So what can those abroad, whose own prosperity and national security owe much to American power, do in the meantime? For one thing, American allies and trading partners need to begin to position their own nations for the changes to come. In the Middle East, Europe, and Asia, the day of reckoning for those depending disproportionately on American power for their survival is coming. The time to get real is now.

Indeed, the "reckoning" of this book's title can also be thought of as a financial term of art recently very much in vogue: an "unraveling." As anyone who followed the 2008–2009 financial crisis will know, in this context, unraveling referred to the nearly impossible task of identifying the true value and ownership of financial assets that had grown so complex and detached from reality that no simple accounting formula applied. When Lehman Brothers went bust in September 2008, the rest of the world's large financial institutions were so entangled in the bank's web of opaque trades and securities that the collapse nearly pulled them all down with it. Similarly, America's geopolitical influence and military might consist of an intricate web of relationships, intelligence capabilities, and power balances that would cause global chaos if they unraveled randomly. If the collapse of Lehman Brothers nearly caused a depression, the precipitous withdrawal of American power from the Middle East or the Pacific Rim could spark a major war between Israel and its neighbors, Iran and Saudi Arabia, China and Taiwan, North and South Korea, or even nuclear-armed India and Pakistan.

Yet unravel it must—the math is clear—and this political reality poses the greatest challenge of the coming decade. So how should the United States proceed to unravel its increasingly unsustainable ambitions abroad, while at the same time tempering the promises it made at home to its own citizens? Will it admit it can no longer afford to keep these pledges without tearing asunder the world it helped fashion? In the upcoming chapters, this book will offer some specific prescriptions for policy changes that would help cushion the inevitable deterioration of US dominance. These are not reforms as much as they are breaks from past practices, and they will be neither simple nor painless.[7]

Maintaining the current situation—the status quo ante, where ante = 2008—is not an option. For another few years, the United States, by putting enormous pressure on its balance sheet, can impersonate the omnipotent superpower it was during the 1990s, but the strain is showing. In the next decade, the assumption that the United States can afford to act as the world's policeman will and should be challenged by those in America who resent the tax burden and by those nations—from friends like Turkey and Germany to rivals like Iran and China—who are tired of having no real say over US-led military interventions. Already, a bipartisan coalition in Congress that opposed the US role in Libya has suggested the outlines of future debate on this topic, focusing on costs as well as strategic goals. The opposition of large North Atlantic Treaty Organization (NATO) nations to the mission, including Turkey, Germany, Sweden, and Spain, also raise questions about the post–Cold War consensus that, until now, provided legitimacy for such missions (as Iraq so clearly demonstrated, shrugging off the importance of such legitimacy is a mistake). If the United States moves to aid the repressed citizens of a Libyan-style regime ten years hence, it could conceivably face China or Russia on the other side, putting the final nail in the coffin of the transatlantic alliance. The fact that captured Libyan documents showed that China was trying to sell Qaddafi weapons only days before his ouster should drive this point home.

THE GREAT ENABLER

Ironically, it was the success of US foreign and economic policies in the twentieth century that created the environment for the rise of India, China, Brazil, and others. This led three billion people to join the international job market since 1989 and brought new prosperity to formerly destitute nations, which bolstered their political and military capabilities. Thus, Washington's ability to maintain military primacy across the planet was bound to slip eventually. But the fiscal mess, largely of America's own making, has greatly accelerated the speed of that decline.

The United States cannot infinitely sustain the current burden alone. Even a short list of US military and intelligence operations must include the following: keeping the world's sea lanes open, providing most of the air and sea transport for international peacekeeping or disaster-relief missions, maintaining satellite surveillance of the world's trouble spots, ensuring various regional

Military Spending in Dollars and As Percent of GDP

Rank	Country	Military expenditures, 2010	% of GDP, 2009
1	United States	698 billion	4.70%
2	China	114 billion	2.20%
3	France	61 billion	2.50%
4	United Kingdom	57 billion	2.70%
5	Russia	53 billion	4.30%
6	Japan	51 billion	1.00%
7	Germany	47 billion	1.40%
8	Saudi Arabia	39 billion	11.20%
9	Italy	38 billion	1.80%
10	India	36 billion	1.80%
11	Brazil	27 billion	1.60%
12	Australia	27 billion	1.90%
13	South Korea	26 billion	2.90%
14	Spain	26 billion	1.10%
15	Turkey	25 billion	2.70%
16	Canada	22 billion	1.50%
17	Israel	16 billion	6.30%
18	UAE	16 billion	7.30%
19	Taiwan	15 billion	2.40%
20	Netherlands	12 billion	1.50%

Figure 1.2   The top twenty countries ranked by military expenditures in 2010 and showing the percent of GDP this spending consumes.
Source: SIPRI Military Expenditure Database, Stockholm International Peace Research Institute, http://milexdata.sipri.org/ accessed December 8, 2011

balances of power stay intact from Northeast Asia to the Indian Ocean to the Middle East to Europe, and maintaining military bases on every continent except Antarctica (and even there a research station supplied by the US Air Force, Camp McMurdo, flies the stars and stripes).

To avoid a global collapse of this web of stability, the United States must convince the most responsible of the world's rising powers to take a broader view of their own interests and to help shoulder these burdens. Europe's unwillingness to pay for credible military capabilities is a case in point: spending less than 2 percent of GDP on defense is unconscionable when your prosperity is based on the stability provided by those forces. Former US defense secretary Robert Gates told his NATO counterparts as much just before retiring in June 2011: "The blunt reality is that there will be dwindling appetite and patience in the U.S. Congress...to expend increasingly precious funds on behalf of nations that are apparently unwilling to devote the necessary resources or make the necessary changes to be serious and capable partners in their own defense."[8] It is high time that the United States shutter most of the bases left in

place since Patton's Third Army established them in the mid-1940s, with the
financial burden shifted to the EU. But there, as in so many similar instances,
Washington plays the role of enabler. Why would Europe raise defense spending from the current levels if the United States is willing to cover it for them?
Washington has never failed to make up the difference...so far.

A similar situation exists in Asia. In Japan, the operations of US military units draw harsh criticism: traffic accidents involving American troops
and Japanese civilians often receive the kind of coverage in local media normally reserved for child murderers. Yet Japan continues to cleave to postwar
restrictions on its military that only make sense if one assumes the enormous
American presence—forty-seven thousand strong in 2011—will remain there
forever. In South Korea, huge protests against the American military presence
of over twenty-seven thousand troops flare every few years, and politicians
cynically avoid mingling with local US commanders for fear of being branded
"warmongers," in spite of the threat posed by a nuclear-armed North Korea.
In both cases, there are bluffs to be called, and the United States, for its own
sake and the long-term sake of the allies it has defended for decades, needs to
call them.

During the Cold War, these deployments made a certain strategic sense,
when none of the aforementioned countries had the economic resources to
suddenly replace the deterrent value of US troops. That simply no longer holds
true. By maintaining these expensive forward bases, the United States has
allowed its allies to forestall difficult decisions (and, not incidentally, nurture
industrial powerhouses like Kia in South Korea and Toyota in Japan that have
hurt its own manufacturing base). Each of these nations has legitimate security concerns, yet the presence of Uncle Sam has ensured they could be met
without diverting domestic resources. To this list could be added many others,
including Taiwan, Colombia, Israel, the Philippines, Saudi Arabia and other
Gulf emirates, the vast majority of NATO nations, and even the relatively
plucky Australians.

Changing regional realities, and the relative decline of the United States
and its geopolitical power, will force all of these nations to adjust their own
national security policies. As the crumbling of the pro-American regime
in Egypt demonstrated, policies not based firmly on regional public opinion will inevitably fail. Turkey's foreign minister, Ahmet Davutoglu, is perhaps the world's leading practitioner of what I'm calling "the post-American
hedge" in foreign policy. Davutoglu has gradually steered Turkey away from

the faithful pro-American stance it maintained all through the second half of the twentieth century and into a more independent position, keeping with Turkish sensibilities but unsettling Washington. "If your foreign policy, however sophisticated it might be, doesn't have a ground in public opinion, then that foreign policy is not sustainable," Davutoglu told reporters recently.[9]

In an age when an enterprising seventeen-year-old can, with a Facebook account or a well-placed Tweet, bring thousands into the streets, the United States can no longer stake its regional interests on police states. Nor can it promise its allies in dangerous neighborhoods that American power will cement in place their preferred status quo ad infinitum. For certain of America's allies, getting ahead of this wave is tantamount to national survival.

THE SILVER LINING

For all the doom and gloom, the United States looks nothing like the twilight empires to which it's often compared. For one thing, in this age of globalization, a far greater swath of the planet—including some surprising nations like China and Saudi Arabia—wish America well, albeit for their own, selfish reasons. Why would either country, in spite of what it may think of American culture or foreign policy, want to upset a status quo upheld, at great expense, by American power that enriches them more each and every year? From the US perspective, this should be an advantage. It creates stakeholders all over the planet that genuinely hope Washington can solve its current fiscal problems. With the exception of the British Empire, which had a relatively benign replacement lined up when it ran out of steam, history offers no other example of a waning empire whose most obvious potential rivals—China, India, the EU, to name but a few—all have good reasons to want to help arrange a long, slow approach to a soft landing.

"I have no objection to the principle of an American Empire," writes Niall Ferguson, the Oxford historian. "Indeed, a part of my argument is that many parts of the world would benefit from a period of American rule." Ferguson and others like him recognize the importance of the role the United States has played, a role that "not only underwrites the free exchange of commodities, labor and capital but also creates and upholds the conditions without which markets cannot function—peace and order, the rule of law, non-corrupt administration, stable fiscal and monetary policies—as well as public goods."[10]

Ironically, many would-be topplers of American hegemony no doubt feel the same way.

Another key difference from the decline of Europe's imperial powers is that while America's relative decline is underway, the United States hardly looks likely to sink quickly to second-class status. In other words, the current trajectory would see the United States settle into a kind of parity with emerging powers. In instances where the changing of the guard occurred with amazing speed—Spain after Philip II, the Dutch after the Napoleonic wars, France after World War I, and Britain after World War II—the declining powers were exhausted, attempting to cling to far-flung colonies because their imperial economic models depended on extracting every last ounce of labor and resources to prop up the home country. The United States has something none of them ever enjoyed—the world's largest domestic consumer market, as well as a commanding lead in many of the disruptive technologies that still drive product innovation. So absolute decline appears only a distant prospect—unless Americans badly fail at the polls, inviting another decade just like the one just finished.

EVERYTHING'S RELATIVE

Relative decline for the United States is hardly the worst possible outcome, if Washington and its allies can fashion a post-hegemonic system as resilient as the US-dominated one launched by Roosevelt and Truman in the mid-1940s. And Americans may find that, after decades of superpower headaches, they kind of enjoy being mortal again.

But this will require some serious repair work, and not just to the national balance sheet. Americans are right to take pride in their country's achievements, but at times this pride looks, from the outside, a lot like arrogance or even racism. "Brazil, China, India, and other fast-emerging states have a different set of cultural, political, and economic experiences, and they see the world through their anti-imperial and anticolonial pasts," says G. John Ikenberry, a Princeton professor of international relations and former State Department official. "Still grappling with basic problems of development, they do not share the concerns of the advanced capitalist societies. The recent global economic slowdown has also bolstered this narrative of liberal international decline. Beginning in the United States, the crisis has tarnished the American model of liberal capitalism and raised new doubts about the ability of the United States to act as the global economic leader."[11]

Removing the stain of financial fundamentalism should be a priority of US foreign policy, too, and I believe it to be achievable. In spite of the financial charlatanism that prevailed in the first decade of the century, the American economy is sputtering but not crumbling. American innovations still drive progress in many fields of science and technology, even if some of its most innovative software—Facebook, Twitter, the Internet generally—occasionally undermine its own interests abroad. American manufacturing, recently written off as a legacy of a bygone age, is mounting a comeback as the costs of labor in the emerging world rise, along with the costs of transporting products back to the home market. At some point, the political risks of a factory in China or Bangladesh might just outweigh the incremental labor cost savings. For these and other reasons, then, the United States is hardly a "spent" power. A more apt word might be *winded*, like an aging runner who ate, smoked, and drank too much over the Christmas holiday. The United States struggles today to call up the old reserves of strength that seemed to power growth and job creation effortlessly through the preceding two decades. This is partly because the "steroid" of the housing bubble that fueled its irrational exuberance during many of those years has turned into a weight around its neck in the form of slow, excruciating deleveraging of household debts. But the runner lives and still has a few marathons left in him.

This is the time for America and its friends to face reality. These may not be the best of times, but with some planning and hard work, they do not have to become the worst of times, either.

CHAPTER 2

AS THE WORLD TURNS, GRAVITY BITES

The great challenge of the next 20 years will be neither military nor economic, but political. This is true across the ailing developed world—in the prideful capitals of the EU, the halls of power in economically stagnant Japan, and, of course, in Washington DC. Most politicians in Europe and Japan will likely choose muddling through over decisive action (though Britain, as we shall see, has opted for a radical and highly risky bout of austerity). But nowhere else does the political dysfunction carry the full weight of global expectations as it does in the United States. Today, virtually everyone across the American political spectrum agrees that something must be done to whip the country back into shape. The question of the moment—indeed, the question that will dominate the campaign debates of the 2012 election—is how best to do it. How soon should the crash diet begin and what side effects should be tolerated along the way?

Economists, with the exception of a few outliers on both the right and left, agree that no short cut or easy plan exists to restore Uncle Sam to fighting trim. GOP politicians pandering to the Tea Party voters in the primary season proscribe a bout of draconian spending and tax cuts that would pitch the United States back into a deep recession, probably dragging a good chunk of the world with it. The Democrats argue that the reason the economic recovery faltered in the summer of 2011 is that government stimulus spending in 2009 was too small and wasn't followed in 2010 with a similar measure. President Obama's "jobs bill" speech in September 2011 called for $447 billion in stimulus, mixing tax cuts and infrastructure spending in about equal amounts. Even with the unprecedented offer from a Democratic president to negotiate a restructuring of the American social safety net, the GOP leadership's inability to control its own congressional caucus has left it with a tactical approach that gives no ground—a reckless stance that dares international markets to punish America. The result is a standoff that makes it unlikely that a true blueprint for medium-term debt reduction and logical, short-term stimulus could be enacted until after the 2012 election. The result of that delay is depressingly predictable: severe stagnation economically and the risk of a dive back into recession.

IRON LADY OR IRON MAIDEN?

If the to-and-fro of the austerity vs. stimulus argument leaves you cold, one need only look at the British economy for a living, bleeding case study of radical austerity's effects if implemented into the teeth of a global economic downturn. Citing the reforms of Margaret Thatcher in the early 1980s, the Conservative-Liberal Coalition government of Prime Minister David Cameron in late 2010 passed radical cutbacks in public spending, on average 20 percent across most government ministries.[1] The result was predictable (and predicted by many, too): a nascent economic recovery stalled and Britain dove once again toward zero-growth and "double dip" recession. British debt problems mirror those in the United States in many ways: for decades, governments in London have spent far more than tax revenues could raise, making up the shortfall by selling "gilts," the British equivalent of Treasury bonds. Once the 2008-2009 financial crisis hit, the need to produce a sustainable medium-term fiscal blueprint in Britain was even more pressing than in the United States: British debt—at 62 percent of GDP as of September 2011—would reach 100 percent of GDP by the end of the decade if no action were taken, and global markets would be far less forgiving of a mid-sized former hegemon than they have been to date of the current reserve currency-wielding superpower.

Even under Cameron's current plans, however, British debt would not stabilize until 2015, where with some luck a debt-to-GDP ratio of around 60 percent might begin to be whittled away by stingy government budgeting. But "front-loading" the austerity so radically also offset the benefits of lower government borrowing. Britain's public sector is huge compared with most developed economies. Since the 1960s, government spending has accounted for about 40 percent of British economic activity—a figure that swelled to 47 percent as post-crisis bank bailouts took effect in 2010. (US government spending, by comparison, historically drives about 30 percent of economic activity, though in 2010, TARP and other recession-related spending programs caused a temporary spike at 33 percent). In effect, by strangling the British public sector at precisely the time when British consumers and corporations felt most distressed, Cameron has guaranteed a deeper downturn, gambling that long-term economic balance is better served by a smaller public sector, with all the sacrifices that implies, than by policies that stimulate GDP growth.

Among critics of this approach, David Blanchflower, arguably the world's leading labor economist, had warned in 2010 that deep austerity on the heels of a deep recession was a historic policy mistake that could permanently lower the "speed limit" of British GDP growth. He accused David Osborne, the top policymaker in Cameron's government, of engaging in a short-term accounting trick to make Britain's national accounts look better, all fueled by Thatcherite ideology rather than economic reason. By the middle of 2011, with his nightmare prediction unfolding as expected, Blanchflower chronicled the results in the *New Statesman and Society*, writing that "Osborne's policies will be responsible for the worst recession in a century—and maybe it should be named the 'Second Great Depression.'" Britain's post-crisis recovery stalled to near-zero growth, effectively a double-dip recession, and by December 2011 was on course to become Britain's worst-ever post-crisis recovery, supplanting the long, Depression-era slog of 1930 to 1934.

In the United States, the lesson has failed to take.[2] Even before US growth began to flatten out once again in the autumn of 2011, the "recovery" that allegedly began in late 2009 had become the weakest of any since World War II.[3] But the parallels are rejected on the right. With the silly season of primaries underway, when rational thought takes a back seat to appeasing the zealous base, the GOP appears unwilling to address the British debacle. Instead, an intellectually dishonest ditty from the Grand Old Hymnal, "What Would Reagan Do?," wafts up from the party's rank and file. Whether the 1980/2012 comparison is relevant or not (the case is dubious at best), contemporary Republicans seem unable to grasp what Reagan actually did in practice as opposed to the sepia-toned remembrances of party lore. So thick is the propaganda around the Gipper that no one recalls how, faced with a difficult economy and divided

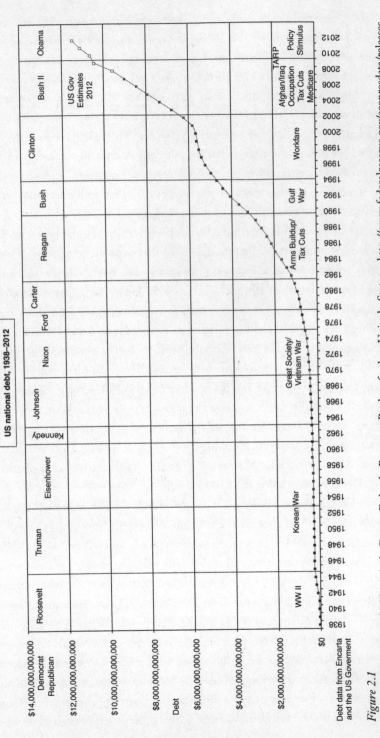

Figure 2.1

Source: Statistics and Historical Data, Federal Reserve Bank of the United States, http://www.federalreserve.gov/econresdata/releases /statisticsdata.htm, accessed December 6, 2011

government himself in the 1980s, Reagan chose to mix tax cuts with stimulus spending and, yes, tax increases, too. Bruce Bartlett, an economic advisor to Reagan and a Treasury official under George H. W. Bush, professes amazement at the twisting of the historical record by those who allegedly idolize his former boss. Bartlett reminds us, "The cumulative legislated tax increase during his administration came to $132.7 billion as of 1988 [$367 billion today]. This compared to a gross tax cut of $275.1 billion. Thus Reagan took back about half the 1981 tax cut with subsequent tax increases."[4]

Sadly, many Democrats, too, prefer fantasy to fact—though perhaps more as political strategy than economic concept. In early 2011, Democrats dropped feelers on how to put Medicare's trust fund on a sustainable course when polls revealed that the GOP's proposal to reform it, penned by Representative Paul Ryan of Wisconsin, was political poison. Talk of compromise on this vital topic was replaced by tongue-in-cheek bumper stickers like *Vote Republican, End Medicare*. While Ryan's plan does indeed ultimately end Medicare in its current form and represents a radical view, it could have also been the basis for a real discussion of how to save Medicare. No one should operate under the illusion that the program—or, for that matter, Social Security and Medicaid—can continue unreformed without destroying the US economy's ability to grow. But politics, even two years before the 2012 presidential election, won the day.

ROMAN HOLIDAY

Again, we need only look abroad to another major developed economy to see what happens to countries in which such huge questions are regarded as politically "off-limits." Italy, the world's eighth-largest economy and a major exporter of high-end industrial goods, luxury items, sports cars, and design concepts, has grown its economy on average a paltry 0.25 percent in the ten years from 2000 to 2010. Pursing short-term policies favored by entrenched interest groups, Italy borrowed until its national debt topped 120 percent of the GDP in 2011, and its anemic growth rates suggest that problem is not going away.[5] In spite of warnings from global markets and economists over the past several years, Italy's government, led until recently by Silvio Berlusconi, did little to curb the gargantuan entitlements doled out by the state or free its labor markets to tackle high youth unemployment. With an unwillingness to face the future worthy of a septuagenarian playboy, Italy sold enormous sums of its government bonds on international markets—so much so that the market for Italian bonds ranks as the third largest in the world after those of the US and Japan. "Italy has become a place ill at ease with the world, scared of immigration and globalization," writes the British reporter John Prideaux in a recent issue of *The Economist*. "It has chosen a set of policies that discriminate heavily in favor of the old and against the young." This unwillingness to face the long-term consequences had, by the end of 2011, brought Italy to the brink of bankruptcy, imperiling not only the euro zone but global growth in general. Italy is, by any measure, too big to fail without serious global consequences.

Happily for Americans, their economy still retains the vitality needed to grow at a reasonable rate—perhaps 3 percent or slightly more annually on average. However, if problems like Medicare continue to be regarded as political weapons instead of economic threats, Italy's fate beckons. Certainly, Prideaux's description of Italian society on its way down the bobsled run of sovereign debt should ring a bell with Americans. But for all the talk of "grand bargains" and putting entitlements on the table on the Democratic side in the United States, politics has prevented any real progress. When the GOP embraced Representative Ryan's "end of days" reform for Medicare, Democrats chose to hang it like a yoke around the necks of the 235 Republican House members who voted in favor of it rather than taking it as the opening bid in the "grand compromise" Obama keeps talking about. As one party fervently digs America's economic grave, the other whistles in the graveyard.

So do all America's current roads lead to Rome? Not necessarily. Serious economic thinkers believe that in the short term—perhaps until 2014—the US economy remains too fragile to be subjected to severe austerity. Some advocate a massive new infusion of stimulus spending. The economist Paul Krugman, for instance, has long argued that the first round in 2009 was too small, and that a second is needed to cut into the structural unemployment rate that has grown into yet another drag on recovery, hovering insistently around 9 percent. Krugman, who now writes a column for *The New York Times*, is often dismissed as a left-wing ideologue by critics of Keynesian economic policy. This cannot be said of Mohamed El-Erian, the highly respected economist who runs PIMCO, the world's most successful investment fund, who agrees with Krugman that unemployment must be tackled. But El-Erian also worries that a huge new bout of deficit spending could invite disaster, with America's credit rating already downgraded. He argues convincingly for a longer-term approach to unemployment that targets the quality of workers—what economists call "human capital"—rather than make-work government-funded jobs.

At its root, America's jobs crisis is the result of many years of under-investment in human resources and the social sectors. The education system has lagged the progress made in other countries. Job retraining initiatives have been woefully inadequate. Labor mobility has been declining. And insufficient attention has been devoted to maintaining an adequate social safety net. These realities were masked by the craziness that characterized America's pre-2008 "Golden Age" of leverage, credit, and debt entitlement, which fueled a gigantic but unsustainable boom in construction, housing, leisure, and retail. The resulting job creation, though temporary, lulled policymakers into complacency about what was really going on in the labor market. As the boom turned into a prolonged bust, the longer-term inadequacies of the job situation have become visible to all who care to look; and they are alarming.[6]

Krugman, El-Erian, Nouriel Roubini and others—including the economists Robert J. Schiller and Joseph Stiglitz—all support the view that the United States needs a mix of medium-term austerity and new government tax revenue to reverse the course of US debt and calm nerves among both creditors and bond markets vital to future US borrowing. As the "V-shaped" recovery predicted by many on the right failed to materialize, this list has grown to include previous skeptics, including Harvard's Kenneth Rogoff and Carmen Reinhardt of the Petersen Institute of Economics. While there is no way to be sure, many believe that the medicine prescribed by either major tribe in Washington—the Tea Party's hyperaustrity without revenue increases or the hard Left's megastimulus without fiscal reform—would be dangerous if not suicidal at the moment, the first prompting a deep double-dip recession, the second a collapse of the country's credit rating and, ultimately, a loss of economic sovereignty.[7]

Washington's ideologically driven political games have prevented sound policy from taking hold, though some smaller efforts have helped prevent the double-dip in the US. The Federal Reserve Bank's quantitative easing, or "QE," has cranked up the printing presses to inject of cash into the economy; historically low interest rates have encouraged lending to large companies, though credit remains difficult for smaller firms and individuals. But to date, more needs to be done to provide employers with an incentive to spend some of the huge reserves of cash they have built up protectively since the near-death experience of the fall of 2008, when short-term credit markets froze up and even enormously successful companies found they were only hours from insolvency. Here, short-term government stimulus could be useful in small doses. In November 2010, Roubini and I proposed that for two years, the administration should reduce payroll taxes for both employers and employees—a measure that could have been funded by allowing the Bush tax cuts for the wealthiest Americans to expire.[8] Politics, again, blocked progress back in 2010, but by mid-2011, with the economy again stalling, the idea was revived and added to Obama's September jobs speech. The reduction for employers would lower labor costs and allow the hiring of more workers; and increased take-home pay would get people spending again. It's not just about increasing foot traffic in the mall; households need to pay down the burden of credit cards, second mortgages, and other unfortunate legacies of the years of easy credit. Whether even this modest measure can survive the brimstone of Capitol Hill in an election year, however, remains questionable.

Such incentives will help, but they will not solve what ails the world's most important consumer market. *America must deleverage.* No amount of ideological posturing will change this reality. Deleveraging—the slow process of paying down all those credit cards, auto and college loans, and first and second mortgages—will prevent robust economic growth any time soon. It will also deaden the effect of "stimulus" measures structured as income tax cuts, since those tax cuts disproportionately benefit the well-off, and the research establishes that the better-off tend to make more prudent use of such windfalls: inevitably, most will be used to pay down debt rather than purchase consumer goods or, say, a basket of groceries. That's good news in the long term, but it is not going to help reignite growth.

In November, 2011, a study by the Center for American Progress, a think tank, argued that household debt—and particularly mortgage debt—will doom the economy to Japan-style stagnation in the coming decades if government fails to intervene and help get distressed homeowners into mortgages that frees up the disposable income that is the life blood of the American economy.

It could take many more years for debt to reach sustainable levels if the decline in household debt is left to market forces alone. Debt levels could reach the levels of the 1990s, which went along with a fast growing economy and strong financial markets, only by the end of 2017 if after-tax income continues to grow at the rate of last year and debt stays flat. This "do-nothing" scenario means prolonged foreclosures and tightening lending standards. It could alternatively take until September 2036 to reach the debt-to-after-tax-income ratio of the 1990s if income growth stays moderate and [household] debt starts growing at the modest rate of 3 percent per year.[9]

Americans, who recall the 1990s as a time of relative prosperity without the excesses of the housing bubble, should be gasping right now at the thought that it will take until 2036—under optimistic conditions—to heal the damage caused by the first decade of this century. This is a terrible penance for American households and one that will lower growth prospects across the planet as the US consumer suffers through this sentence. All the more reason why the solution must look beyond the country's borders and include a new examination of the burdens—and costs—of American hegemony.

LIGHTENING THE GLOBAL LOAD

An American Century's worth of overseas commitments, doubled down during the post–Cold War years when America thought itself all-powerful, will make the deleveraging process at home even harder unless, here to, deleveraging becomes policy. The line item costs of sustaining American dominance, as Johns Hopkins professor Michael Mandelbaum has argued, have been treated as little more than a rounding error in the annual debate over federal spending.[10] These problems cannot be tackled consecutively—all of this must be dealt with urgently and simultaneously to avoid creating the kind of downward momentum that could permanently erase the advantages the United States still holds over other powers that have faced life after hegemony.

But can American politicians, notorious for their inability to put simplistic ideological biases aside, diagnose and treat these diseases? Political instincts will prevent Obama or his GOP opponents from stating America's problem clearly. Each will woo voters with platitudes about a new American Century or American exceptionalism, and some will even believe it. American voters know these rituals all too well—the flag-draped backdrop, the frequent references to the "American people," the historical anecdote about past crises overcome (the Depression and FDR for Democrats, the Cold War and

Reagan for the GOP). None of it matters a lick to US creditors, nor should it to American voters.

In the search for a cold, clear-eyed navigator of the rocky shore ahead, Americans ought to examine a candidate's relationship to the "free market." The market is neither the religious force described by many Republicans, nor the pit of evil and corruption portrayed by many Democrats. It is, for lack of a more scientific phrase, a force of nature. Fanatics who insist on full exposure to nature's tempests—the fundamentalist, GOP approach to market economics—will live a short, brutish life. Consider the recent "exposure." By 2007, even American regulators—the people charged with tracking and planning for approaching economic storms—had instead joined the naked fools dancing in the rain. When the storm hit in 2008, the results were all the more catastrophic because the overseers had gone native.

Yet the Democratic approach is only slightly more rational. Rather than bare themselves to the ups and downs of the economic weather, Democrats cower before it, alternately praising the free market in good times and vilifying it when the downturn comes, demanding that it then be blunted and controlled. The financial reforms that followed the last crisis wound up doing little to address the main problems: American financial institutions that had grown so large that they could not be allowed to go bankrupt, and markets for derivatives, like those that brought the banking sector to its knees, were unchecked by regulation. The financial reforms of 2009 and 2010 left both of the dangers unchanged. Instead of tackling these thorny, complex problems, the Dodd-Frank financial reforms[11] treated symptoms, targeting the consumer end of banking by creating the Consumer Financial Protection Agency. This is not necessarily a bad idea—it's merely an irrelevant one, a weapon with which to fight the last war. The banking industry, predictably, passed on the extra costs to its customers and launched a titanic lobbying battle to kill the new agency. The "victory" was Pyrrhic, and an important industry must now deal with reams of new rules that may not prevent future abuses.

For too many Democrats, the free market remains a dangerous, rather than a beautiful, mystery. It needs to be respected, not feared; it should be harnessed (think TVA—the great Tennessee Valley Authority that brought electricity to the rural south), not walled off like some kind of economic Superfund site. Too often, postcrisis Democratic policy seeks to stifle, rather than channel, the market's power. After four years in office, Obama can no longer blame the miserable economy solely on the mistakes of his predecessors. He will need to demonstrate that he understands the need for the government to police the markets without dictating outcomes, because when it tries, too often the result is precisely the opposite.

Writ large, these differing conceptions of the "free market" have profoundly distorted the discussion about how to repair the US national balance sheet. Plans drawn up by GOP leaders and the White House rely on what many economists believe to be wildly optimistic assumptions about the US economy returning to a consistent 4 percent annual GDP growth rate after 2014 or so. Tim Pawlenty, a short-lived candidate for his party's presidential nomination in 2011, argued at a June 2011 GOP debate that targeting US growth at 4 percent is timid. "This idea that we can't have 5% growth in America is hogwash. It's a defeatist attitude. If China can have 5% growth and Brazil can have 5% growth, then the United States of America can have 5% growth."[12] His basic misunderstanding of numbers, of course, is that for the United States to grow by 5 percent annually, it would have to grow three times as much in real terms as China (which is three times smaller) and seven times as much as Brazil (which is that much smaller than the United States in terms of GDP). Pawlenty's candidacy failed to catch on, but his belaboring of this fallacy forced other campaigns to counter with fallacies of their own; Mitt Romney, a former Wall Street fund manager who should know better, quickly rolled out his own promise—albeit only for "four percent year-over-year growth."[13]

In fact, neither the White House blueprint nor the current GOP plan holds water. But both provide good reasons to be concerned about the competence of US economic thinking. First, some basics: The total size of America's national debt in mid-2011, according to the Congressional Budget Office (CBO), was $15 trillion and climbing.[14] The United States and virtually all developed economies run some level of debt, which is not in and of itself dangerous. But starting in 2001, America's debt began a steep climb (see figure 2.2). The accelerating debt was driven by many things, but four loom largest: the Bush tax cuts, the wars in Afghanistan and Iraq, the Bush expansion of prescription drug benefits for Medicare recipients, and the Troubled Asset Relief Program and other bailouts necessitated by the global financial crisis, including Obama's stimulus spending. So, the aim of the furious fiscal debate in Washington is not necessarily to eliminate national debt but rather to stop it from reaching destabilizing levels. A recovering US economy and smaller annual federal budget deficits would eventually achieve this.

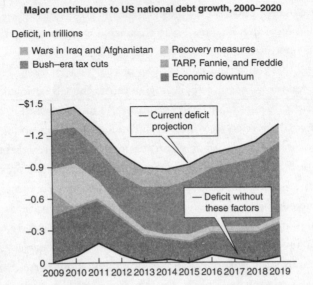

Figure 2.2
Sources: Congressional Budget Office, Center for Budgetary Policy Priorities, http://www
.cbpp.org/cms/index.cfm?fa=view&id=3252, accessed Dec. 6, 2011

Both parties offered "blueprints" for fixing America's fiscal mess in 2011,
each updated again and again in rounds of fruitless budget and deficit reduction negotiations, as well as the give-and-take of the GOP presidential primary
debates. None of these plans would actually reduce America's national debt:
the debate is entirely about slowing its growth so that America's credit rating
will remain intact. Nor will any of these plans ever become law—at least not
until after the 2012 election clears the air, briefly, for a round of non-electoral
bargaining. But the basic philosophy of each party remains a constant, so they
bear examination.

President Obama's approach to slowing the growth of this debt mountain, initially spelled out in his 2012 budget,[15] conceded that entitlements—
the huge, built-in "nondiscretionary" costs of Social Security, Medicare, and
Medicaid largely created and defended by Democrats over the years—must be
on the table. He has received scant credit for this small act of bravery. Obama
also proposes reforms to corporate tax laws that would force big businesses to
pay more of the 35 percent rate they currently dodge via a host of loopholes,
along with cuts to transportation, arts, foreign aid, defense, and other so-called
"discretionary" spending. Obama had also hoped to phase out the Bush-era
tax cuts for the richest Americans by 2014—in effect, a tax hike for the upper

middle class during his last years in office, though this was hardly bold. The CBO estimates[16] that federal deficit spending, if unchanged from current levels, would add $9.5 trillion to that $15 trillion national debt by 2021. Overall, Obama's plan would have reduced those projected deficits by $2.51 trillion, though the federal government budget would remain far from balanced. This would still add $6.99 trillion to the top of that mountain.

Republicans, on the other hand, richly embraced a plan written by Wisconsin House Budget Committee chairman Paul Ryan, a Republican, which bases its savings largely on the privatization of Medicare, along with a Congressional repeal of the Obama health care reform plan passed in 2010.[17] "Revenue enhancement" had no place in Ryan's calculation; the Bush tax cuts would remain in place, and further cuts would be pushed through. Ryan's plan also spares defense spending and projects to prevent $4.05 trillion from being added to the national debt (in effect, neither actually reduces national debt— debt would just grow more slowly than under the Obama plan). But while the crowd-pleasing lack of taxes and defense cuts won applause from the GOP's Tea Party faction, the Medicare plan quickly turned into a political problem. Ryan's plan would have replaced Medicare coverage for anyone under 54 in 2011 with a voucher to purchase private coverage. That voucher, economists quickly noticed, would be indexed to inflation. The problem is that medical costs rise much more quickly than inflation, and many elderly voters quickly concluded this was a prescription for eroding the health of their golden years away.

The inability to square these two approaches—*neither of which, again, would actually reduce the size of the national debt any time soon*—led directly to the S&P downgrade of August 2011. A host of subsequent "bipartisan" efforts at compromise failed, primarily due to the GOP's inability to enforce discipline in its ranks. GOP candidates, meanwhile, offered their alternatives, ranging from the sublimely optimistic (Romney)[18] to the downright ridiculous (Herman Cain's "9-9-9").[19] By autumn, with the economy faltering, the numbers that actually do register with American legislators—opinion polls—reported a deep, abiding disgust with the GOP for its summertime performance, and precipitous slippage in Obama's approval ratings as well.

LEGENDS OF THE FALL

For Americans, the budget calculus—and the contradictory claims surrounding it—can seem hopelessly confusing. It doesn't help that neither side will face reality. The truth is, everyone is lying. Of course, the smartest politicians, including Obama and senior GOP leaders, know that the old elixirs—the GOP's supply-side tax cuts or Democratic "revenue enhancements"—won't delay the approaching fiscal juggernaut. But politics, not economics, is what America's leaders have been bred to practice. Most, remember, are lawyers by training—not financial experts and certainly not economists. In fact, most appear to have no idea what "foreigners" on international bond markets have to do with America's economic health.

David Stockman, who as Ronald Reagan's budget director and father of the 1981 tax cut is something of a patron saint of budget cutting, warned the GOP of a "conflagration"[20] unless Republicans allowed the Treasury Department to honor American financial commitments. Apparently unbeknownst to many in Congress—even those who voted time and again throughout their careers to pass deficit-laden budgets—the practice is only possible because countries (and large individual investors) all over the world purchase US Treasury bonds. Stockman, of course, agrees that balanced budgets would be preferable, but he also knows that suddenly halting payments on the national debt would be a devastating mistake. Imagine an environmentalist whose solution to global warming is for the United States to simply stop using gasoline, and you have some idea of the logic at work here.

Average Americans shouldn't need to understand the intricacies of the international bond markets and how they underpin US government operations, from the wars of 9/11 down to the salary of the local mail carrier. Unfortunately, the people they elect (and pay) to explain it to them apparently don't know either. The problem is so widespread and obvious that I hesitate to single someone out, but for the sake of demonstrating the point, let's take Representative Adam Kinzinger, a freshman Republican from Illinois who voted against raising the federal debt ceiling when it first came to a vote on the House floor in May 2011. Explaining his vote in a statement, Kinzinger said,[21] "It is high time that we cut up the government's credit cards and draw a hard line to stop the government from overspending, which is hampering its economy's ability to grow and thrive."

Equating US national debt with "credit cards" illustrates a misunderstanding not only of basic financial realities but also of the English language. It is not "the national credit cards" being shredded if the United States defaults on its national debt; it's the national mortgage. As any ailing homeowner can tell you, when you "cut up" your mortgage and stop making payments, the bank stops lending you money and takes your house! While average folks may not understand interest rate spreads and bond yield curves, they certainly know what foreclosure means. Americans elect representatives in part so that someone outside their own busy lives has the job of locating the edge of the national cliff and steering clear of it. Instead, their elected officials have plotted a course right over it, and apparently those with a hand on the wheel would be halfway to the bottom before they even knew what was happening.

And the rest of the world has certainly noticed. Already, it is demanding a greater voice in shaping the global agenda, from international trade to nuclear proliferation to global health programs. China, in mid-2011, repeatedly urged the United States to get its fiscal act together. "The U.S. government has to come to terms with the painful fact that the good old days when it could just borrow its way out of messes of its own making are finally gone," China's state-run Xinhua News Agency said after the S&P downgrade. "China, the largest creditor of the world's sole superpower, has every right now to demand the United States to address its structural debt problems and ensure the safety of China's dollar assets."[22]

For all its shrill hypocrisy, China is right this time. The "wars of 9/11" eventually will end, but the challenges they were launched to address will remain. At home, even the current best-case scenario for the US economy is one of anemic growth and government austerity that staves off a downgrade to its national credit rating. The disastrous financial crisis of 2007-2009 left the US economy's potential annual GDP growth rates diminished in real terms, perhaps 2.5 percent on average in the next few decades rather than the 3.4 percent that had prevailed since the 1870s.[23] High unemployment—in the 7-to-8 percent range—will persist, while a desolate housing market forces a large percentage of Americans to tread water. Meanwhile, the banking sector continues to hide an enormous quantity of bad assets; and higher costs for staples like fuel, food, and health care will make social mobility harder, at least in the upward direction.

Herein lies the most painful truth for average Americans: coping with the realization that, for the first time in US history, it may be more difficult for their children's generation to make its way in life than it was for their own. This runs against the great American narrative, the immigrant story—one I feel personally in the figure of my father, an Irish immigrant who clawed his way from the windowless thatch hut of his birth to a four bedroom colonial in the leafy Connecticut suburbs. But the world will be a bigger, more competitive place for the next American generation of strivers. The benefits of having won World War II from across two oceans—and of emerging as the only significant economy that wasn't in ruins—brought advantages that lasted right through to the end of the twentieth century. That's all history now. Those who deny it do great harm to Americans by offering them a delusional excuse to avoid the hard work of adjusting to the world that looms just ahead.

As a nation, the United States needs a frank talking-to: America must "rightsize" its commitments, globally and domestically, and demand more of its educational system. It must also enact a more transparent tax system, raise the skill levels of its workforce, and stop the double-standard that applies to crimes committed in the corporate sector versus those committed by the average citizen. At the global level, the United States should lead a reform of international institutions while it remains at the top of the heap—locking in the huge gains in international law and stability its investments in national blood and treasure affected since World War II. As part of this last process, Washington must demand more of its allies, who have every reason to want to preserve the benefits of the American Century, even if they would be glad to see America itself taken down a peg.

Common sense adjustments by US households will not only contribute to rebalancing the distortions of late-twentieth-century US economic policy, but will also create a more accountable political system. No household following a careful budget will countenance the kind of charlatanism that has passed for economic leadership in Washington in recent years. The votes of those households that manage to live within their means should make a difference. Again, persistence, patience, and caution—unsexy but rational—are the bywords. For the mountain of money owed to various foreign and domestic creditors by the US government, US households look almost thrifty by comparison. Under three GOP and two Democratic administrations since 1980, the national debt has ballooned from about 32 percent of the annual GDP in 2008 to about 62 percent at the end of 2011. Federal spending grew at a slower pace until the end of the 1990s, but since then, fed by expensive wars, lost revenue from the Bush tax cuts, Bush's expansion of Medicare, and—most of all—the disastrous financial crisis and subsequent bailouts of Wall Street's gambling bets, has increased in size and pace. At 62 percent, the United States is just over halfway to the 1946 Truman-era debt record of 109 percent of the GDP that piled up by the unavoidable expenses of World War II and was all but eliminated by a postwar boom that lasted to the end of the 1960s.[24] That boom won't be repeated in the competitive global environment of the early twenty-first century. Some dismiss the gravity of these issues, pointing out that other advanced economies—both Italy and Japan, for instance—run deficits well above US levels. This should hold little solace for Americans. Japan's debt is held primarily by domestic sources, allowing its government to manage interest rate payments and other potential problems without worrying about international markets. Italy, meanwhile, discovered where political paralysis, questionable government accounting, low growth rates, and uncontrolled borrowing leads. In November 2011, its borrowing costs skyrocketed above 7 percent as international bond markets finally woke up and smelled the prosciutto.

The United States, however, has even more baggage. About a third of America's debt is held by foreign sources that may not have Washington's best interests in mind—some 26 percent of that by China alone. Another 11.5 percent or so is held by Russia, Hong Kong, and various Gulf Arab states. For those not steeped in economic policymaking or the workings of Wall Street banks and sovereign wealth funds (SWFs)—the investment arms of foreign nations—much of this may seem arcane. After all, the larger the investments a nation holds in the US economy, the more it should fear causing a precipitous drop in the value of that stake. Think of it as an updated, economic version of the Cold War doctrine of mutually assured destruction, or MAD, the nihilistic gamble that kept the United States and Soviet Union from launching sneak attacks. If one launched, the theory went, both went up in flames. To date, this dynamic appears to have helped keep the Sino-American relationship on a relatively even keel, even through some tricky moments—the accidental bombing of China's embassy in Belgrade in 1999, for instance, or the collision over the South China Sea in 2001 that resulted in the downing of a Chinese fighter jet and the brief internment of an American spy plane. China had the excuse it needed in both cases to react quite aggressively on international financial markets, but the relatively careful moves Beijing made suggest that Chinese leaders saw much greater value in maintaining their passive leverage over US economic policy than in wielding its investment portfolio as a weapon.

Two important caveats apply here. First, China and America, while hardly close friends, have not faced a major international crisis in which their interests are diametrically opposed since the Korean War. There is no telling what a Chinese government might do if, for instance, the United States came to the aid of India in a future Indo-Pakistani war, or to Taiwan's aid in an invasion by mainland China. Certainly, it must be assumed that Chinese think tanks and war colleges have gamed scenarios that include a mass selloff of US Treasuries in order to determine whether Beijing can minimize the self-inflicted damage such a move would cause. In practice, even the threat of such a move could be sobering enough to prevent China from carrying it out. Then again, it could also be enough to stay America's hand in a regional conflict.

Those who see such thinking as doom-saying should consider recent history. Former Bush administration treasury secretary Henry Paulson has written that, during the 2008 meltdown of the mortgage lenders Fannie Mae and Freddie Mac, China revealed that it had turned down a plan offered by Moscow (then embroiled in a war with a US ally, the Republic of Georgia) to conduct a coordinated Russian-Chinese mass dumping of more than $100 billion in Fannie and Freddie securities—a move that might have significantly deepened the distress in the US financial systems.[25]

Secondly, the use of such financial leverage as a weapon has a powerful precedent. In 1911, Germany and France nearly went to war over control of Morocco. After a few weeks of standoff, however, the Banque de France, the country's central bank, engineered a financial panic in Germany, sparking a bank run that drained the Reichsbank of a fifth of its gold reserves—in those days of the gold standard, a near catastrophe.[26] France took Morocco.

An even more dramatic example took place in July 1956, when the Egyptian government of Gamal Abdel Nasser nationalized the Suez Canal soon after inviting the USSR and communist China to establish diplomatic relations. France, Britain, and Israel attacked, planning to seize the canal and, they hoped, precipitate Nasser's overthrow. But US president Eisenhower, furious at being surprised and already dealing with the 1956 Hungarian uprising against the Soviet occupation, demanded that Britain, France, and Israel withdraw. When they resisted, Eisenhower threatened to sell a large part of the US Treasury's holdings of pound sterling,[27] Britain's currency, and also refused to allow American oil companies to replace supplies for Britain and France that were being embargoed by Saudi Arabia. Britain and France quickly relented, and neither ever acted again on such a scale without a deferential call to Washington.

If the US national debt continues to expand, however, it will not take a shadowy plot by Moscow and Beijing to bring America to its knees. A continued failure to address the gap between revenue and spending ultimately will sap the country of financial vigor, harm its ability to act internationally, and, ultimately, compromise its economic sovereignty. Writing to describe the last great transition in international power, the British historian A. N. Wilson noted that in the 1940s, the US strategy for displacing the British was subtle and effective. "For some American statesmen and politicians at least, the expansion of their power seemed to depend on the diminution of the British…for a large, rich, patient nation like the United States of America, willing to bide its time, there were very many factors which could help their purposes. Sometimes it would be necessary to shake the branches, sometimes the fruit would fall off of its own accord."[28] Chinese leaders, understanding their own dependency on US economic well-being, have apparently read Wilson's book. So far, they refrain from shaking the branches.

FROM MACRO TO MICRO

As the US seeks to adjust national and international policies to these new realities, as individuals, too, Americans must rethink their economic behavior. The changes that make sense at the personal level will sometimes clash with the efforts of national policymakers, particularly the short-sighted ones, who would like nothing more than to inflate a new asset bubble of some kind in order to put off the more serious, structural reforms that long-term economic health require.

Happily, average people, unlike nations, tend to act rationally when confronted with bills they cannot pay. Data since 2008 show that Americans continue to deleverage by paying down mortgages, increasing their savings, diversifying retirement plans away from the volatility of the stock and real estate markets, and readjusting overheated material aspirations. They must also demand that their children attain the most advanced degree possible if they are to compete against the tens of millions of PhDs, engineers, and business school graduates that will emerge from the improving universities of Asia, Latin America and Africa over the next several decades.

Something is clearly wrong not only with the US tax code but also with the philosophy of those who defend it. Warren Buffett, the legendary investor and second-richest man in America, noted in a recent *New York Times* op-ed that in 2010, he had paid "only 17.4 percent of my taxable income—and that's actually a lower percentage than was paid by any of the other 20 people in our office. Their tax burdens ranged from 33 percent to 41 percent and averaged 36 percent."[29]

The presidential election of 2012 offers an opportunity for a talented leader to emerge and speak frankly about these issues—to highlight the kinds of absurdities that see billionaires pay less of a percentage of their income in taxes than their hired help, or America's largest corporations, like General Electric, pay no taxes whatsoever.[30] Whether the zeal of the right or the eloquence of the incumbent will allow room for harsh truths is hard to say. As the next chapter outlines, the emergence of the Tea Party movement and Occupy Wall Street—similar expressions of raw outrage from right and left—suggest the middle class may be unwilling to be bought off with the same old marketing ploys. The world must hope that America's middle-class voters, whose relative share of the national income has fallen steadily for three decades even as their numbers have expanded, will assert their interests more intelligently at the 2012 polls, rejecting the protectionist populists of the left and especially the straightjacket, fundamentalist antigovernment bromides of the right.

CHAPTER 3

A "BOILING FROG" MOMENT FOR AMERICA'S MIDDLE CLASS

The leveling of the global playing field—the realization that the United States, while blessed and beautiful and unique in many ways, is not divinely anointed to lead the planet—will be bitter medicine for many Americans. The United States is accustomed to thinking in exceptionalist terms, of being told for generations that nothing is beyond America's capabilities. This already creates a kind of cognitive dissonance wherein Americans can empathize deeply with victims of genocide in Darfur or Rwanda, yet regard the near-destruction of Native American societies at our own hands as nothing more malignant than a regrettable by-product of its "manifest destiny."

As argued in the last chapter, the greatest challenge facing both the government of the United States and its individual citizens is devising a political plan to tame its national debt, which now casts an Everest-like shadow over future growth, not to mention future generations. The debt is on a trajectory to soon reach 109 percent of GDP—the historical high reached at the height of World War II—by 2021, according to the more realistic scenario applied by the government's General Accountability Office.[1] In effect, the country, like so many of its homeowners, will be under water.

While short-term spending to prevent the economy from returning to negative growth makes sense, ultimately America must take a long, hard look

in the mirror. Debt of such magnitude, particularly for a nation with plenty
of enemies in the world, will show up on more than the balance sheets of the
Treasury or its banks. It will invade every aspect of American financial life,
from the caverns of Wall Street to school construction bonds to college loans.
Americans can hope that their leaders will head off these worst-case scenarios,
but they should also think through the implications of failure ahead of time.
Politicians of various stripes put their special hue of gloom on these predictions, but the GAO—the US government's official nonpartisan auditing arm—
describes the peril in terms not normally found in dry government accounting
reports:

> Debt at these levels also would limit budget flexibility, affecting the fed-
> eral government's ability to respond to a future economic downturn or
> financial crisis. The longer action to deal with the nation's long-term fis-
> cal outlook is delayed, the greater the magnitude of the changes needed
> and the risk that the eventual changes will be disruptive and destabiliz-
> ing.... This means that on average over the next 75 years revenue would
> have to increase by more than 50 percent or noninterest spending would
> have to be reduced by about 35 percent (or some combination of the two)
> to keep debt held by the public at the end of the period from exceeding its
> level at the beginning of 2011 (roughly 62 percent of GDP). Even more
> significant changes would be needed to reduce debt to the level it was
> at just a few years ago or the 40-year historical average....Policymakers
> could develop a plan in the short term that could be phased in over time
> to allow for the economy to fully recover and for people to adjust to the
> changes. However, with the passage of time, the window to develop and
> implement such a plan narrow.[2]

Chilling prose indeed coming from a department filled with certified
public accountants. Americans will need time to "adjust to the changes."
Delayed action will result in a situation that is "disruptive and destabilizing."
Destabilizing! Ponder that term in the context of the world's most powerful
nation.

A certain numbness might be expected here. After all, the "changes"
Americans are getting used to exists at the personal level, not at the macroeconomic plane and certainly not the global geopolitical realm. But the crisis
has provided the American middle class will an opportunity to avoid a "boiling
frog" moment. As any high school lab student can tell you, a frog placed in a

pot of water that slowly warms to a boil will sit patiently as the temperature rises and the creature ultimately dies. The experiment neatly approximates the incremental loss of household wealth and relative share of GDP that has afflicted the American middle class since the 1970s.

Starting in 1980, about 5 percent of annual national income has shifted from the large middle class to the tiny fraction of a percent who make up the nation's richest 6,000 households. The results of the 2008-2009 downturn exacerbated the trend. In fact, according to the Bureau of Labor Statistics, the 2010 median income of $49,445 remains 7 percent below peak level of $53,252 from 1999.[3] The longer-term trend regarding the top 1 percent of earners is even starker: Census data indicate this group controls 49.3 percent of the nation's wealth, up from 41.8 percent in 1976. This is the most unequal distribution of wealth since 1928, the year before the stock market crash plunged the country into the Great Depression.[4] The response of both left and right has been anger. If the Tea Party and Occupy Wall Street movements find little to agree upon over policy options, at their core both sprung out of an outraged sense that the country was no longer being governed on behalf of the middle class.

By now, five years after the Lehman moment, the narrative of the global economic crisis for most Americans is well worn: a worker, perhaps in the manufacturing industry or in an office, who was laid off from a job that appears unlikely ever to return—at least not anywhere within the borders of the United States. The narrative also includes some who have lost their homes, victims of the public/private Ponzi scheme that was the American mortgage banking industry from the late 1990s onward. Others took jobs at half their former pay or less, or, having run through savings, moved in with relatives or friends. Still others would have retired once the downturn hit, if it had not taken most of their market-pegged 401(k) savings with it. And the truly unlucky endured the humiliating anxiety of raising a family without health insurance or the prospect of saving for retirement or to educate their children beyond high school.

Yet even in these hard times, most Americans remained employed. For that majority, these are merely cautionary tales. From 5 percent at the start of 2008, unemployment shot up to 10.1 percent by the end of 2009 and has stayed stubbornly close ever since, settling at 8.5 percent as of this writing in December 2011. When you include those who have given up looking for work—about six million people who have been dropped from the official Bureau of Labor Statistics method of reporting joblessness—the rate rises to about 12.5 percent. This is very bad news, but it's not yet catastrophic. (The jobless figure during the depths of the Great Depression was 25 percent—or 37 percent, if those who gave up looking are included.) For the vast majority of Americans, the 2008-2009 crisis was a bullet narrowly avoided. And for most average families (those who do not command vast hordes of capital to invest around the globe) the lesson is personal prudence: work harder if you have work, get out of risky investments, pay down credit cards and that second mortgage if at all possible, rent rather than own for the time being, save a little bit if you can, and insist that your kids learn something useful if you're planning to spend $20,000 to $40,000 a year on a college education—all easy to say but hard to accomplish.

These kinds of sacrifices have always accompanied hard times. This time, however, these belt-tightening measures may be too little, too late. Writ large, the challenges facing the United States mirror that of a distressed family: spending (federal outlays) has been vastly greater than income (i.e., tax revenues) for years, and bills (servicing the national debt) demand a greater and greater proportion of income and will rise further still before reaching a plateau. A lack of job security (uncertainty) and fears about irrational moves in Washington (political risk) sour the dinner table conversation. Deleveraging—the long, hard slog out of debt—is under way, but devoting too much to paying down debt might mean ignoring a leaky roof (infrastructure) or forcing a child to transfer out of an expensive degree program to a less prestigious institution (support for education, science, and research and development).

Families in the United States understand all too well that the mortgage and other monthly bills must be paid. No family would choose suddenly to devote so much to paying down credit cards that it could no longer afford food and shelter. And they would always find a way to invest in the future, even if it meant borrowing in the short term to pay college tuition or home repairs.

As with these families, only drastic fiscal consolidation can ultimately protect the economic reputation of the United States and avert a downward spiral of worsening consequences. The simplistic response to this fact would be immediate, sharp budget cuts to shrink the size of the federal government. Of course, government spending can always be trimmed. But mindless austerity, in this case, is just as dangerous as the mindless borrowing that preceded it. Austerity, as the troubles in Britain demonstrate, brings economic activity to a screeching halt—the worst thing that could happen in the current crisis.

Indeed, S&P's downgrade of the US sovereign credit rating in August 2011, from the coveted AAA to AA+, was based not on the size of its national debt burden—though that played a role, of course. Rather, S&P singled out the inability of American politicians to agree on a reasonable plan to tackle it. "The downgrade reflects our view that the effectiveness, stability, and predictability of American policymaking and political institutions have weakened at a time of ongoing fiscal and economic challenges," the credit agency wrote in its statement, adding it was "pessimistic about the capacity of Congress and the Administration to be able to leverage their agreement this week into a broader fiscal consolidation plan that stabilizes the government's debt dynamics any time soon."[5]

The "agreement" in question—the result of the debt ceiling talks that saw the United States flirt publicly with defaulting on its debts—was really no agreement at all. It merely kicked the can down the road to yet another congressional "super committee," adding an absurd provision that mandates automatic cuts if the politicians cannot agree to rational ones. That anyone even complained about S&P's downgrade is laughable. Imagine this scenario: You help subsidize the monthly costs for your 20-something son. He's working, but he lives in an absurdly expensive apartment and his monthly costs keep rising, demanding ever more of your money. Some of those costs represent interest payments on big credit card bills he's run up buying furniture, electronics, and traveling around the world acting like a big shot. He collects expensive guns and trades stocks online. Last month, in a desperate bout of tough love, you threatened to cut him off if he didn't get his act together. "Draw up a budget, show me where you can cut, what you really need for your business, and let's talk," you said. A month goes by, then two, then three. "I'm working on that budget," your son says, even as costs continue to rise. Finally, he turns up at your door with his plan. He's going to quit his job to spend more time trading stocks online because his gains will be taxed at only 15 percent. He's already stopped paying his credit card bills—"Let them sue me," he says—but don't worry: he's hidden his guns in your basement in case the collection agencies come sniffing around. And if all else fails—or if you don't agree to his plan—he has set in motion a plan to have his apartment burned down so he can collect the insurance money.

Would you lend money to this kid?

So why have the global markets not flattened us already? In the wake of the S&P downgrade, they gyrated but held their nerve. Paul Krugman and other economists of the left argue that the threat of default is vastly overstated[6] and that in spite of its problems, America still enjoys unique economic advantages that have warded off what economists call "bond market vigilantes"—the huge international financiers, pension funds, investment banks, and others that trade in government bonds. Over the past few years, these heavyweights have forced ill-timed austerity on the likes of Britain, Greece, Ireland, Portugal, Italy, Spain, and many others. Indeed, most of these market players—big international banks, sovereign wealth funds of countries like China, Japan, Taiwan, Russia, and Saudi Arabia—would react in a panic if the United States launched into euro-style austerity, because they know it would doom the world's largest economy to a decade or more of stagnation (the "lost decade" scenario that undid the Japanese economic miracle during the 1990s).

Still, Americans need to heed this danger and not take their unmatched economic advantages for granted, lest they disappear. These advantages come in several forms, starting with the American currency. Because most of the world's trade is denominated in US dollars, the price Americans pay for most commodities (oil, for instance, or food) is just a bit lower than elsewhere, even if they may be subject to a little more volatility as part of the deal. Similarly, because the US Federal Reserve controls the number of dollars in circulation, America can sustain policies—like the near-zero federal funds rate that has prevailed since the financial crash—that would have global bond markets baying for the blood of any other nation. These low rates effectively lower the ultimate return-on-investment foreign creditors will receive for purchasing American debt through the sale of US Treasury bonds and other government securities. With US national debt heading into record territory versus annual GDP growth, the ability to keep interest rates artificially low is no small advantage. But these perks of global dominance will erode along with America's hegemony, and erratic policy measures in Washington will speed the arrival of that day. Already global markets are chirping, and China, Russia, and other economic rivals have demanded that the dollar be supplanted as the global reserve currency by something else. This will not happen quickly unless American politicians, by strangling growth with budget cuts in the midst of a downturn, stupidly force the issue.

There is precedent for such stupidity, even outside David Cameron's Britain. In 1937, the US economy had finally, after nearly a decade, matched its size in 1929, the year the stock market bubble popped and the world cascaded into the Great Depression. Then, the deleveraging process was even longer and harder in every measure than it is today. By 1937, modest growth had returned, and while unemployment remained stubbornly high at just under 10 percent, that was down from a peak in 1932-33 of 25 percent.[7]

At this point, both the Fed and the Roosevelt administration—giving in to orthodoxies that still haunt US economic thought—made terrible, independent errors. FDR acceded to Treasury advisors who declared the recovery self-sustaining and pushed for spending cuts. FDR, by now in complete control of the congressional agenda after a landslide reelection in 1936, duly cut government spending by 10 percent in an effort to balance the federal budget. The Works Progress Administration (WPA), which had employed three million in 1936, was sharply curtailed, as were other "emergency programs." The Federal Reserve, meanwhile, had been rattled by recent gyrations in commodity prices, particularly in corn and wheat—crops devastated by the Midwestern Dust Bowl. Acting to tame what it saw as the threat of hyperinflation, the Fed raised interest rates sharply. Various economic schools assign different weight to these two decisions, but the overall math is devastatingly clear. By 1938, joblessness had shot back toward 15 percent, industrial production fell by 37 percent, and the worst double dip in US history had begun.

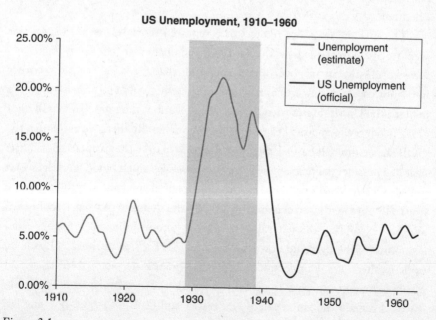

Figure 3.1

Source: Statistical Abstract of the United States, http://www.census.gov/prod/www/abs/statab.html

Could the mistake of 1937 be recurring as we speak? Ben Bernanke, who as chairman of the Federal Reserve bank has a relatively free hand in interest rate policy, has spent his career promising it would never happen. "Regarding the Great Depression. You're right, we did it. We're very sorry. But thanks to you, we won't do it again," Bernanke said back in 2002 at a conference honoring the ninetieth birthday of economist Milton Friedman, godfather of the monetarist school and a man whose scholarly work contends that it was the Fed, not FDR, whose error threw the country back into the Depression in 1937.

Yet Bernanke, who has also made the unprecedented promise to the market that the Fed will keep real interest rates below 1 percent until at least 2013, could still repeat the mistake—or rather have it imposed upon him by the more orthodox members of the Fed's policy-making board, which consists of the chairmen of regional reserve banks. For instance, St. Louis Fed president James Bullard has been agitating for changes in the way inflation is computed to take greater account of spikes in energy and food prices. He also agrees with Dallas Fed president Richard Fisher, an inflation hawk, who has opposed Bernanke's policy of "printing money" to stimulate the economy—a technique known as quantitative easing or QE. Should these voices come to dominate the Fed's board of governors, Bernanke could be forced to swallow his promise to Friedman.

The mistake far more likely to be repeated, however, is FDR's. In this scenario, Congress—led by the GOP's fundamentalist Tea Party faction— forces a drastic cut in government spending that turns an anemic recovery into another steep downturn. Automatic spending cuts and other gimmicks may see the United States through the 2012 election, though Obama will once again need to win approval to raise the debt ceiling. By then, we can hope, the GOP leadership will have regained some control over their caucus. But in the heat of a presidential primary season, they may also smell blood, and the worst political instincts will prevail. If so, the prospect of a default greatly increases, ironically threatening to accomplish exactly the opposite of what Republicans aim for: expanding the federal government. Simon Johnson, a former chief economist of the IMF and now a professor at MIT's Sloan School of Business, explains that a US debt default would cause the private sector to collapse and unemployment to surpass 20 percent. So while the government would shrink, it would remain the employer of last resort and thus get larger, not smaller. "The Republicans are right about one thing: a default would cause government spending to contract in real terms," Johnson says. "But which would fall more, government spending or the size of the private sector? The answer is almost certainly the private sector, given its dependence on credit to purchase inputs. Indeed, take the contraction that followed the near-collapse of the financial system in 2008 and multiply it by ten. The government, on the other hand, has access to the Fed, and could therefore get its hands on cash to pay wages."[8]

AVOIDING A SECOND "GREAT RECESSION"

All of this has the average American's head spinning. Whom should they believe? Distinguished economists? Politicians? Radio talk show hosts? Amid all the blather about defaults and inflation, monetary policy and sovereign credit, one uncomplicated fact looms: a national debt that will soon be larger than the annual output of the world's largest economy. It's as firmly lodged in American minds as the Soviet Union after Sputnik. It's not surprising that well-meaning citizens are falling prey to ideologues. It happened in the 1950s, and it is happening again today.

But this is not a Chicken Little moment; the sky will not fall if economic policy is driven by reason, rather than panic. The "debt scare," like the Red Scare of the Cold War, is all too easily leveraged precisely because it *is* based in reality. Politicians who advocate swift, searing solutions are focused solely on short-term impact—that is, electoral politics. If ever there were a moment in American history to focus on the longer term, this is it. The solutions to America's debt problems will take much longer than a two-year term in the US House of Representatives.

Indeed, it took the United States 235 years to amass this debt. "With the brief exception of the peak years of World War II, the United States have never had a debt-to-GDP relationship of that level in the history of the United States since record keeping began in 1792," says Roger Altman, chairman of Evercore Partners.[9] At such levels, it is widely agreed, the current 1 percent interest rate paid on money the United States borrows in the future will rise—possibly to around 4 percent. Already, at 1 percent, "interest on the federal debt" equals $169 billion dollars annually—more than the federal government spent on education, homeland security, and highway construction and other transportation projects in 2011. Add 3 percent more to borrowing costs—certainly possible given what Greece, Ireland, and others have experienced—and the annual interest payments begin to rival the US Navy's budget ($215 billion requested for 2012)[10] or Medicaid outlays ($269 billion). Put another way by the GAO, by 2020, the cost of interest, plus Social Security, Medicare and Medicare, will barely be covered by tax revenues. All other governments spending, from defense to scientific research to transportation and infrastructure, would need to be borrowed on global markets.[11]

"PREFERRED CUSTOMER"

Since World War II, the United States has enjoyed "preferred customer" perks around the planet, its credit hovering well above the 720 rating that the most valued American consumers generally enjoy. But a credit rating is a delicate thing—even a small error or oversight can have negative consequences. Most Americans know how frustrating it can be to deal with one of the seemingly faceless, supposedly omniscient agencies that rate consumer credit. If Equifax, Experian, or TransUnion suddenly decides you no longer deserve a high credit rating, good interest rates on your car or home loan suddenly are out of reach. For an individual, the difference over the life of a loan can be tens of thousands of dollars, or a realization that the purchase is simply out of reach.

Governments, too, as America learned in the summer of 2011, are subjected to credit ratings. As in consumer life, three supposedly all-knowing firms rate the likelihood that, say, Nigeria will repay a ten-year loan represented by the sale of a $500 million government bond. S&P, one of those firms, gave a B+ rating to one such bond offering in January 2011, which may sound good to those who happily accepted that grade to get through high school chemistry but is actually a long way from the AAA rating the US government bond offerings enjoyed until recently. Nigeria had to promise to pay almost 10 percent interest on that bond in order to sell it—a very steep cost and a burden on the national budget for the life of that loan. But the United States borrows frequently and freely, and even with its diminished AA+ rating, other factors—like the reserve currency status of the dollar—allow it to sell a similar US Treasury bond and pay just around 3 percent interest.

Now imagine if, after a second go-around between Congress and the administration, S&P and the other ratings agencies downgraded Uncle Sam's credit rating to, say, A from AA+ because of politicians who still think they can use the threat of default to get their way. From the equivalent of 790, America now drops to 660—not quite Nigeria (perhaps a 590) but certainly enough to be a high-risk client. The cost of borrowing $1.645 trillion (the difference between what the federal government collects in revenue and what it spends) could triple—or worse. And an involuntary default on debt payments would be a disaster requiring almost all the money left in the federal budget that is not already earmarked for Social Security, Medicare, and Medicaid, and probably some that is, too. This would leave nothing for education, job training, emergency relief, highway and infrastructure construction, scientific research, space exploration, or even defense. Admittedly, this is a worst-case scenario, but then the probability of an earthquake touching off a tsunami large enough to crest the retaining walls at a Japanese nuclear power plant also seemed remote. If humanity knew how to avoid such devastating natural disasters, surely we would plan carefully to do so. Yet in the United States, politicians who know all too well where the trip wires are seem determined to dance on them.

For any nation-state, or sovereign, as financial experts call them, the prospect of national bankruptcy means losing control over important elements of national policy making. If creditors stopped purchasing America's debt, it would force cuts that even the Tea Party would blanch at. Interest rates on everything from mortgages to student loans would skyrocket, and many middle-class families and small businesses would be shut out of the credit market. Before long, roads and railways would deteriorate, federal prisons and hospitals would teeter, public schools and universities would slide in quality, border controls and customs would lose integrity, and mail would be delivered weekly rather than daily. Local governments, already stressed, would lay off police officers, firefighters, and other civil servants in droves. Military and civil service pay and pensions would be radically curtailed, and the size of the armed forces would be pared back. Small business loans would dry up, and a black market would emerge for many of the services formerly funded by taxes—all of it acting as a drag on the kind of economic growth vital to breaking the downward spiral. Here, in detail, is the "disruptive and destabilizing" results of a failure to act rationally described by GAO's audit.[12]

Then there is the intangible influence of politics. Anger and economic dislocation raise crime rates and fray civility. The natural turning inward in such circumstances only adds to the spiral of decline, and once that spiral begins the bottom is hard to define. None of this may loom ahead for the United States, yet something disconcertingly similar appears to be stalking the nations of the EU's euro zone—those countries that use the euro as a common currency. Anger runs high in northern Europe's stronger economies—Germany, the Netherlands, and Finland, in particular—about the funding they have extended to Greece, Ireland, Portugal, Spain and Italy to help those high-debt countries stave off default. This resentment has vaulted elements of the far right to power in these countries around the continent, from Umberto Bossi of Italy's surging Northern League, which would like to separate the wealthy north from the rest of the country, to the Dutch Freedom Party leader and anti-Muslim agitator, Geert Wilders, now leading a major parliamentary force in the once ultratolerant Netherlands. It has also fueled a violent backlash against immigration. Indeed, a very similar combination of economic collapse, diminishing global power, debt payments for foreigners, and national humiliation helped fuel the rise of Adolf Hitler in the 1930s, as well as the earlier crises that toppled Tsarist Russia, China's Nationalists, and Spain's monarchy before its bloody civil war.

America has nothing yet to fear from peasants with pitchforks, but well-organized digital insurgents selectively quoting from those revolutionary eighteenth-century texts are their equivalents in the current crisis. The modern Tea Party movement offers no thoughtful solutions; their modus operandi is anger mixed with raw austerity, a perfect prescription for the economic death spiral just described. Yet the movement may come and go without leaving too much of a mark on the country's politics—it is too early to tell. Certainly, the difficult times ahead will make it easy to sow discontent. As life's luxuries move out of reach of the US middle class, the backlash against those who continue to prosper will be profound. Anti-immigrant sentiment will grow, too, and populism will undermine the remaining free trade consensus in Congress, insisting that America's ailing industries be protected with tariffs. (For a sense of why this would be disastrous, examine what happened during the Great Depression when a trade war touched off by the notorious Smoot-Hawley Tariff Act added years and untold depth to the crisis.) Structural unemployment that remains at around 9 percent will have social ramifications, too. Young people unable to find work tend, fairly quickly, to add to crime statistics. This is a dangerous place to be: if the difficult decisions about repairing America's fiscal ailments are put off and its global credit worthiness lowered, its decline will have become irreversible. In such a political atmosphere, reason loses its hold, leaving anger and passion alone to drive the debate on national destiny.

STUPOR-POWER POLITICS

Americans are accustomed to reveling in the unassailable might of their military, the superiority of their technology, and the centrality of their country to the world's great issues. We are, after all, the people who would "pay any price, bear any burden," in the words of John F. Kennedy from his inaugural address,[13] and the "last best hope of man on earth," as Ronald Reagan put it not long afterward.[14] How, then, can America's political leaders begin to explain to average citizens the importance of unraveling these titanic, unsustainable burdens at home and abroad?

A good start would be a simple, nonpartisan exercise in public education. Pose the question, What has underpinned America's enviable standard of living since World War II? and see how many Americans attribute it to "hard work" or "innovation" or "the genius of the free market," or even "manifest destiny"—understandably, given that these are the primary explanations offered by its politicians and high school history teachers. But, as any real friend or qualified therapist will tell you, believing your own bullshit is dangerous. Americans must come to terms with the extent to which their living standards—measured by such factors as salary growth, material possessions, expendable income, and life expectancy—have depended on their nation's place at the very top of the geoeconomic food chain, and its relatively competent management of that position until, roughly, the late 1990s. It is ironic that precisely at the moment the US government's budget finally moved into surplus—1997–2001—the most disastrous financial policy decisions were made. In November 1997, the Gramm-Leach-Bliley Financial Services Modernization Act partially repealed the Glass-Steagall Act of 1933, eliminating the restrictions that kept commercial banks separate from brokerages and insurance companies. In 2000, Congress followed up with the Commodity Futures Modernization Act, which deregulated credit default swaps (CDSs)—a kind of insurance on bad investments—and also prevented government from regulating trading on electronic energy commodity markets. The final nail in the economy's coffin was hammered home in 2004, when the Bush administration lifted leverage restrictions on broker-dealers and investment banks. In effect, the Securities and Exchange Commission (SEC), created to prevent Wall Street from ever again taking the economy to the brink of collapse, told Wall Street brokers they could make bets with potential losses many dozens of times the size of the actual cash and assets they had on their books. Not surprisingly, that's precisely what all of them did.[15] Within four years, Bear Stearns and Lehman Brothers had effectively bankrupted themselves, and only the quick action of the federal government prevented the rest of the banking system from going down with them.

SURFING THE BIG WAVE

So what should Americans do to prepare for the tectonic changes looming ahead? Here, what is good for the country (the goose) may diverge somewhat from the interests of the individual households (the gander). Whatever reforms are eventually implemented on Wall Street, one thing remains indisputable: growth in the United States still depends too much on consumption—on consumers who spend money to purchase things. The conventional business school wisdom over the past two decades—until Wall Street nearly killed the goose—held that the way to increase US economic growth, about 70 percent dependent on consumption by the time of the crisis, was to stoke this consumption by finding new ways to provide credit to the American middle class. This is akin to concluding that the way to make your unhappy, overweight teenaged child happy is to provide unlimited ice cream. The huge spending binge that resulted mixed easy credit with ridiculous incentives and practices that encouraged lenders to dole out cash with very little concern about its ever being repaid. The script by now is well worn: most lenders, from the banks who issued credit cards to the mortgage companies that executed home loans, quickly sold those loans onto larger companies, who from there backed all those obligations into tangled, impossible-to-value "CDOs"—collateralized debt obligations—which became heavily traded investment vehicles. Ratings agencies—the same ones now threatening to downgrade the United States—competed for the fees they were paid to stamp these pieces of financial excrement with "AAA" ratings. On this shaky ground the boom years of the last decade rested until the subprime mortgage crisis, a mere tremor in any well-regulated economy, brought the whole rotten house down.

CONSUMPTION JUNCTION

The implications of all this for average people in the United States and other advanced economies depend on many factors. In the United States, for instance, with its unique overreliance on real estate and consumer spending and underreliance on savings and pensions, individuals will need to make fairly substantial adjustments. Even economists measure progress largely by metrics such as consumer sentiment, housing starts, and retail sales, reinforcing the extent to which American economic activity depends on more and more material consumption. But economic activity and economic health are not synonymous.

Over the long term, only restoring balance to individual American household budgets—less debt, more savings, and investments other than real estate—can create a sustainable foundation for economic growth.

The recession pushed the US savings rate—the percentage of income saved per month on average—up to 4.9 percent, a nearly fivefold increase over 2005, when wildly reckless incentives led Americans to save just over 1 percent. That progress may not continue, however, since the short-term political incentive is to show economic activity rather than shore up macroeconomic problems. Americans can do themselves and their country a favor by pushing that savings rate up further, back toward the roughly 8 percent range of recent decades (as recently as 1983, just after the 1981 recession, the figure was over 10 percent). They must also resist the temptation to divert that money to stocks, where share prices have all but detached from the actual performance of the economy, since fundamentals suggest a sustained period of volatility, making gambles as likely to fail spectacularly as payoff.

In Europe and Japan, household savings rates are much higher—more in the range of 10 percent (the average in 2010 was 11.2 percent). Except in Britain, where recent personal savings lows near 2 percent have bounced back toward the 5 percent range, and in a couple of other countries (Ireland, where

Figure 3.2
Source: A Guide to the National Income and Product Accounts of the United States (NIPA), http://www.bea.gov/national/pdf/nipaguid.pdf, accessed December 6, 2011

rates are around 3 percent, and Greece, where rates have been sharply negative for over a decade), the problem in the EU is precisely the opposite. This is part of a problem economists refer to as "global imbalances," whereby countries that generate high trade surpluses tend to have high household savings rates, while the opposite is true in countries like the United States and Britain, which run trade deficits. This situation puts too much emphasis on consumer spending in nations that need to borrow to sustain it (namely, the United States). Thus, by definition, it represents an unsustainable way to run a world economy. Households in the export powerhouse Germany save over 11 percent a year; in Switzerland, the figure is 13 percent; Italy's rate is over 7 percent; and the rate in the Netherlands is close to 9 percent.[16] Governments in these places, where the need for personal pensions or educational savings is far less pressing than in the United States, Britain, or developing nations, should stoke consumption with tax incentives that get some of this money producing jobs and tax revenues.

The problem is even more apparent in the so-called BRICs,[17] but for very different reasons. Credit Suisse, a Swiss bank, estimated in 2011 that Chinese households saved 31 percent of income; even in Brazil, where the bank quipped that households show "an appetite for life," savings represented 10 percent of income, the lowest among the BRICs. In these societies, such statistics cannot be compared one-to-one with figures in advanced economies; for instance, banks may not always be trusted in emerging nations, so savings rates may actually be higher. Alternatively, households in India and China often need to save to cushion against the lack of state services in health care and education. Still, only a slow opening up of consumer spending in these countries has been seen, though it could accelerate as these economies grow. The dilemma is poignant: if China lent less to the United States and Chinese households spent more, the resulting consumption would fuel global economic growth. But if that pattern changed too quickly, the American debt bomb could detonate.[18]

And what of personal investments? Again, the picture for portfolios varies across the advanced economies. In places where disposable income exists—that is, outside the United States, Britain, and the euro zone's PIIGS, all of which have a decade of debt deleveraging ahead—personal investments in companies of value and selected commodities make sense to a point. Most European households are free of the nightmarish overreliance on real estate that afflicts the United States, Ireland, Spain, and Britain. Freeing up some of what currently goes into savings and investing in long-term growth will raise all boats.

However, the euro zone has its own nightmare in the form of failing peripheral economies—Greece, Ireland, and Portugal—which will need to be bailed out in order to prevent the collapse of the common currency. One way or another, this translates into higher taxes for high-performing euro zone economies—in effect, transfers of wealth from the rich EU north to the poorer periphery. This will be discussed further in a later chapter, but allowing defaults among the more severe cases, particularly Greece, may be necessary to prevent the crisis from devastating larger, more important debt-laden euro zone countries like Spain and Italy. Given this reality, it's understandable that households in the euro zone might want to get some of their money offshore.

The challenge in the United States, and in the European countries that rode real estate booms during the bubble years, will be a dual process of paying down debts and rethinking the overreliance on the family home as the household's most important asset. This is easier said than done, and it will be difficult at a time when economic growth remains relatively low (economists I speak with believe 2.5 percent annual US GDP growth to be a far more realistic average for the second decade of the century than the 4 percent both Democrats and Republicans want to bake into their "deficit reduction" plans). Another issue is the lack of growth in salaries relative to inflation. This is nothing new: real wages for American workers, except the lucky few in the top 5 percent of earners, have gone virtually nowhere for decades. Growth in median income in the United States, which rose sharply after World War II, petered out in 1969, with many studies indicating a net loss since then.[19] This situation may worsen in coming years. Bill Gross, founder and leading investment strategist at PIMCO, one of the world's most respected asset management firms, believes the politically driven prescriptions of both American parties doom US workers to lose ground. "Because policy stimulus is focused on maintaining current consumption as opposed to making the United States more competitive in the global marketplace, American workers' real wages will almost necessarily lag historical norms," he says.[20]

This bind may tempt US households to take precipitous moves to readjust their balance sheets. Financial advisors with strong macroeconomic credentials have been offering some basic rules: be open to renting, avoid speculative investments, take advantage of tax-free savings plans like IRAs and health savings accounts, continue to upgrade your own skills to avoid falling behind the technological curve at work, be open to relocating for advancement, and place more emphasis on the stability and career growth opportunities of your job situation than the immediate financial return. This may sound like a doleful commencement speech, but for overburdened households in a low-to-moderate growth economy, options are not plentiful. Caution, persistence, patience are the bywords.

For those ensnared in a real estate liquidity trap—a house so under water that servicing its mortgage debt is nearly ruinous—traditional remedies may fail. In such cases, more radical moves make sense. The federal program encouraging banks to recalibrate mortgage debt—the Home Affordable Modification Program (HAMP)—is a failure, having done little to clear out the pipeline of bankruptcies and potential bankruptcies. Campaign-year promises to do more should inspire little confidence. Banking industry lobbying, aided by the GOP, blunted the government's ability to force such modifications, and timid Democrats, when deciding precisely how to structure financial reform legislation, did not reverse it. Over the next several years, as more and more distressed households finally give up the ghost, they will feed the downward cycle of home prices, preventing the rebound so many US households are praying for. Some, facing the need to relocate or simply unable to pay their ballooning mortgage bills, have rented out their primary residences and obtained rental housing for their families. In some instances, particularly in cases where relocation for a job is involved, the difference between the money the home brings as a rental and the mortgage payment can be a tax deduction, though not indefinitely. A more radical move—walking away—should not be ruled out in dire circumstances, where legal. The psychological and personal financial ramifications are daunting and should not be underestimated.

"Failure" comes with consequences that can take many forms. But lingering in the real estate equivalent of a corpse doesn't benefit the long-term financial health of the household, the national economy, or the US banking sector, which remains dangerously undercapitalized and burdened with toxic assets hidden by accounting tricks and a deliberately liberal interpretation of the rules by regulators who fear sparking a panic.[21]

PROGRESS BY DEGREES

Franklin Roosevelt, in even more trying times, said, "We cannot always build the future for our youth, but we can build our youth for the future."[22] Households in the developed economies of Europe and the United States need to heed these words. Unfortunately, for those at the start of a career or still pondering the best course to chart, despair is prevailing. The job market looks daunting, and the *zeitgeist* inspires little confidence. For those whose memories barely reach back into the 1990s, this is a devastating turn of events. Not long ago, US youth culture lionized "slackers," the derogatory/hip 1990s term for Generation Xers who preferred skateboarding and body art over a place in the booming economy of their day. That all looks rather quaint to today's young people.

In the United States, at least, Gen Y, as the post-9/11 crowd was quickly dubbed, looks back on the spoiled Gen X phenomenon with the same kind of disdain that kids from the Reaganite 1980s heaped on their hippie parents. "I've had three internships in the three years since I got out of school and not one of them paid me a dime," Dylan Byers, a bright young journalist and former student of mine at Bard College told me during a job interview. "I just can't take another internship."[23] These students, graduating into the world wrought by the Great Recession, place huge value on practicality. Already, universities report a shift away from some liberal arts majors toward disciplines with a more obvious career application. From 1971 to 2008, the period covered by the latest report on bachelor's degrees by discipline by the National Center for Education Statistics, the number of English literature degrees has risen only slightly, far less than necessary to keep up with the huge increase in the number of students enrolled in four-year college programs. A similar downward trajectory afflicts social sciences, library sciences, and philosophy. Indeed, another liberal arts staple, education, is one of the few fields of study that suffered major real declines during this period. In 1971, over 176,000 students graduated with a BA in education. The figure in 2008, with a far larger sampling, had fallen to just above 102,000, and the assault on public employee pensions and unions since surely won't help.[24]

Contrast that with career-oriented degrees. Predictably, computer science degrees skyrocketed, but this result can be put down to what economists call the "zero effect"—that is, measuring something that barely existed (prior to 1971) and being impressed by percentage increases. More tellingly, other "practical" degrees also grew: graduates with BAs in business, psychology, health sciences, and public administration doubled and, in some cases, tripled over the same period. This suggests that students, and their parents, have been paying attention to shifts in the US job market for some time—but not necessarily enough. If money is the goal, students should be paying far more attention to the sciences. PayScale.com, an online payroll assessment company, suggests that those seeking the highest pay upon graduation should pursue majors ending in the words *engineering* or *science*. These majors include computer science, electrical engineering, computer engineering, mechanical engineering, civil engineering, and mathematics. (Also in the top ten are economics, finance, marketing, and—oddly enough—my own major, political science.) Interestingly, business administration, the ultimate "parents forced me to" major, ranks thirteenth, with graduates bringing an average of about $40K in their first job, as opposed to $60K for computer engineers. And psychology, the country's most popular major, according to the Princeton Review, ranked nineteenth, below history and sociology majors, netting graduates a mere $34.7K in their first positions.[25]

A "first job salary" is hardly a scientific way to plan a child's future, let alone a country's. But other studies have found that, even among workers who choose blue-collar careers, a huge gap in pay exists between those who do or do not have a college degree. Georgetown University's Center on Education and the Workforce noted in a 2011 study that a college degree helped the average hairdresser make 69 percent more than a nondegree colleague. For plumbers with a four-year degree, the average salary was $52,000 compared with $39,000 for nondegree fitters. Even the humble dishwasher, the avocation famously described as "a thoroughly odious job" in George Orwell's classic *Down and Out in Paris and London*,[26] gets a huge bump out of a four-year degree, gaining 83 percent on a nongraduate *plongeur*.[27] Some social scientists posit that self-esteem plays a role here. An educated dishwasher, for instance, is more likely to be regarded as having a career path. He or she may even have taken the job on the promise of future advancement, whereas someone less educated might simply be happy to have the job at all. Some reasons remain statistically unknowable.

Still, a deeper look—attempting to match job skills with the jobs experts believe will be available in ten, twenty, or thirty years—paints a similarly science-oriented picture, though the need for vocational skills also comes through clearly. A 2010 study by the consulting group McKinsey and Company concluded that the mismatch in jobs and skills will only widen.

"Under current trends, the United States will not have enough workers with the right education to fill the skill profiles of the jobs likely to be created [by 2020]," the report warns, with "a shortage of up to 1.5 million workers with bachelor's degrees or higher in 2020. At the same time, nearly 6 million Americans without a high school diploma are likely to be without a job."[28]

For parents and students, and those with time to change career paths before life's burdens and blessings—from mortgages to credit card debt to children—begin to close off options, this is invaluable intelligence. Whether seeking technical vocational skills for high-end manufacturing jobs or advanced degrees in biotechnology, it's more important than ever for those living in advanced industrial economies to make clearheaded choices about education. Low-wage jobs will not come back (though there is evidence that US, Japanese, and European manufacturing in important value-added areas will survive and, in some cases, thrive thanks to the skills necessary to produce some modern goods).[29] The future will involve compromises and possibly an adjustment of the ambitions some families harbor for their children. But growth will return to the innovative sectors of the US economy if the country works to reverse the mistakes of the past two decades. This process starts with American households making intelligent choices with their money, their education, and their job skills. The competition for jobs, thanks to technology and America's own successes in the twentieth century, is now global.

CHAPTER 4

FROM SHORTWAVES TO FLASH MOBS: TECHNOLOGY SPEEDS THE MARCH OF HISTORY

Like many Egyptians, Ramy Nagy learned about the uprising against Hosni Mubarak and his regime through Facebook and Twitter. A Cairo-born Internet entrepreneur, Nagy runs an Arabic-language video-sharing start-up, Medeo, whose website suddenly blossomed with videos of antigovernment protests posted by cell-phone-toting Egyptians. Unlike some, Nagy does not claim that social networks like his own mobilized or sparked the revolution that ultimately toppled Mubarak's oppressive rule. "People needed to make real, dangerous decisions for any of this to happen," he said. But social media did offer a crucial way around the censored state media, which downplayed and even ridiculed the early crowds gathering in Tahrir Square.

"Social media—Facebook, Twitter, and sharing sites—played a significant role in spreading news about the protests, violence, and violations in a real-time fashion that was not available through traditional media within the 18 days of the uprising," he said. "This fast, widespread reporting influenced people's perceptions of how to gauge the success and influence of the protests. The traditional outlets reported things like 'a few people protested at Tahrir Square today,' but you got a very different story from the thousands of people on Facebook and Twitter who were posting real-time images and information. This invited people in to participate."[1]

Other Egyptians piled on quickly. Those without Internet or smartphones found people who did have them, and informal digital revolutionary cells formed to follow events in Cairo. Many expressed the same simple, powerful sentiment. "For the first time in my life," said Ayah El Said, an Egyptian economist working for Roubini Global Economics, "I am truly proud to be an Egyptian. But nobody was fooled by Obama," she added, referring to his eleventh-hour decision to back the demonstrators' demands for Mubarak's resignation. "After 30 years of paying the jailer, you can't expect the people who pulled off a prison break to say, 'Thanks, America.'"[2]

America, the Great and Powerful, meet Dorothy and the gang. Their walk down your Yellow Brick Road has been eventful, brimming with dangers just as you warned. But they no longer want your gifts. Hearts, brains, courage—they found them in the streets of Tunis, Cairo, and Manama. What's more, they saw you, Uncle Sam, behind the curtain, pulling levers and selling wings to the very monkeys that repressed them all these years. They no longer quite trust your talk about freedom and liberty; neither are they impressed by your Emerald City. At this point, you barely warrant a tweet. In the language of the revolution, in short, the message for America was something like this:

> @Sam. Go back to Kansas. We freed ourselves and don't need you telling us what to do (or pretending to care).—Egypt

The digitally fueled overthrows of two pro-American dictators in early 2011—first in Tunisia and, more dramatically, in Egypt—represent a tremendous comeuppance for the Great and Powerful Oz. They were not the first upheavals aided by the new social networking and Internet technologies sweeping the planet, and they will not be the last. Yet they marked the maturing of an important trend: nothing—not Gutenberg's Bible, Marconi's radio, nor the satellites enabled by Goddard's rockets—has empowered individual people like the mass availability of Internet-capable cell phones and laptops. The "smart" phone in particular, a relatively simple device, places the combined power of the printing press, broadcast television, radio, spy satellites, and all the world's libraries in the hands of the average people, all of it moving at incredible speed.

The resulting shift in political power from government to the masses has surprised even digital evangelists. Jared Cohen, the director of Google Ideas, the in-house think tank of the software giant, was running social media policy for the State Department's Policy Planning Staff when the Jasmine Revolution in Tunisia kicked off in early 2011. He says events across the region since have revised his view of the role technology can play in the overthrow of repressive regimes. Modern social networking technology, accessed through simple but widely available cell phones and computers, he says, "makes weak ties stronger. So in a place like Tunisia, where [former president Zine el-Abidine] Ben Ali was very repressive, individuals who otherwise would find it too risky to organize offline are able to use technology as an additional tactic. It's not a silver bullet, but it is an additional tool that allows them to build stronger ties."[3]

Consider the old model of organizing and propagating revolution. As recently as the late 1990s, back when "revolutions were televised," mobilizing thousands of people to oppose a repressive government involved months of furtive meetings, any one of which might be penetrated by the regime's security services and lead to sweeping arrests; the loss of jobs; or in the most brutal cases, jail, torture, and death. Even if you successfully brought demonstrators into the street, there was considerable risk that the protests would be crushed without the outside world ever knowing. Even today, large uprisings and demonstrations that occur in China's vast interior can take weeks or months to make the news. One has to assume that many over the years were simply crushed before coming to light.

To some extent, beginning in the late 1980s, the widespread adoption of satellite broadcasts by news networks changed this a bit, but only if the network had sophisticated equipment based in the country and access to the event in question. When CNN beamed back live images of the Tiananmen Square massacre in 1989 and the first Gulf War in 1991, it profoundly changed the way the public, governments, the military, and the media approached global crises. Satellite broadcasting (and the gutsy decision by CNN to ride out each event in a local hotel room) changed the relationship between media, government, and protester and made CNN the envy of its competitors. CNN's unique ability to show what was happening in real time transformed its journalists into the arbiters of international opinion in times of crisis. Washington says Saddam has fled Baghdad? What does CNN say? Saddam claims last night's raid killed civilians and destroyed a "baby milk factory?" What does CNN say? They didn't always get it right, but CNN—and later the BBC World Service, Al

Jazeera and others—changed the dynamics of international events. For those attempting to challenge a tyranny, it was essential that the images be seen via satellite.

Still, CNN and other broadcasters represented a single, unidirectional node: their cameras showed live images in real time, but the audience was still in passive spectator mode. Also, the networks still had to kowtow to authorities, lest they lose satellite uplinks or have their visas revoked. Ultimately, the world's governments and military commanders learned to manage the problem—throwing CNN and Al Jazeera out as soon as trouble started in some cases, jamming their signals, or, more subtly, insisting on "embedding journalists," as in the case of the US military in Iraq, a practice meant to provide some access while preventing them from roaming all over the battlefield.

Compare this approach to the avalanche of information that now quickly accompanies any major international event. Since roughly the start of the twenty-first century, major events—the 9/11 attacks, the 2004 South Asian tsunami, the railway bomb attacks in Madrid in 2004 and London in 2005—were all captured instantaneously in eyewitness video and text accounts that were rushed to the world via cell phone, Internet, and social networks. Every person with a phone becomes the world's witness, if not a journalist. From one node in the Gulf War, or a dozen in places where other major news outlets take to the field, the number of nodes now hits the millions. And unlike television, radio, and print reports, which still flow mostly toward the mass audience, filtered through editors and producers charged with ensuring the reliability of what they send, the new template elevates the "conversation" above the level of information. Viewers and readers now see the raw data as it streams in and can engage in conversation with those sending it, cheering them on or arguing against them. Only occasionally do the posters of these many nodes of information step back and consult a less breathless report from a traditional outlet before diving back into the fray.

Even before would-be revolutionaries applied these new capabilities, the cell phone made its mark thanks to people victimized by disasters, both man-made and natural. Cell phones raised the first unheeded warnings of the 9/11 hijackings, as terrified airline passengers reported flying below skyscraper level moments before meeting their fate. Once the attacks began, even though many cell phone networks went down due to the volume of calls, tens of thousands of images, videos, and text reports of the unfolding nightmare became instantly available, even if the means of harvesting it all had yet to be invented. The 2004 tsunami—perhaps the ultimate international demonstration of the cell phone effect before social networking sites joined in—indicated the extent to which the traditional vetting and production systems of both journalism and government intelligence agencies had been overtaken by technology. The dispersed nodes of hundreds of thousands of people proved adept at providing rich detail very quickly about events that overwhelmed the information-processing ability of even the biggest and best traditional outlets—the BBC, CNN, and the New York Times, for instance. All three quickly ran up the white flag, bowing to the new reality, and put their "citizen media" output front and center in their coverage.

Whatever hand-wringing this caused among journalists regarding their duty to provide editorial judgment, it was the right thing to do. From cell phones and laptops in disparate corners of the ten thousand square mile zone affected by the earthquake and tsunami flowed desperately important information, ranging from the conditions of remote villages and the damage caused by aftershocks to photographs of children who had been separated from their families. Quick-thinking bloggers harvested these nodes into a single blog, the *South-East Asia Earthquake and Tsunami Blog* (http://tsunamihelp.blogspot .com/), and eventually convinced Google to provide gratis a featured "ad word" that would bring it attention. "We realized that people were looking for information and there was not much out there," said Indian blogger Rohi Gupta, one of the organizers of the blog, in an interview with Online Journalism Review. "Our idea was to set up a clearinghouse for all the information that we were collecting."[4]

No government bureaucracy anywhere, let alone South Asia, could have provided as rich a source of intelligence on the disaster or as compelling a view into the tragedy. Neither could any media outlet. Steve Outing, a columnist for *Editor & Publisher*, an industry magazine, called it a "tipping point" for citizen media—news for digital democracy.[5] While many journalists still harbor deep reservations about the lack of fact-checking and editorial prioritization that "citizen journalism" entails, opposing it at this point would be like complaining about the earth's rotation around the sun. Adjusting to it makes a good deal more sense.

In instance after instance, technologies designed for daily communication or research have adapted to a new task—exposing the malfeasance and incompetence of governments and the increasing irrelevance of traditional media to the average person. In the past decade, this has proven true in natural disasters (Hurricane Katrina in 2005, the Sichuan earthquake in 2008, and the 2010 quakes in Chile and Haiti), at war (the hanging of Saddam, the brutalities of Abu Ghraib, the WikiLeaks video of a US army helicopter killing a Reuters cameraman), and in moments of revolution (Iran's suppressed Green Revolution of 2009, Ukraine's 2004 Orange Revolution, the Tulip Revolution in repressive Kyrgyzstan in 2005 and its follow-up in 2009, and the so-called Twitter Revolution in Moldova in 2009). Most relevant was the seminal uprising in Tunisia in December 2010, which followed the WikiLeaks release of secret US diplomatic cables barely a month before that detailed the appalling extent of official corruption in Tunisia's dictatorial regime.

These events occurred in vastly different countries with a variety of political and economic systems ranging from free to dictatorial. Yet none of these governments could play by the old rules, leveraging access to power or remote disaster zones to "manage the story." The indomitable power of information straight from a source has undone centuries of government news management (or, in some cases, censorship) capabilities.

TAKING IT TO THE STREETS

While the uprisings and crackdowns continue to flare in the Middle East, an earlier technology-fueled uprising, in the post-Soviet Balkan nation of Moldova, provides important lessons on how average people who might never, under normal circumstances, risk life and limb in antigovernment protests are inspired and incentivized by social networks.

Dana Muntean was a 19-year-old university freshman in Moldova's capital, Chisinau, when the governing Moldovan Communist Party announced it had overwhelmingly won the April 2009 parliamentary elections in spite of polls showing it with only tepid support. "After the results were announced, I was in my class...no one wanted to talk, everyone was thinking, 'What the hell?' and saying 'I am leaving this country!'" After class, she and several classmates checked their Facebook accounts. "We saw all these messages, and by 6 pm we had made our way to the main square, armed with candles, to show the communists their time was past."[6]

What international media soon dubbed "the Twitter Revolution" had begun, but at the time it seemed like a novelty, not the start of a trend. The deeper global implications were lost on both the international media and the young Moldovans who pressed their case and ultimately forced a recount.

"Looking back, I'm very proud today that Moldovans were the first to use social media this way," Muntean says. "I think Iran, and Tunisia and Egypt, they all learned from us."[7]

DIGITAL TRUMPS ANALOG DEMOCRACY

Moldova's digital dissenters failed to dislodge their government, and plenty of other movements had previously used text messaging to rally troops and coordinate responses, including anti-Bush protesters during the 2004 presidential nominating convention in New York and demonstrators protesting the policies of Spain's conservative government immediately after the Madrid bombings in 2004.

But developments between 2004 and 2009 added a new sophistication to these techniques. Sharing services like Flickr and the photo-uploading capabilities of Facebook meant images and videos of events could be broadcast to a broad, self-selected audience nearly instantaneously. Owing to the quality of phone cameras, the duration of modern battery charges, and the new ubiquitous existence of the phones themselves, governments—particularly resource-poor ones like Moldova's—were powerless to control the conversation.

If Moldova set the example, it was Iran and Syria that proved the rule: even in the face of violence, arrests, and a sophisticated state security apparatus, Iran's Green revolutionaries in the summer of 2009 and Syrians facing down tanks and infantry got their message out to the world. Syria's regime, unaccustomed to having its lies disproven so decisively by hard video evidence, quickly discredited itself—so badly that it lost its most important ally, Turkey, and even the Arab League, with its history of moral relativism, suspended Syria's membership. In 2009, millions viewed, via YouTube, the death of an unarmed young woman, Neda Agha-Soltan, who was shot in the chest by Iran's fanatical Basij militia. Many millions more saw other atrocities committed against peaceful protesters. While Iran cracked down hard and averted regime collapse, it teetered very close to the edge, and the fissures that opened between various factions in the regime may yet prove its undoing. At the very least, the publicity emboldened prodemocracy activists elsewhere and badly undercut Iran's campaign to portray itself as a force for liberating other Muslims from their governments. It also foreshadowed the dilemmas to come for the United States, which twisted and turned before denouncing Tehran's crackdown, worried about the administration's policy priority of engaging Iran in productive talks on its nuclear weapons program.

As Iran demonstrated—and uprisings against similarly violent regimes in Syria, Libya, and Yemen showed two years later—social media cannot control events; rather, as Ramy Nagy said, it accelerates them. Clearly, media of all kinds—principally Al Jazeera's satellite broadcasts, but also radio and print outlets—spread word of the Tunisian uprising and the Egyptian revolution that followed, stoking the courage of angry Arab citizens elsewhere who longed to claim their share of human dignity. Media hype about Twitter or Facebook "revolutions" may overstate the role of technology, as the Google's Cohen and others, including Facebook founder Mark Zuckerberg, have suggested. Yet the extent to which technology has undermined a government's ability to control its citizens cannot be overstated. As a historical milestone, the digital revolution is profound. Even World War I, which spelled doom for absolute monarchies from Germany to Russia to the Ottoman Empire, did less to empower average citizens than Nokia, Motorola, Blackberry, and Apple did—not to mention Facebook, Twitter, Google, and the legions of young activists determined to put all that power to use. After all, those early twentieth-century monarchies simply gave way to new elites—industrialists, military men, and left-wing ideologues, most of whom employed the same levers to control their populations as their royal predecessors: police forces, censorship, assassinations of troublemakers, bans on political gatherings, and when useful, beatings, torture, and death.

Even shutting down the Internet, which the security services in Syria, Libya, and Egypt all tried at various stages of those uprisings, cannot prevent determined cyberdissidents from organizing. In Libya, rebels used satellite telephones to upload videos of violence by Qaddafi's government against protesters. In Egypt, software developers managed to cobble together an alternative Internet—a peer-to-peer network that bypassed the state-controlled one—when the regime began blocking access. And from China to Belarus to Cuba, dissidents have used updated versions of time-tested samizdat methods developed to smuggle prodemocracy writings out from behind the Iron Curtain, downloading videos, images, and text onto tiny USB flash drives and mailing them or smuggling them abroad. Syrians smuggled USB drives across the northern border to Turkey and, thanks to robust connections with relatively free Lebanon, kept a steady flow of images and information streaming into cyberspace even through the darkest moments of the Assad regime's crackdown. With the US government and other public and private entities funding research into ways of keeping such dissidents just ahead of the censors, the information "arms race" between regimes and their subjects so far appears to give a lopsided advantage to the people.

Even in China, where the state meticulously censors websites and blocks foreign web domains in order to keep a tight lid on topics like Tibetan independence, challenges to the Communist Party, and environmental disasters, the state has lost several recent battles. When the state reacted to the derailing of a high-speed train in the summer of 2011 by censoring coverage and actually burying entire train cars to cover up the evidence of shoddy construction, the social network Sina Weibo, set up by China's government as a controllable alternative to microblogging sites like Twitter and Facebook, exploded with outrage. The government quaked as citizens engaged in a full-throated denunciation of mind-control techniques, along with accusations of lies and corruption in the high-speed rail network, one of China's showcase technology projects. This flexing of microblog muscles forced China's Ministry of Railways into a rare apology, and the level of anger directed at China's senior leader, Premier Wen Jiabao, was unprecedented. Conservatives in the ruling communist party demanded censorship of the microblogs, and voices within Sina Weibo and its main rival, Qzone, suddenly began agitating for an end to anonymous posting—the main thing allowing frank conversation about politics on the platforms. These "voices" were shouted down, branded state agents. Said one response on Sina Weibo: "Let's crowd around the rapist who issues appeals against sex before marriage."[8] As of this writing, the microblogs continue to grow both in size and influence, as do China's Facebook equivalents, Kaixen and Renren.

BIG BROTHER'S LOST LEVERAGE

For America, on one level, this represents an enormous victory. About half the world's population—some five billion people—possess either a cell phone or a computer with some form of social networking capability or access to the Internet, according to the OpenNet Initiative, a nonprofit project devoted to helping users in repressive countries circumvent government efforts to control Internet usage. Facebook, along with Twitter and blogging, texts and cell phones, satellite news broadcasts and the Internet itself, began in America. The democratization of politics that each of these technologies and software innovations has unleashed is truly a Jeffersonian moment—a world free to seek life, liberty, and the pursuit of happiness.

From my own experience in the technologies of a previous restive age—the 1989 revolutions in Eastern Europe—I know the potential benefits that might flow to the United States if it can harvest due credit from today's information revolution. Listeners in the former Soviet bloc in Eastern Europe and the USSR itself paid close attention to outlawed foreign broadcasters like the BBC World Service, Voice of America, or Radio Free Europe/Radio Liberty, where I worked at the time. In societies that long ago lost faith in their own government-run media, a looming international crisis or rumors of unrest at home sparked a stampede away from local sources to the crackling shortwave broadcasts of the West. People in the millions risked very real consequences—jail and, in some places, worse—to hear uncensored reports of the events shaping their lives. How else would a young democracy activist in Hungary or Bulgaria follow the groundbreaking work of Poland's Solidarity movement? If state media mentioned such a development at all, it was in the language of propaganda, labeling the protestors "dupes of the West" or "class criminals." Throughout this period, in Berlin, Warsaw, Prague, Bucharest, and other places, the awareness that the outside world knew and cared about acts of popular resistance in these police states sustained the morale of those inside.

"People will surprise you," said Nick Kaltchev, a prominent Bulgarian broadcaster at Radio Free Europe/Radio Liberty from the 1970s until his retirement in 1997. "I know how Americans viewed people behind the Iron Curtain before the Wall fell—robots, can't think for themselves. But they could, and they did. And when they got an opening, even after 45 years of communism, they seized it. They knew that America was not perfect, but because the news they heard from America admitted as much, it gave you great credibility."[9]

Yet the United States, by virtue of the fact that it has more interest than most in maintaining the current status quo, will struggle with the aspirations its creative side has unleashed this time around. Twenty-three years after the Wall fell, the Arab world's Jasmine Revolutions will be a good deal harder for the United States to co-opt. Unlike the Cold War, which pivoted on an existential ideological conflict between democratic capitalism and repressive communism, the currents of opinion in the Middle East vary enormously, and US policy there has been as cynical as any it has ever put forward. If hard-core

Polish nationalists or Russian democracy activists resented the fact that the United States allied itself with Stalin during World War II, they at least recognized the practicality of American motives: defeating Hitler's Germany. But Arabs take a far less forgiving view of US motives in their region. At best, Arab opinion regards the United States as naïve in policy and captive to a powerful Israeli lobby in Washington. More commonly, however, Arabs view the United States as a racist, Machiavellian giant thirsting after the Arab world's petroleum resources and bent on thwarting the efforts of Islamic Arab culture from taking its rightful place in the world. This, in short, is the "Great Satan" cited so often by Ayatollah Khomeini, the driving force behind Iran's Islamic revolution in 1979.

Some—including me—had hoped that a regime change in Washington in 2008 might provide an opening to address these misconceptions. But the changeover from George W. Bush to Barack Obama, which struck many Americans as profound and even historic, barely registers in the Islamic world, a region where the most palpable results were an increase in troops in Afghanistan and a stepping up of the use of drones to seek out terrorists hiding in the Pakistani tribal lands. And the lack of progress, after decades of talks, on the Israeli-Palestinian front has soured the well considerably. Indeed, a poll by the venerable Pew Global Attitudes Project in the spring of 2011 indicates that, well into the Obama presidency, American policy is seen as a cause of, rather than a solution to, the region's problems. "In key Arab nations and in other predominantly Muslim countries, views of the U.S. remain negative, as they have been for nearly a decade," the Pew report concluded. "Indeed, in Jordan, Turkey and Pakistan, views are even more negative than they were one year ago."[10]

Americans, accustomed to living at the top of the food chain, have traditionally shrugged off such attitudes. Arab views, in particular, are dismissed as expressions of resentment by a culture seeking to blame its own failings on others, particularly the United States and Israel. In historical terms, the Arabs strike many Americans as "the culture that peaked in high school," as one waggish friend of mine once put it. Yet to believe such a generalization repeats the key mistake of the Cold War—in effect, lumping Egyptians, Syrians, Moroccans, and Saudis together the way America once generalized about the Warsaw Pact. As Arab populations emerge from the rocks their dictators kept them under, they force the United States to reassess. Americans find good television irresistible, and very few live events since the Wall came down made for more compelling video from abroad than the spectacle of a people-powered, social-networked, nonviolent revolution in Cairo's Tahrir Square.

In spite of the "Made in America" labels on Facebook, Twitter, and other accelerant technologies, or the fact that many Egyptians and Tunisians looked to the US civil rights movement and its constitutional guarantees as a model, a generation of cynical, self-interested US policy in the Middle East ensures that the United States itself gets little credit. The technology revolution has, indeed, empowered the weak, and one of the powers they chose to exercise immediately was to snub the hegemon. Secretary of State Hillary Clinton, the first high-level American official to visit Egypt after Mubarak's ouster, got the cold shoulder from Egyptian youth movement leaders, who posted on their powerful Facebook page that their refusal was "based on her negative position from the beginning of the revolution and the position of the U.S. administration in the Middle East."[11] The days when American diplomats could ignore popular sentiment and cut deals with a detached, autocratic elite are numbered. In this new, networked age, the views of common people matter nearly as much as those of their government. Strange as it may sound to the citizens of a country that has spent billions proselytizing democracy, this will turn out to be a nightmare for America.

CARRYING THE TORCH

At the base of this dilemma is the fact that the America that emerged from World War II inherited the British Empire's job of keeping global trade routes open and mustering coalitions to face down challenges to capitalism or illegal invasions. In the US interpretation, this meant guaranteeing "stability" for markets, diplomats, and allies even if that meant enormous disruption, repression, and instability for the local inhabitants. As such, deep down, postwar America, while opposed to colonialism of the European variety, had a rather dubious interest in the spread of democracy across the planet. In Europe, Japan, and newly independent European colonies around the world, democracy was the preferred solution. But in the old Third World, democracy got one shot. If democracy failed to take root quickly and easily, or flirted with state socialist solutions to the crushing poverty most suffered from, the dynamics of the Cold War and the necessities of global capitalism conspired to instill in the United States a nearly infinite tolerance for coups and the autocrats they empowered, even if they were murderous (like Argentina's military junta and

Haiti's Duvalier family) or religious fanatics (as in Saudi Arabia).[12] This moral ambiguity, encapsulated in the old Cold War saying, "He's a bastard, but he's our bastard," fell away in many regions after 1989. But it persists to this day in some nasty corners of the planet—and the Middle East is arguably the nastiest of all.

Whether Americans like it or not, much of what these newly freed people want to change is the world America itself fashioned over the past 70 years. The evidence of the terribly misguided assumptions behind US policies can be read all over the Arabic-language Internet today. In a world without "liberation technology," as some have dubbed it, the reimposition of a US-enforced stability based on "bastards" like Mubarak or Yemen's longtime President Ali Abdullah Saleh might be possible. Certainly, Israel would prefer the devil it knows, even a bloodthirsty one like Syria's President Bashar al-Assad, to the devil it does not know. Europe's governments, too, for economic purposes, might be tempted to conspire with Russian, Chinese, and other interests to keep governments that have granted oil exploration rights to their national monopolies in power.

But the world expects as much of second-tier powers. The United States, through its own rhetoric, has raised the bar of expectations. For the Obama administration, the Arab Spring, as the movements across the region came to be called, created a "whack-a-mole" problem—as soon as US policy was adjusted to rationalize one challenge (Tunisia), a new one emerged (Egypt) followed by a third (Libya) and a fourth, fifth, and sixth (Bahrain, Yemen, Syria), each one raising the stakes and stretching the fabric of rhetorical logic to the breaking point. Washington has responded by drawing very clear, quite ignoble lines when it comes to backing popular uprisings. Washington was only too happy to pile on against the distasteful, violent Qaddafi (as long as the French and British agreed to lead the police action) but was slow to criticize Syria's vicious crackdown on its own restive population due to Israel's fear of unrest on its borders and Syria's strategic position as a known, if inert, quantity in Arab-Israeli peace diplomacy. More importantly, Washington remained almost silent when Saudi Arabia and its Gulf emirate allies sent tanks to suppress an uprising against the Sunni minority monarchy, which rules over the largely Shia island of Bahrain. These moves, described by administration officials in off-the-record comments as hard-headed realism or realpolitik, in fact suggest something else: a lingering, wistful longing for the certainties of what might be called the pre-Jasmine world, a world that no longer exists. To put a technological spin on it, Washington still lives in a pre-Facebook world. These inconsistencies only reinforce Arab impressions of moral relativism in Washington and, on a deeper level, reveal a superpower reacting opportunistically, with no clear strategy, to events it can no longer hope to control.

BEYOND THE SANDS

The growing irrelevance of the United States cannot be pinned on technology alone, of course. Missteps in Iraq and the global financial crisis play a large role. But technology greases the skids, making it very difficult to reverse the decline of America's reputation for omnipotence. Consider US policy toward China and, in particular, its human rights record. This is an area one might have expected would get serious attention in an Obama presidency. From the start, however, the administration, burdened as it was with two wars and an economic crisis, has paid little more than lip service to human rights. With economic ties now the foremost concern in US-China relations and worries about the possibility of armed conflict never far behind, China's treatment of its own citizens has fallen down the agenda. Today, Washington rarely criticizes China's crackdowns, whether aimed at prodemocracy dissident bloggers or ethnic minorities whose grievances have burst into violence regularly of late, including Tibet in 2008, Muslims in Xinjiang in 2009, and ethnic Mongols in Inner Mongolia in 2011. Hillary Clinton gave voice to this new reality on her first visit to Beijing as secretary of state in 2009, saying that while she would bring up issues like Tibet and jailed dissidents, "our pressing on those issues can't interfere on the global economic crisis, the global climate change crisis and the security crisis."[13]

This is a source of deep unhappiness in the human rights community, where groups like Amnesty International, Freedom House, and Human Rights Watch (full disclosure: I serve on HRW's communications advisory board) are disappointed at the second-tier treatment human rights have received during Obama's presidency. Yet the technology story offers a ray of hope. While American rhetorical support and diplomatic pressure remain important, they are no longer the only means of pressuring recalcitrant tyrants. Indeed, from China to Saudi Arabia to Cuba, these regimes have shown far more fear of bloggers and shadowy social networks than any pronouncement from Washington.[14] Not long from now, political dissidents may find themselves increasingly abandoned by the traditional government diplomatic pressure they courted in the past. Yet technology may counter this by bringing their ability to defy, shame, and organize against central government to an all-time high, and empowering the NGOs that support their right to speak freely, too.

The risks remain, of course, for the dissident. China still locks up people who challenge the political monopoly of the Communist Party, and Cuba tolerates virtually no serious criticism of its dysfunctional police state. In the best-case scenario, the United States and other nations that traditionally lend at least moral support to such dissent would continue to do so, occasionally acting with tangible punishments in the case of egregious abuses. But authoritarian states will strive to adapt to these new challenges, too. Already, there is plenty of evidence that such efforts are regarded as the most important and serious challenges to one-party rule in China, Cuba, Iran, Saudi Arabia, and Uzbekistan, and as a challenge to the monopoly on information held by dominant political parties in slightly less repressive societies like Russia or Venezuela. Even in Britain, during a spate of urban rioting in the summer of 2011, police and some members of parliament asked Twitter and Facebook to "black out" local networks that authorities felt were helping spread violence from one city to another.

Thankfully, Twitter and Facebook can reject such nonsense in free societies. But despots will not take this sitting down. Besides enforcing punitive and deterrent measures like jail and internal exile, all such governments work feverishly to filter and censor Internet sites and other communication networks accessible from their territory.

"The Chinese government has already made clear its intention to declare sovereignty over an Internet of its own. Other authoritarian states have every incentive to follow its lead," writes Ian Bremmer, president of the political risk consultancy Eurasia Group.[15]

Bremmer's right, and all too often, American and other Western technology companies seeking to protect their access to lucrative high-growth markets like China or Russia have provided the filtering software that enables these regimes to achieve their goals. Yet attempting to halt the free flow of technology is a losing game. Homegrown ingenuity and assistance from nonprofits in the free world continue to defeat filters, though they are still effective at keeping less ambitious people—essentially, the masses—from accessing censored information or foreign websites. Yet in the lengths China's thin-skinned ruling party goes to prevent free speech—it banned the term *jasmine* from Chinese search engines in 2011 and even removed the ubiquitous flower from market stalls—one can see how much a humble tweet can spook even a dragon. They cannot hope to defeat technology indefinitely. Their loss will be civilization's gain.

THE OTHER SIDE OF THE COIN

Degrading the control mechanisms of a dictatorship is the easy part. In coming years, democratic societies, most of all the United States, will also struggle in this new environment. For as in America itself, where everything from the Socialist Workers Party to the Aryan Nations to illegal groups trading child pornography have popped up online, the democratization of technology will give voice not only to altruistic young Egyptian students and Chilean mothers angry at shoddy construction in an earthquake zone, but also to vehemently anti-American terrorist organizations like Al Qaeda or nationalists and racists pressing each and every complaint against their enemies.

For the United States, which has already spent tens of millions monitoring Al Qaeda chat rooms and other places where militant Islamists gather to fulminate against the Great Satan, the first real damage to its national agenda came instead from an Australian expat named Julian Assange and his now-famous disruptive technology, WikiLeaks. In April 2010, Assange released secretly obtained gun camera footage from a US Army Apache helicopter in Iraq as it gunned down a Reuters news agency videographer under circumstances that led many viewers to conclude it was deliberate. Having earned the ire of the US military, WikiLeaks followed up in July with over forty thousand pages it dubbed the "Afghan War Diary," almost all of which had previously been classified. In October came four hundred thousand classified US military documents on the Iraq War, followed the next month by a similarly huge tranche of secret US State Department diplomatic cables.

Much of what WikiLeaks released during this period allegedly came from a single source: a disgruntled Iraq War veteran private in the US Army named Bradley Manning. As a member of the US military, Manning will be severely punished if his alleged decision to leak tens of thousands of classified documents is proven. His mistreatment before trial—unusually harsh confinement conditions—led the State Department spokesman P. J. Crowley, a veteran Washington flack, to resign in protest. Charges against him include treason, a capital offense technically punishable by the death penalty, although prosecutors have said they will not seek it.

Whatever the ethics concerning Manning's fate, and whatever sentiments motivated him to violate his oath as a soldier, military justice will inevitably seek to make an example of him. The larger question for the US legal system, and indeed for the United States, is what to make of WikiLeaks. Is it an "enemy"? Charges against Manning refer to it as an "unauthorized source," rather than a foreign power or enemy. Is it a legitimate journalistic organization, as its supporters insist, and if so, where does one mail the subpoena? (Where, for that matter, does the US Air Force send its Predator drone?) The "stateless" nature of the organization, founded in 2006 by Assange but staffed by volunteers from all over the world, including the United States, adds to the dilemma. Laws governing the publication of classified information remain tremendously vague, though clearly the government has decided to raise the stakes for those who leak it. In addition to Manning's treatment, the Obama administration's recent use of the 1917 Espionage Act to pursue charges against more conventional leakers—including a former National Security Agency whistle-blower, Thomas Drake, who told the New York Times in 2009 about the Bush administration's illegal wiretapping of American telephone communications—make this clear. Drake ultimately pleaded guilty to a far lesser charge in exchange for having espionage accusations dropped.[16]

But WikiLeaks' "activism," if that is the right term, has exposed an even larger gray area regarding the nature of leaking and WikiLeaks' stateless status. "Appealing to national traditions of fair play in the conduct of news reporting misunderstands what Wikileaks is about: the release of information without regard for national interest," wrote Jay Rosen, a New York University journalism professor. "In media history up to now, the press is free to report on what the powerful wish to keep secret because the laws of a given nation protect it. But Wikileaks is able to report on what the powerful wish to keep secret because the logic of the Internet permits it. This is new. Just as the Internet has no terrestrial address or central office, neither does Wikileaks."[17]

It has also upset long-held beliefs, both in media and government, about the constitutional protections "the press" enjoys in the United States. Most legal scholars, at least until recently, argued that publishers were virtually immune from prosecution or prior restraint by government as long as the information involved was not obtained illegally. This was always a hazy line, and while the 1971 Pentagon Papers case (*New York Times v. United States*) suggested a very high standard for the government—"Only a free and unrestrained press can effectively expose deception in government," wrote Justice

Hugo Black, denying the Nixon administration's desire to halt publication of the secret Vietnam War history—others have pointed out that the laws that might have been used to prosecute the leaker, a former National Security Council aide named Daniel Ellsberg, were never tested.[18] The received wisdom in the media—that a leaker acting on conscience is blameless and a publisher is protected by the First Amendment—is flawed, according to Gabriel Schoenfeld, a scholar and national security expert at the Hudson Institute. The Nixon administration, he notes, enmeshed in its own ultimately fatal Watergate legal wrangling, chose not to prosecute Ellsberg or the New York Times under espionage statutes for its own reasons.[19] Fast forward four decades, and it appears that the US government, this time headed by a Democrat and professed advocate of government openness, might revisit that strategy.

Clay Shirky, a leading thinker on the evolution of the media, Internet, and law, believes a kind of gentlemen's agreement, rather than a precedent, emerged after the Pentagon Papers episode. That deal, he argues, is now obsolete.

> Sometimes a bargain is so robust it lasts for centuries, as with trial by jury, but sometimes it is so much a product of its time that it does not survive the passing of its era. I think that this latter fate has befallen our old balance between secrets and leaks. This does not mean that the Pentagon Papers precedent shouldn't free Wiki Leaks from prosecution, but it does mean the old rules will not produce the old outcomes....Like the music industry, the government is witnessing the million-fold expansion of edge points capable of acting on their own, without needing to ask anyone for help or permission, and, like the music industry, they are looking at various strategies for adding control at intermediary points that were left alone under the old model.[20]

Disruptive activism of this kind on the Internet is not entirely new. Starting in the 1990s, ideologically minded hackers began attacking websites and even penetrating the databases of governments and major corporations, including US agencies like the CIA, FBI, National Security Agency, and the US government's nuclear laboratories. In 1998, my msnbc.com colleague Brock Meeks and I were contacted by shadowy representatives of a group called AntiOnline, which claimed to have hacked into the database of India's primary nuclear weapons laboratory.[21] It sounded unlikely, yet India confirmed the security breach, and while the extent of the data theft remains secret, it was an early indication of the potential impact smart individuals, be they activists or terrorists, could have on careless government bureaucracies.

Hacks and security violations continued in the intervening years—some, no doubt, the work of foreign intelligence agencies in China, Russia, Iran, and elsewhere. The United States dropped all pretense in late 2011 when a report to Congress by the US intelligence community accused China and Russia of hacking into US government networks and private-sector corporate and research computer systems. In an unusual step suggesting a deliberate decision to embarrass the two nations, the report was released publicly and included detailed accounts of infiltration efforts and methodology. While the report also noted that "friendly" nations, too, engage in some of this behavior, "Chinese actors are the world's most active and persistent perpetrators of economic espionage [and] "Russia's intelligence services are conducting a range of activities to collect economic information and technology from U.S. targets."[22]

This isn't news, of course, just confirmation of what most who follows these issues already knew. Russian hackers almost certainly hacked into Estonia's government servers in a dispute over a Russian military memorial. The extent of Chinese and Russian efforts to penetrate sensitive US databases, both corporate and government, suggested considerable resources devoted to the efforts, including reports that both hacked deep into servers that control the US national power grid.[23] Clearly, the ability to undermine the US economy by dumping dollars isn't enough: they want to be able to turn off the lights, too, after doomsday is over. China, which denied the public accusation, embarrassingly confirmed much of the activity to its own media in a television program aired by China Central Television in August 2011, including the capability of planting "data bombs" inside US government computers.[24] Just before stepping down as the head of cybersecurity at the Pentagon a few months earlier, William Lynn III, a US deputy defense secretary, revealed that over twenty-four thousand classified documents had been lost in a single March 2011 intrusion.[25]

Americans need not hyperventilate over such reports, however. American cyberwarriors—based both in the intelligence agencies and the military—are unrivaled in the scope of their activities. William Arkin, an expert on US intelligence efforts and digital warfare, says foreign governments probably feel even more embattled. "Any progress China or Russia has made to map US digital infrastructure is just a game of catch-up," he says. "We've been mapping their electronic DNA for years."[26] In other words, to paraphrase Carl von Clausewitz, the great Prussian military theorist, the cyberwarfare activities of governments are just war by other means and, in the course of human history, hardly surprising. Invent a new technology, and the military will adapt and hone and improve it into a weapon within a generation.

Perhaps more notable is the proliferation of hackers pursuing political agenda outside the employment of governments or even stateless political movements like Al Qaeda or Greenpeace. These digital activists, like Assange, tend to hold up complete transparency as an ultimate good, a debatable proposition in a world where nuclear secrets, or simply the financial information of average individuals, are held in countless databases. But, short of dispatching Navy SEALs to silence them, the United States may have to learn to live in a world where secrets are regularly revealed, where dishonorable motives or cynical calculations are exposed for what they are. This might not be all bad.

CELL CULTURE

Like the other adjustments the United States must make, rethinking its approach to global information will not be easy. In many ways, American intelligence agencies, political communications, and global public diplomacy outlets, like the Voice of America and federal websites, still bear the unmistakable imprint of the Cold War. "If it's not broken, don't fix it" sufficed for a few decades. But events as far back as the 1990s should have suggested that US thinking on this front is profoundly broken.

While the global media has showered attention on the potential for the digital disruption of dictatorships since the Arab Spring began, as far back as 1989 shortwave and ham radio broadcasts, samizdat newspapers, and other methods began wrestling control of information from central governments in Eastern Europe and the former Soviet Union. During the 1990s, the advent of satellite television networks and e-mail accelerated the process. In April 1999, when NATO began a bombing campaign to dislodge Serbian troops from the province of Kosovo, State Department spokesman James Rubin claimed that the Serbs had rounded up thousands of men in a football stadium in the Kosovo capital, Pristina, in what appeared to be a prelude to executions. Within minutes, an e-mail arrived in my msnbc.com in-box from Pristina with a time-stamped photo of that soccer stadium—empty. The information wasn't confirmable, but it was enough to prompt questions about the State Department's sources (and ultimately, a retraction from Rubin). Later in the conflict, a Pentagon spokesman denied that bombs had fallen in a residential area of Belgrade, the Serbian capital. Again, an e-mailed photograph—this from an activist working against the Serb government of Slobodan Milosevic—arrived within minutes, showing a bomb crater in the yard behind the photographer's building. Two episodes within a few weeks showed that it would no longer be enough for government spokespersons to pronounce on things. We would need to directly engage people on both sides of any issue.

The challenge for the United States is to embrace this wave of democratization without sowing anarchy or undermining its legitimate interests and those of its allies. This will require Washington to begin conversations with a much broader range of people overseas—not just the elites who happen to be in power or opponents amenable to American goals. It will also mean rethinking America's own overseas information strategies—Voice of America, Radio Free Europe/Radio Liberty, and particularly the misguided US-funded Alhurra network in Arabic. Such "top-down" organizations, even when maintaining high standards of journalism, simply have limited credibility in a world of social media. The hundreds of millions of dollars spent on their prodemocracy missions will pale next to the far less expensive efforts of individuals like Wael Ghonim, the Egyptian Google executive whose Facebook page helped organize the overthrow of Mubarak.

A final note: the time will come when these despots and terrorist groups learn to more effectively harness these technologies for their own purposes. Right now, Al Qaeda, for instance, remains stuck in the "broadcast" world—releasing crude propaganda videos but showing little ability to profit from new technologies that, by their very nature, fly in the face of its centralized, undemocratic doctrine. In fact, reliance on this analog technique turned out to be the Achilles's Heel that led a US Navy SEAL team to Osama bin Laden's villa in 2011; intelligence agents traced a suspect courier who, among other jobs, ferried the infamous Bin Laden videotapes out to Al Jazeera.

Al Qaeda and other groups will internalize this failing, as will state security forces inside tyrannical regimes. Among the surprises of the Egyptian uprising, given the size and funding of Mubarak's security apparatus, was the fact that so little disinformation about protesters appeared to be inserted into cyberspace. Egypt's security services showed a complete inability to use Twitter, Facebook, or text messaging to exploit the many fears of the country's eighty million people. It is worrisome to consider the havoc a few well-placed posts by such moles might have wreaked as events built to a crescendo in Cairo. A savvy cyberintel unit might have, say, donned the mantle of a protester online and boasted about beheadings of Muslim policemen by the Coptic minority, or the desecration of the Koran by young secularists behind the uprising. Luckily, Mubarak's goons stuck to camels and truncheons. But you can be sure that Iran's Revolutionary Guards, China's police, and others have taken the lesson. Next time may be different.

Indeed, post-Mubarak, one of the first things Egypt's military did was create a Facebook page.

"When you watch the television news and see the spokesperson make a statement, it gets lost in memory and what is recollected is the different news sources' commentary about these statements with select 'quotes' to make a point," said Nagy, the Egyptian Internet entrepreneur. "This is ultimately what creates the damaging 'he said / she said' in politics. By having direct open channels between regimes and their people in a way that is documented and available to share, it makes the regimes a lot more human, approachable, and believable, but it also makes them accountable."[27]

Dictatorships, which by their nature maniacally seek to control the very forces that produce innovation, should be doomed to remain permanently behind the technology curve. Happily, that does not have to be the fate of the United States, the nation that hatched these technologies and has the most to gain in the long run from their widespread adoption. That the old levers of American dominance will begin to fail in the face of this digital onslaught is all the more reason for the United States to embrace the new digital reality. It would be wrong for Americans to think, after 40 years of helping prop up dictatorships all over the Middle East, that Arabs will shower us with thanks for our last-minute decision to throw Mubarak or Qaddafi under the bus. But programs like the State Department's nascent "suitcase Internet" project can, in the long run, do more than change regimes: they can change minds.

CHAPTER 5

IN THE MIDDLE EAST, THE WRITING IS ON THE WALL

America, most of its citizens would quickly tell you, is not an empire. "Some nations achieve greatness, the United States had greatness thrust upon it,"[1] wrote the historian Ernest May in 1961, four decades before he served as a senior advisor to the 9/11 Commission. For many, May's neat formulation squared an uncomfortable contradiction: the United States, born of a revolution against imperial tyranny in 1776, had by the height of the Cold War stationed troops and warships in every corner of the planet, and its military, intelligence, and diplomatic institutions were constantly in overdrive. It was, admittedly, a "reluctant empire"—the recklessness of European and Japanese behavior in the twentieth century, and then the aggressive decision by the Soviet Union to tacitly absorb Eastern Europe into its empire after World War II, made leaving the world to its own devices virtually impossible. Mainstream political thought in the United States still held that American foreign and economic policy aimed to liberate, not colonize. Thus, if some nations had come to depend on Washington for protection or financial aid, history had shown that failing to provide it—within reason—would only cost more American blood down the road.

But never was this mid-twentieth-century formulation less convincing than when applied to the Middle East. To be sure, the United States supported tyrants everywhere in the name of anticommunism during the Cold War, and even today, it makes common cause with repressive regimes in places like Ethiopia, Vietnam, and Kazakhstan when its strategic interests are at stake. But the end of the Cold War eradicated that practice in most of the world. In the Middle East, however, the collapse of Washington's anti-Soviet excuse changed nothing. Aid and weapons sales to Egypt, Algeria, Morocco, Yemen, Saudi Arabia, Jordan, and other repressive governments continued unabated after 1989, with few strings attached. This did not go unnoticed by those living under the thumbs of US-backed regimes. Aid to Israel increased, too, and while attempting to broker a settlement to the conflict over the Holy Land, Washington continued to shield Israel from censure at the United Nations (UN) with its Security Council veto. Washington also refused to apply determined diplomatic pressure even when peace talks reached the final, conclusive stages. In effect, the United States created an Israeli veto that hangs over all such efforts, resulting in a long, bloody stalemate. This has been a boon to Israeli settlers and US weapons contractors, and a useful distraction for Arab dictators from their own corrupt failings, but it has also been disastrous for the world at large.

CONFRONTING THE *E* WORD

America, the power that has called the shots in the Middle East for decades, must like it that way. You don't need a PhD in international affairs to see the advantages.

"Three decades ago, the radical left used the term 'American empire' as an epithet," wrote Joseph Nye, an author, Harvard professor, and former assistant secretary of defense under Clinton. "Now that same term has come out of the closet: analysts on both the left and right now use it to explain—if not guide—American foreign policy."[2]

In the Middle East, this reality is stark. While American military and intelligence activity diminished everywhere else after the Cold War, in the Middle East it expanded exponentially—roughly doubling during the 1990s and then exploding in the early 2000s (see figure 5.1). In 1989, the US military's "footprint" in the Middle East was confined to a US Navy base in Bahrain, a NATO air wing in Turkey oriented toward the USSR, and a 750-man contingent of US Army peacekeepers in Egypt's Sinai Peninsula, a legacy of the 1979 Camp David accords. Then, after the Gulf War, a network of new air bases and supply

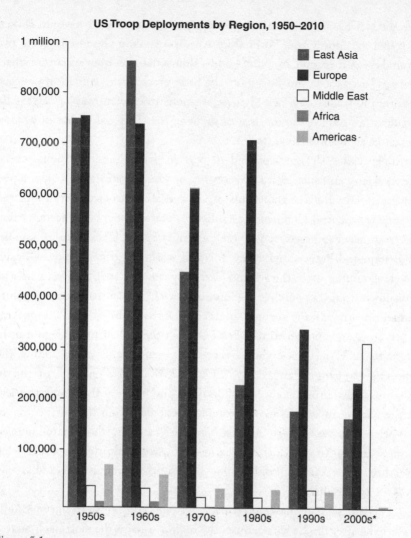

Figure 5.1
Source: GlobalSecurity.org, Where Are the Legions? http://www.globalsecurity.org/military
/ops/global-deployments.htm; Tim Kane, Troop Deployment Dataset, 1950–2005, The
Heritage Foundation, http://www.heritage.org/Research/NationalSecurity/troopsdb.cfm

depots sprang up around the Persian Gulf, along with new army facilities in
Saudi Arabia, Kuwait, and Djibouti. The buildup, all ostensibly to protect the
Gulf's oil sheikhdoms from Saddam Hussein's Iraq, continued throughout the
decade as "pre-positioned" ammunition dumps were established in Oman and
Kuwait, US air and ground bases expanded in Saudi Arabia, and the US Navy
presence in Bahrain upgraded to include a permanent carrier deployment. To

the north, US and British air operations out of the NATO base in Turkey patrolled the "no-fly zone" over Iraqi Kurdistan, adding hundreds of air and ground crews there and dropping bombs almost daily on Iraqi antiaircraft batteries. The tit-for-tat no-fly action got little press in the United States, but because the Iraqis often placed these weapons in civilian areas, Arab media broadcast a steady stream of images showing the shattered bodies of women and children for over ten years.

Then came 9/11, precipitated in part to drive "infidel" troops out of the Arabian peninsula, at least according to Osama bin Laden's videotaped demands.[3] Hundreds of thousands of US and allied troops poured into the region. US Central Command established forward-operating headquarters in Qatar, new bases were constructed not only by the United States but also by Britain and France, and a new form of warfare—armed drones—began hovering ominously in the region's skies. By the end of 2010, even with the drawdown from Iraq nearly complete, some 195,000 American military personnel remained in the region,[4] augmented by as many as 100,000 military contractors and another 41,000 NATO and other allied forces deployed in Afghanistan.[5] And this excludes the 4,000 airmen and sailors aiding the bombing campaign against Libya's Colonel Muammar Qaddafi, or the 36 warships and approximately 150,000 sailors and pilots of the US Sixth Fleet in the Mediterranean. Is it any wonder, then, that from the perspective of Egyptians like the feminist novelist Nawal El Saadawi, who suffered imprisonment under Anwar Sadat and exile under Mubarak, the revolution that overthrew the regime not only ended a dictatorship but also marked an end to "U.S. imperialism."[6]

The United States has good reasons for remaining engaged in the Middle East. Even after Bin Laden's demise, the region remains the most likely source of what the military calls "asymmetric threats" to the US mainland—that is, terrorism. And perched atop two-thirds of the world's proven petroleum reserves, the Middle East also controls the price of the most valuable commodity on earth.

Additionally, for reasons of both strategy and duty, we cannot leave Israel to fend for itself. However one may feel about Israel's posture and conduct, it has been encouraged and enabled by a consistent message of support from Washington and a decided lack of candor about long-term prospects for success. With American power and influence in decline, resetting Israel's expectations may be the single most challenging task facing the United States outside its own borders. So the United States is likely to strain every fiber to remain engaged in the Middle East, even as its influence declines. At the same time, oil-dependent emerging powers like China and India will inevitably protect their own interests—namely, keeping the flow of oil secure. It is no coincidence that the first post–World War II deployments of Japanese or Chinese armed forces outside East Asia were to the Middle East—for Japan, a 2004 deployment of troops to Iraq; for China, a warship to evacuate Chinese oil workers from war-torn Libya.

In the face of these challenges, the means by which America has maintained its dominance in the Middle East since the middle of the twentieth century—raw military brawn, coercive diplomacy, economic incentives, and support for Israel—will no longer suffice. Other players—some benign, some not—have increased influence and interests in the region and will insist on displacing Washington from its central role in the region's diplomacy. The relative shrinking of US economic and military muscle will coincide with increasing credibility and competence among states hostile to, or at least at odds with, Israel. These include Iran, Egypt, Turkey, Saudi Arabia, Iraq, and Syria—some of whom have governments in flux, many of whom are potential forces for reforming the region's poisonous politics if things go well, and all of whom may stand to acquire nuclear weapons in the coming decade. For both the United States and Israel, clinging to policies formulated during a period of brief, unrivaled American hegemony is a prescription for disaster. Even as US troops draw down in Iraq and Afghanistan, the United States must begin to invite other, friendly regional powers—especially Turkey and Egypt—into a more diversified conversation on how to resolve the Israeli-Palestinian conflict and prevent the growing Saudi-Iranian / Sunni-Shia rivalry from turning into the scourge of a new century.

CONFRONTING OLD MYTHS

Adjusting to the "new" Middle East will start with a sober look in the mirror. Most Americans view the post–World War II history between their country and the Middle East as a one-sided tale of hostility to the United States, with the natural exception of Israel. Why do they hate us? was the question on the lips of many Americans after the 9/11 attacks. The answer, delivered on the nation's behalf by President George W. Bush in an address to Congress on September 20, 2011, was this: "They hate our freedoms—our freedom of religion, our freedom of speech, our freedom to vote."[7] Americans largely agreed and reelected him to four more years in office in 2004.

Yet if America's freedoms so offend Muslims, how do Americans explain the tens of thousands of Arabs who have faced down tanks and machine guns (often sold to their tormenters by the United States) seeking precisely those same freedoms? Since 2009, Arabs young and old, male and female took to the streets of Cairo and Tunis and the towns and villages of Syria, Libya, Yemen, and Bahrain demanding—for lack of a better term—freedom. And what of those millions who volunteered to serve in the US-backed police and armed forces of democratically elected governments of Iraq and Afghanistan? Were none of them impressed by the elections and relative free speech that followed the trauma of American occupation? Polls by the Pew Research Center, al-Jazeera and the Arab-American Institute, among others,[8] indicate that Arabs and Muslims beyond the Arab world have no less interest in a government that respects their dignity than Americans. Just ten years after 9/11, these facts stand as a complete repudiation of the *casus belli* offered by Bush and widely accepted by Americans in 2001.

In retrospect, at the turn of the century, America was uniquely ill-equipped to answer a question like, why do they hate us?" In the election of 2000, before 9/11, Bush won the presidency in part by criticizing the amount of time his predecessor in the "Clinton-Gore administration" had spent on world affairs. "If we're an arrogant nation, they'll resent us; if we're a humble nation, but strong, they'll welcome us," he said in a debate with Al Gore less than a year before the attacks.[9] Bush had, in fact, channeled the *zeitgeist*. During that time, I was international editor at msnbc.com, and starting in the late 1990s, following the suicide bombings of the US embassies in Kenya and Tanzania, my NBC News colleague Robert Windrem and I agitated internally for more coverage of Osama bin Laden, who was regularly threatening to strike at the United States in his rambling video releases.[10] Yet we confronted enormous resistance at the time; Americans simply wanted to enjoy their millennial prosperity. In the summer of 2001, as 19 Arab men infiltrated the United States and prepared to hijack four airliners, citizens of the greatest power in history were engrossed in the salacious coverage of the search for a missing congressional intern, Chandra Levy, and terrified by wildly exaggerated news reports of shark attacks off the East Coast. Windrem and I were ridiculed for pushing the "downer" topic of some far-off Islamic zealot. The head of NBC Nightly News at the time, David Doss, referred to my friend derisively behind his back as "Robert bin Windrem." After we pitched a story about Bin Laden's role in helping the African embassies return to Pakistan and elude justice, Phil Griffin, then a senior producer at msnbc, bluntly said no. "Unless bin Laden is training killer sharks to attack young American girls in Florida, our viewers aren't interested," Griffin quipped.[11] Like Bush, Griffin, now president of the MSNBC cable network, was dead right about how his target audience viewed the world.

For those outside this American bubble, the self-interested attitude America projected, even as its military regularly dropped bombs in the Iraqi no-fly zone, confirmed a long-held suspicion that Americans cared little for the opinion of anyone outside their borders, much less non-American lives. Superpowers are doomed to struggle when trying to understand how they appear to smaller nations—the familiar Gulliver effect. Yet that should not excuse US policy makers from trying. Each and every nation views America through its own parochial historical prism—a prism that assumes, however unfairly, that a country as powerful as the United States does nothing by accident. The assumption regards every swipe, slight, or snub from Washington as carrying the force of full intent. Just as neighbors packed onto a middle-class suburban street will have widely different opinions of each other, often based on fleeting encounters or hazy memories of something they saw, heard, or smelled from across the fence, so, too, do the nations of the world carry their own eccentric reference points for assessing the United States. They may be half-truths, but they become received wisdom. Here are some examples:

- Most Iranians, whether they support the Islamic state or revile it, condemn the 1953 CIA-backed overthrow of their democratically elected president, Mohammed Mossadegh, as a disaster for their nation that led to repression under the US-backed shah and, ultimately, to the rise of the ayatollahs.
- Syrians remember the 1949 coup organized by CIA agent Miles Copeland[12] to overthrow the elected parliamentary government left behind by the French when they granted the country independence in 1946. Democracy would never return.
- Saudis fume at the planting of a democracy in Iraq that almost invariably will be dominated by Iraqi Shia groups sympathetic to Iran, as well as the Obama administration's decision to cut Egypt's Hosni Mubarak loose rather than help keep a faithful ally in power.

- Across the region, generations have grown up being constantly reminded by their media outlets that the bombs, missiles, and warplanes used by Israeli forces are made in the United States. Whether or not one regards this as relevant to a particular news story or a result of anti-Israeli propaganda, the cumulative effect of a lifetime of footage showing dead civilians killed by "US-supplied Israeli F-16s" cannot be wished away.

The list goes on and on—many Bahrainis resent the influence the US Navy wields in their country, Algerians blame the United States for buying oil from their military regime during the bloody civil war of the 1990s, and Turks resent that their warning against the Iraq War in 2003 was not only ignored but ridiculed as cowardly by overconfident American officials. Some of these perceived slights are inevitable in a complex world, and some were arguably the right thing to do. (For instance, if the Saudis disagree with the decision to cut ties with Mubarak, the real lesson for them is about their own repressive tactics, not the quality of US alliance.)

But perceptions matter, and the scant regard the United States has paid over the decades to the opinions of local inhabitants (as opposed to corrupt elites) means that, for all intents and purposes, it has acted as an empire. By valuing oil supplies over all else, supporting friendly regimes no matter how vile, and defending the conduct of Israel in every instance, Washington has acted exactly like every other conquering empire in history—intervening militarily, exploiting the region's energy resources, establishing a network of military bases, backing local favorites, and punishing anyone who dared give challenge.

If one accepts the notion of an American Empire, at least in the narrow context of the Middle East, it's easier to imagine how hollow Washington's claims to "essential global leadership" sound to Arab, Persian, or Turkish ears today. Since 2000, the region has witnessed the failure of the US-brokered Oslo peace process (2000), the attacks and retaliations of 9/11 (2001), a discrediting of Washington's weapons of mass destruction theories in Iraq (2003), and a global economic meltdown caused largely by US financial malpractice (2008). The successive collapses of American-backed regimes in Tunisia, Egypt, and Yemen followed by Washington's sheepish acceptance of a Saudi invasion of Bahrain to put down peaceful protesters are the coup de grace, confirming what most in the region had decided long ago: America's rhetoric about freedom and democracy, in the Middle East anyway, is merely the window dressing of empire.

AN APPOINTMENT IN EGYPT

Did America create this baggage, or was it thrust upon it? Even a cursory look at the modern history of US ties in the Middle East reveals that from the start, the United States has aggressively pursued its own interests in the region. Its hyperinvolvement began in 1933, when Standard Oil of California (later Chevron) won the world's first concession to drill for oil in Saudi Arabia.[13] From that point onward, Washington treated Saudi Arabia, and eventually all Arab states, quite differently than its allies in any other part of the world. It refrained from the prodemocracy message it pushed in Asia, Africa, and Latin America. It's no coincidence that there's no such thing as Radio Free Arabia. In the Middle East, where the bulk of the world's oil and natural gas reserves are located, the usual messianic agenda of the United States was supplanted by a quest for "stability." This stability remained the paramount goal of US foreign policy well after the Cold War ended and the presumed threat of Soviet penetration disappeared, despite allowing for dictatorial regimes that tortured and killed political foes and human rights activists, disenfranchised women, and in the worst cases, funded radical groups whose offshoots planned terrorist attacks on the United States.

Standard Oil's Arabian venture failed to make much of an impression on the wider Arab world in the years prior to US entry into World War II. The region was ruled as a series of colonies controlled by the British, French, and Italians before the war. American views of Arabs and their lands were shaped largely by Hollywood; Arab views of America were shaped by the tales of the trickle of immigrants there—mostly Orthodox Christians from the Levant, or the broadcasts of the BBC and other European colonial powers. Then in 1942, the American Army joined the fight between Germany and Britain in North Africa, invading Morocco and Algeria to help relieve pressure on the British in Egypt. The British Empire was fighting desperately to prevent German field marshal Erwin Rommel from taking the Suez Canal and possibly rolling on to the oil-rich Gulf. For most local Arabs, though, the war was just another calamity visited upon them by Europeans—aided now by their North American offspring. Victors, of course, write the history of such wars, so as nonparticipants, the Egyptians, Tunisians, Moroccans, Palestinians, Algerians, and Libyans

figure very little in the West's wartime literature. But Arab textbooks, naturally, view the war through the prism of their own national independence
movements and note the violence visited upon them by the troops of all sides,
including Americans. Rick Atkinson, in his masterful look at this first stage
of US participation in the European war, *An Army at Dawn: The War in North
Africa, 1942–1943*, details the many documented cases of US troops shooting
Arab civilians for fun as they rolled through North African deserts.[14] These
are mere footnotes in Western history books, but they are central to the Arab
experience, foreshadowing how the West would treat them in the new age of
decolonization.

As mentioned previously, the opinions of Arabs rarely figured in US policy
decisions—it was what lay under their deserts, not in their hearts, that concerned Washington. President Franklin D. Roosevelt was no exception. A senior
official of the Department of the Navy during World War I, FDR knew that
Britain and France had relied almost entirely on oil from American reserves in
the Great War, and that the pattern was repeating itself in the early 1940s once
the United States entered World War II. But this time, FDR's energy advisors
warned him that US reserves were fast depleting. So in February 1945, only
two months before he died, Roosevelt met Saudi Arabia's King Abdul Aziz Ibn
Saud outside of Cairo to lay the groundwork for one of the most important and
controversial bilateral relationships of the century.[15]

So much of what went right and wrong for the United States in the Middle
East since 1945 can be traced to those conversations between Roosevelt and
the Saudi king on the USS *Quincy*, moored in a Nile estuary that day. First
and foremost, the meeting cemented the new US-Saudi alliance, though few
at the time would have used such a grand term to describe a deal between
the leader of the world's most powerful democracy and the king of a dusty,
barely populated desert land. Besides pledging millions in aid to the impoverished kingdom and promising to help Saudi Arabia exploit its oil resources,
Roosevelt also hoped the king "would somehow be helpful in solving a daunting problem that the president knew was coming: the future of Palestine and
the resettlement of Europe's Jews."[16] The Holocaust's full horror was just then
becoming clear, as Hitler's retreat led to the liberation of Auschwitz and other
death camps.

Only 13 years after Standard Oil's breakthrough concession, currying
favor in the Arab world took on new importance. In the midst of global war,
the meeting between FDR and King Saud got little public attention. Yet the

meeting would affect the subsequent events of the century as much as anything FDR, Churchill, and Stalin discussed at the Yalta Conference a few days before. Accounts by officials present, including Roosevelt's translator and emissary to the king, US Marine Colonel William A. Eddy, detail the Saudi monarch's outright rejection of the idea of a Jewish state in Palestine.[17] "What injury have Arabs done to the Jews of Europe?" the king famously responded when Roosevelt cited the Holocaust and pressed the case for a Jewish return to Palestine. "It is the Christian Germans who stole their homes and lives. Let the Germans pay."[18]

Roosevelt was unable to persuade the king that it was impractical for Jews who had barely survived genocide to resettle in Germany. In Eddy's account, he turned instead to the oil question and, in order to secure US access for decades to come, went as far as to pledge that the United States would not support the establishment of a Jewish state in Palestine. Two months later, with only a week to live, FDR confirmed his pledge (though in masterfully ambiguous terms) in a letter to the king written on April 5, 1945.[19] American officials of the day may have failed to appreciate the significance this promise would have to the Arabs; or perhaps they felt that the immense power of the United States in 1945 would spare them from keeping it. Now we know much better.

A generation prior, both Arabs and Jews had felt deeply betrayed after World War I. In the midst of that conflict, Britain had made similar promises about the future of Palestine to the Arabs in order to win their support for an uprising against Germany's ally, Ottoman Turkey. At almost the same time, they offered contradictory assurances to Jewish leaders and then conspired to betray them both by signing the secret Sykes-Picot Agreement of 1916, dividing conquered Ottoman lands between France and Britain. This treaty, followed by the Balfour Declaration in 1917, which promised a Jewish homeland in Palestine, directly conflicted with the promise offered by Colonel T. E. Lawrence and other senior British officers: a united, independent Arab state that included Palestine following the war, if the Arabs would rise and fight the Ottoman Empire alongside British forces.[20] That uprising today is familiar to most through David Lean's masterful 1962 film *Lawrence of Arabia*, and it helped drive the Ottoman Turks out of Jerusalem and eventually much of Syria. Yet by 1917, it was clear that British policy was, at best, at odds with itself and that Palestine's future was up for grabs. In the end, the Europeans brushed aside both their Arab and Jewish allies and ruled the region as colonial possessions and mandates.

We can never know whether FDR understood the emotional freight his promise carried. But to the Arabs, it meant that support for their cause was official US policy. And clearly, American policy was now the only one that mattered. The demise of British and French power in the region was regarded as a *fait accompli* by almost everyone (except, perhaps, the British and the French themselves). The near death of Europe's imperial powers in World War II at the hands of Germany and Japan spurred hopes of mass decolonization around the planet. The United States, through propagation of FDR's "Four Freedoms" speech in 1941,[21] had fanned the flames of such passions, taking great pains to clarify that the independence of colonial peoples was one of its wartime goals. So when, in 1948, Roosevelt's successor, Harry Truman, dramatically reversed course on FDR's Palestine pledge and supported the establishment of Israel, the impact on the Arab world was profound. For a second time in three decades, the promises the West had offered the Arabs proved worthless. To the Arabs, the Israeli state was a colony of Europeans displacing the native Arab population, and the United States' eschewing of FDR's pledge to King Saud confirmed their suspicions that America would be no better than Britain and France. "The Arabs never hoped for much from England or France," Egypt's president Gamal Abdel Nasser, the dominant Arab figure of the postwar era, would tell *Life* magazine in 1955. "But ever since your President Roosevelt spoke of the Four Freedoms, the Arabs had looked to the United States with hope. We had always thought you would help us win our freedom. When you did not—when you took the side of your allies, Britain and France, we felt betrayed and disappointed in you."[22]

Why did Truman support Israel's cause over FDR's pledge to Saud? The topic, as tormented as any in the region's history, has been explored in dozens of books in as many languages. Truman's foreign policy aides, including General George Marshall, for whom Truman had an almost fatherly respect, vehemently opposed the move. Certainly, Cold War calculations about the need to return stability to the destroyed economies of western Europe played some role—by now, the Truman Doctrine of aiding Greece and Turkey to prevent further Soviet gains was in full swing, as was the Marshall Plan's even larger aid transfers to rebuild Britain, France, Germany, Italy, and the rest of the battered continent. In Palestine, meanwhile, the British had announced that they were withdrawing in 1948, and their rule was quickly devolving into Jewish-Arab civil war. Stabilizing that situation, given Soviet inroads in Greece and the rest of the Balkans, was also a strategic US concern.

But in the end, the decision to recognize Israel rested on Truman's own sense of justice. Personally, Truman evinced no innate love for Jews: he was, as subsequent publications of his personal letters and other official documents showed, deeply anti-Semitic.[23] But he did genuinely identify with Israel's cause and, in particular, its aging emissary, Chaim Weizmann. The fact that Jerusalem's most senior Arab official, the grand mufti, had been a guest of Hitler during the war and an enthusiastic supporter of German race laws, and was even made an honorary Nazi field marshal, certainly didn't help. But Truman still might have rejected the United Nations' partition plan for Palestine that ultimately led to Israel's independence had it not been for the intervention of a former army artillery unit buddy, Eddie Jacobson. The two had served in World War I together, and Jacobson, a Jew, was Truman's postwar partner in a failed Kansas City haberdashery. As the debate among Truman's aides raged, Jacobson contacted Truman and urged him to meet Weizmann before making his decision. Weizmann's lobbying did the rest.[24]

On Truman's orders, the United States backed the crucial 1948 United Nations partition. The Arabs, once again stung by the West's broken pledges, immediately rejected the plan to divide Palestine between Arabs and Jews and attacked the new state, ultimately losing what became known as the Israeli War of Independence. Just under a million Arab Palestinians fled or were driven out of Israel in the war's wake, each a living host of the resentment that stalks the region to this day.

THE "STABILITY" TROIKA

Oil, Israel, and the fear of Soviet expansionism: by 1948, the three factors that would drive American policy in the Middle East for the rest of the century were firmly in place. The United States would foster Israel into a regional power with arms and financial aid, even as it continued to court the kingdoms of the Persian Gulf. Slowly, US diplomatic pressure and defeat at Israel's hands peeled some Arab countries off the pro-Soviet, anti-Israeli line, neutralizing their involvement in the region's central Arab-Israeli conflict. Most importantly, the United States helped broker the one lasting bit of progress, the Israeli-Egyptian peace, at Camp David in 1979. That same year, however, the United States lost an equally powerful ally in Iran when the increasingly autocratic shah was toppled by a revolution that began by demanding democracy but was ultimately hijacked by radical Islamic clerics with deep grievances against America.

American foreign policy journals regularly dismissed the idea that Arabs, as a civilization, were even suited for democracy.[25] To the extent that the aspirations of Arabs or Persians or Turks entered into the US policy picture, it was in the context of the lack of real action by the United States when its Middle Eastern allies abused human or political rights of their citizens. The idea of democracy as a right Arabs were worthy of made only a brief, inconsistent appearance during the second Bush administration, and only after the initial rationale for war in Iraq—weapons of mass destruction in the hands of a Saddam allegedly complicit in 9/11—came up short. The Bush policy was long on op-eds and short on reality, and like all previous US administrations, that administration pursued ever-closer ties with repressive strongmen in Egypt, Yemen, Algeria, Saudi Arabia, and even Libya throughout its time in office. This consistently hypocritical stance weighs heavily on US efforts to get ahead of the region's current popular uprisings. What aspiring prodemocracy movement would not suspect US motives? US influence has not been decisive in any of the countries affected by the Arab Spring—even in Libya, where the United States somewhat belatedly backed a British- and French-led air campaign that gave rebels the upper hand.

Surprisingly, America's sagging influence has failed to produce a significant Israeli review of its own security policies. Even before the Arab Spring, Israel's refusal to aggressively press for a negotiated solution to the Palestinian problem bordered on self-destructive. Israel's security strategy rested on three pillars, all degrading fast: peace with Egypt, its alliance with the United States, and its nuclear deterrent. To the west, Israel has banked on the Camp David peace since 1979 to pacify Egypt, the Arab world's most powerful state. To the east, the prospect of a nuclear-armed Iran and the likelihood that such a move by Iran would spark Turkey, Saudi Arabia, and Egypt to seek their own nuclear arsenals mean that others in the neighborhood may soon check Israel's nuclear deterrent. Meanwhile, all around it, the ability of the United States to control diplomatic and military outcomes, too, is degraded. Yet Israel continues to pursue policies based on the false assumption that America will always have the power and diplomatic heft to tip the scales in its favor. The United States still wields a veto at the UN, and that may provide Israelis with some solace. But the days are gone when, because of a phone call from Washington, a Turkish or Egyptian leader would bite his tongue. Israel, like its American patron, has reached a tipping point.

Fiscal Year 2010 Country		Fiscal Year 2011 Country	
Afghanistan	$4,102.1	Afghanistan	$3,923.7
Israel	2,775.0	Pakistan	3,053.6
Pakistan	1,806.9	Israel	3,000.0
Haiti	1,778.8	Egypt	1,558.0
Egypt	1,555.7	Iraq	729.3
Iraq	1,116.8	Kenya	714.0
Jordan	843.0	Jordan	682.7
Mexico	757.7	Nigeria	617.7
Kenya	687.7	South Africa	586.1
Nigeria	614.7	Ethiopia	583.5

Figure 5.2   Top ten recipients of US foreign aid in 2010–2011 (in millions)[26]

Many American allies across the planet will face similar dilemmas as US power wanes in coming years—in Taiwan and Japan, in Southeast and Central Asia, in Europe, and possibly Latin America, too. But for Israel, the threat is far more immediate. Unless American leaders speak frankly and honestly to Israel about the new facts on the ground, the momentum of the Arab Spring will force regional governments to act on pent-up Arab grievances. The United States, and anyone who claims to care about Israel's fate, does that country a great disservice by allowing it to believe that time is on its side. Without a major shift in Israel's approach to the Palestinian issue, to broaden the agenda and enlist supporters beyond Washington, a war that will rattle the global economy and spread tragedy and death across the Middle East is inevitable.

For all these reasons, the US policy of allowing Israel to set the terms of any peace agreement, or declare where and when it can use force against its neighbors, is rapidly becoming unsustainable. Defense Secretary Leon Panetta stated the obvious—though still set something of a precedent for frank speaking on this topic by an American official—when he asked at an October 2011 news conference in Tel Aviv, "Is it enough to maintain a military edge if you're isolating yourself in the diplomatic arena? Real security can only be achieved by both a strong diplomatic effort as well as a strong effort to project your military strength."[27] He might just as well have asked the question of America's foreign policy establishment, which seems flabbergasted that American influence and credibility in the Middle East have deteriorated to such an extent that the agenda is now in the hands, once again, of the UN. The feeble US veto of the UN resolution granting observer status to the Palestinians may be defensible from a tactical policy standpoint, but just how long are the Palestinians to wait? And what evidence would suggest that any American administration, Republican, Democrat, or otherwise, has the political will and stamina to demand concessions on Israel?

The collapse of Washington's ability to set the agenda in the Middle East is the culmination of decades of arrogance. Over the years, Israel's behavior, including the occupation of the West Bank and Gaza, proliferation of nuclear weapons, denial of voting and property rights to Palestinians, and debatably disproportionate force in countering its enemies, has gone unchallenged by the United States, which stresses stability at all costs. Yet change, even for the better, always carries risks. Negotiated solutions to long-running historical conflicts invariably spawn a backlash by violent extremists, usually on both sides. In the past few decades alone, massacres, terrorism, and other abuses followed peace agreements in East Timor, Northern Ireland, South Africa, Bosnia, Kosovo, and Spain's Basque region. Yet in each case, the consensus for peace ultimately held fast.

Unfortunately, deal derailment tactics have proven more successful in the Arab-Israeli context, in part because of the flawed state of Palestinian democracy and the divided nature of Israel's electorate. In both cases, there has been enough defection to enable a relatively small faction of disgruntled militants to blow up the whole peace train, whether driven by Yitzhak Rabin, Yasser Arafat, Ehud Barak, Mahmoud Abbas, or Ehud Olmert. Arab groups that refuse to recognize Israel's right to exist—Hamas, Hezbollah, and smaller Palestinian factions—have grown adept at manipulating Israel's political scene with well-timed atrocities, such as the Hamas bus-bombing campaign in 1996, which sunk the electoral hopes of the prosettlement Labor Party candidate, Shimon Peres. The massacre of 29 Palestinians in a Hebron mosque by a right-wing Jewish fanatic in 1994 is another example, followed the next year by the murder of Prime Minister Yitzhak Rabin by a disgruntled Israeli settler.

In all these instances and others since, Palestinian and Israeli leaders, often acting under public or internal factional pressure, soured on peace talks and concentrated on blaming each other instead. For the Palestinians, the missed opportunities and corruption nearly led to civil war, and a split only recently healed between Hamas, which rules the Gaza Strip, and Fatah, Arafat's old party and head of the officially recognized Palestinian Authority. For years, until the Arab Spring forced the Palestinian factions into an uncomfortable reconciliation, this Fatah-Hamas fissure practically disqualified either side as a negotiating partner, providing a perfect excuse for the risk-averse Israeli government.

Israel, meanwhile, has repeatedly misjudged the strength of its own hand. The assumption from Israel since the victory in 1967, which gave it control of the Gaza Strip, the West Bank, East Jerusalem, and Syria's Golan Heights, has always been that it could take or leave a peace deal—that its military strength and alliance with the United States gave it the option *not* to make peace. Now, suddenly, the ecosystem has utterly changed. America must impress this upon Israel immediately and overcome the inertia bred into policy makers by decades of reflexive support for anything Israel does. With Iran's nuclear programming humming ahead, there's no time to waste.

The outcome of the unrest raging across the Middle East and North Africa (MENA) region remains uncertain. Even in the most hopeful cases—Tunisia, Egypt—things could still go wrong, including a hijacking of the revolution by Islamic extremists as in Iran. Yet one thing is clear: in the Middle East, Western policies that paid lip service to democracy yet poured millions of dollars into the bank accounts of regional despots have been comprehensively discredited. The United States needs to demonstrate that it understands this reality, and the most powerful way to do it would be to take a strong hand in dealing with the Israeli-Palestinian conflict.

THE BATTLE OF THE HOME FRONT

The effort to reshape opinion in the United States will be at least as difficult. Some experts suggest that Israel wields undue influence on US foreign policy. The contrary argument, subscribed to by the vast majority of lawmakers in the US Congress and a good percentage of the US foreign policy establishment, is that US backing for Israel grows out of natural affinities, a history of close cooperation in military and intelligence affairs, and a moral duty to secure the future of a nation founded as a lifeboat for the survivors of Hitler's Holocaust. Meanwhile, outrages like airport suicide bombings and the 9/11 attacks have, to say the least, left the Arab side of the argument with something of a branding problem, particularly in the United States.

Like all arguments on Middle Eastern affairs, the one about the Israel lobby contains plenty of passion and prominent voices on both sides. At the center is a powerful and highly sophisticated force in Washington. While it is not monolithic, it has generally supported a hard line on the central question of a "land for peace" exchange with the Palestinians. The lobby and its activist offshoots are indeed formidable. But its influence is frequently overstated. For instance, AIPAC—the American Israel Public Affairs Committee, by far the most effective arm of the lobby—pales in power and size next to the groups representing Big Oil, elderly Americans, and the ever-resilient American banking industry, to name just a few. In the 2010 election year, AIPAC spent $2.74 million on lobbying, according to US Federal Election Commission data. This is a fraction of the $132 million spent by the US Chamber of Commerce, or the $22 million spent by AARP and the American Medical Association.[28]

Has well-organized lobbying by pro-Israeli groups, along with agitating by Jewish and evangelical Christian members of Congress, helped erode US influence in the Middle East? Has the effectiveness of this powerful coalition led Israeli governments to believe that they can push back forcefully against US pressure to negotiate with the Palestinians? Has it shielded Israel from American criticism when Israeli military actions cross the line? Yes— repeatedly. Is any of this illegal, unethical, or "un-American"? Absolutely not; rather, it's precisely how American democracy works. The United Federation of Teachers does this, Irish Americans and their lobby do it, and so do the coal industry and the Sierra Club. Could we reform the process by preventing organized lobbying groups from using money as a weapon in political campaigns? Perhaps, and if I were king, I'd do just that. But that wouldn't be a democracy. Warts and all, Americans live in the democracy they deserve.

Whether one agrees with the "Israel lobby," sees it as an agent of a foreign power, or believes its influence is overstated is beside the point. It has been tremendously effective as an advocate for Israeli security interests, particularly as defined by the Israeli Right. But today, anyone pinning their hopes for Israel's security on the American Israel lobby has completely lost the script. As the new century unfolds, the lobby's arguments will look increasingly hysterical. The equation is simple:

1. Oil, for another several decades at least, will continue as the underpinning of modern economies. Even if the United States' own oil needs are mostly met outside the Middle East, the price is still set by the predominantly Middle Eastern producer states of the Organization of the Petroleum Exporting Countries (OPEC). As these countries grow more democratic, they will demand that the Israeli-Palestinian issue

be dealt with on terms acceptable to both sides, and they will use oil to pressure the United States.

2. Israel, an emotional and moral commitment the United States has met for decades, has grown into a significant burden for the United States as it seeks to navigate in the new Middle East. Its value as a strategic ally on intelligence and military matters, which has diminished since the Cold War, can't offset the problems that lockstep support for Israeli policies now creates for Washington.

3. As the most influential countries of the Middle East—especially Turkey, Egypt, and Saudi Arabia—decouple further from the United States, they will demand a more aggressive stance against Israel's occupation of the West Bank and Golan Heights. And if Iran goes nuclear, these three regional economic powers—already members of the G20—might also join the nuclear club, creating a dangerous and unmanageable environment for US policy makers and Israelis alike.

For all these reasons, both the United States and Israel should move quickly toward a negotiated solution to the Palestinian issue, lest they face the prospect of being forced to the table by the rest of the world under far less favorable terms. The outlines of the solution have been painfully obvious for two decades—a revised return to the 1967 status quo and a Palestinian capital in East Jerusalem, with land swaps that provide a contiguous Palestinian state in the West Bank and Gaza and allow Israel to retain the inner ring of settlements immediately adjacent to Jerusalem. I've argued that, given the role Britain, France, and Germany played in creating the problem, they should agree to form, or at least fund and arm, an international peacekeeping force to patrol the new borders for a defined period after a peace is signed. (The United States, again, no longer qualifies in most eyes as an "honest broker" in that regard—a boon to those loath to see yet more American troops deployed in the Middle East.)

Today, given the changes wrought by the Arab Spring, progress will require a broader approach that enlists newly assertive allies in the region. The recognition of a Palestinian state at the UN General Assembly, unsupported by the Obama administration, merely underscores how out of touch US diplomacy has become with reality. How, realistically, can the United States ask an elected Palestinian leader to forego that blessing?

THE NEW CALIPH

While the United States retains enormous influence in Israel, the past several years have raised real questions about its ability to convene the kind of peace conference that George H. W. Bush brought together in Madrid after his Gulf War victory in 1991—a seminal moment of Arabs and Israelis confronting each other across negotiating tables for the first time since Israel's creation. The problems his son had 16 years later trying to pull off a similar feat in Annapolis, Maryland, show just how quickly US prestige deteriorated. Bush the Younger may have thought his vanquishing of Saddam would match his father's Gulf War victory as a means of focusing Arab and Israeli minds. But by 2007, with the Iraq War discredited and US forces suffering grievously at the hands of Iraqi insurgents, neither Israel nor the Arabs believed America could deliver a peace deal. And they were correct. Israeli political wrangling over further concessions destroyed the process almost as soon as it started. Prime Minister Ehud Olmert could never forge a consensus within his governing Kadima coalition for anything approaching a comprehensive deal. In particular, the ultraorthodox Shas party and the nationalist expansionists of Yisrael Beiteinu threatened to bring down the government if East Jerusalem was put on the table. The "road map to peace" touted by the Bush administration for years turned out to be a road map to nowhere.[29]

Obama may have better luck, but not without help. He has taken a few modest steps to position the United States—despite its ham-handed prevaricating over the Arab Spring—in a better light. These include the Libya intervention and his decision, belatedly, to push for the ouster of dictators in Yemen and Syria. His decision to risk a daring mission to take out Osama bin Laden, too, bolsters his prestige. As tired as the region may be of American hubris, no actor had worn out his welcome more thoroughly than Bin Laden.

Bin Laden, of course, famously longed for a revival of the caliphate—the Ottoman sultan who once ruled the entire Middle East according to Islamic precepts. Bin Laden lived just long enough to witness the complete repudiation of that dream. The uprisings of 2011 across the region were driven by a desire for "decadent" values like nonviolence, personal liberty, rule of law, economic opportunity, and free speech. To pour salt in the wound, when a leader did finally emerge from the land of the Ottoman sultans, he would not be the fiery advocate of Islamic revolution Bin Laden had prayed for, but rather the leader of a secular democracy with a modern economy, warm ties with the West, a military treaty with Israel, and membership in the very military alliance, NATO, that was battling the remnants of Al Qaeda in Afghanistan.

Not since the downfall of Nasser in the early 1970s has a single figure emerged who could plausibly claim to speak for the Arab world. It is no small irony that the leader in question is a non-Arab: Turkey's prime minister Recep Tayyip Erdogan. Polls show that Erdogan, a practiced juggler of the region's many conflicting passions, is the most admired leader from the Atlantic coast of Morocco to the border of Iran. In the latest Arab Public Opinion Poll conducted annually by the University of Maryland and Zogby International, the Turkish leader was cited by 20 percent of Arab respondents when asked, "Which world leader do you admire most?" Venezuelan president Hugo Chavez and Iran's president Ahmadinejad, at 13 and 12 percent, respectively, were distant runner-ups, and Bin Laden (before his death) languished at 6 percent.[30]

For the leader of Turkey to assume the mantle of leadership in the wider Middle East reversed a century of decline in Turkish influence, dating to the collapse of the Ottoman Empire in 1918. Moreover, it would be a tremendous blessing for the United States and for the wider region if Washington and its Turkish ally act wisely. For starters, Washington could broker reconciliation between Israel and Turkey. One of the rare Muslim nations that recognized Israel long ago, Turkey had close ties with Israel until very recently. Turkey's government was highly critical of the Israeli push into Gaza in late 2008, and goodwill was strained to the breaking point in 2011 when Israeli commandos raided a civilian aid flotilla coming from Turkey to break the UN embargo on the Gaza Strip, where sanctions were causing humanitarian problems. The commandos killed nine Turks under controversial circumstances, and Turkey's criticism of Israel turned poisonous.

A longtime NATO ally of the United States, Erdogan's mildly Islamist government has drawn criticism at home for undoing some of the stricter tenants of Turkey's secular constitution—most famously, allowing women who so desire to wear the Islamic head scarf. This hardly qualifies Erdogan as a militant, though his political opponents in Turkey, centered in the army, would argue otherwise. More importantly, in recent years, Erdogan charted a much more independent course in foreign policy, led by his foreign minister, Ahmet Davutoglu, whose doctrine of "no problems with Turkey's neighbors" provided the justification for its sometimes uncomfortably close ties with countries like Syria and Iran, as well as the Palestinian movement Hamas. Nonetheless, the fact that Erdogan's government has proven its independence from Washington has won him great credibility in the Arab world at precisely the moment when such a voice is desperately needed. Realistically, if there were any rival at all for Erdogan's influence, it would probably be another non-Arab: Iran's unpredictable Ahmadinejad. This is all the more reason, then, for the United States to offer a serious partnership on regional economic and security issues to the ambitious Turkish leader.

This could be worrisome: Turkey has found it no easier to suddenly turn its back on despots than Washington has, and with regard to Libya and Syria in particular, Turkish policy has verged on the bizarre since the Arab Spring began. Turkey's opposition to a no-fly zone over Libya, even after the normally quiescent Arab League demanded one, perplexed admirers of Erdogan, particularly those risking their lives to challenge Qaddafi. Turkey also prevaricated horribly on Syria, even as Assad's tanks drove civilian refugees over its border seeking shelter from the violent crackdown. "As a result, at a moment of unprecedented regional change, when people power and democracy is sweeping the Middle East, the Turks look timorous, maladroit, and diminished—not at all the regional leader to which Ankara has aspired," says Steven Cook, a fellow on Middle East studies at the Council on Foreign Relations and author of books on Turkey and Arab military regimes.[31] But here, too, Turkey reversed course, and by late 2011 were hosting an armed group, the Syrian Liberation Army, dedicated to Assad's overthrow.

Erdogan also has been slow to mend ties with Israel since the Gaza flotilla killings. Yet there was no formal breach in Turkish-Israeli relations, and in fact, Turkish-Israeli trade has surged ahead, growing at a pace of 40 percent annually in recent years. The fact that diplomatic and economic ties remain in place, even if Israel's ambassador was asked to leave in a renewed spat over Turkish demands for an "apology" in August 2011, suggests that the Turks know a total breach will undermine their own unique influence and the role of "regional superpower" to which they aspire. The Turks clearly covet a major role in brokering peace in the region—they tried repeatedly to do just that between Assad's Syrian government and Israel over the Golan Heights. By inviting Turkey to cohost talks between the Israelis and Palestinians, the United States would acknowledge that it is not regarded as a fair mediator of the conflict. It would also put the Saudis on notice that the days of kowtowing to their interests are over, and raise the stakes considerably for all sides—for Israel, which wants to repair damaged ties with Turkey; for the United States, which is eager to harness Turkey's new assertiveness; and for Turkey itself, as a measure of its arrival on the world stage.

A US-Turkish partnership would also have enormous strategic benefits beyond the Israeli-Palestinian conflict, specifically enabling a more realistic approach to Iran's nuclear program. The current UN sanctions and other unilateral moves aimed at pressuring Tehran have been more effective recently, but given the high oil prices buoying Iran's economy, sanctions alone may not force hard bargaining. Turkey already tried, in partnership with Brazil in 2009, to broker an agreement with Iran on uranium enrichment. It failed largely because of US opposition. Forging a truly joint Turkish-American approach could break the deadlock.

Turkey is also the only power in the region to combine industrial capabilities with sophisticated banking and corporate sectors that enable it to turn Gulf money into useful infrastructure. Its growing economy and world-class construction and engineering firms, coupled with investment from Saudi Arabia and the Gulf emirates, could remake neighboring countries where roads, railways, and housing still largely consist of what the French and British left behind a half century ago.

None of this would be simple. Turkey's recent spat with Israel and its independence on foreign policy issues has earned it enemies in Washington. Yet down the road, drawing Turkey deeper into the politics of its former empire will be key to creating a lasting security structure—a kind of Middle Eastern NATO—to keep the peace as American power wanes and other interested players, from China to India to the oil-thirsty EU, move to secure the region's vital resources. With Washington's help, and the addition of Egypt and possibly the Saudis, the Turks could help create the first truly regional security collective in the Middle East.

American policy makers seem to have given little thought to this possibility, again assuming Washington itself would play the role of "balancer." But history shows that leaving such details to chance invites chaos. The United States should begin planning now for the orderly unraveling of US influence in the Middle East in the out-years—2025 and beyond—when geopolitical and economic physics will truly come to bear. Unless we expect American taxpayers to forever sustain the current constellation of American military bases and naval flotillas in the region, some alternate system of managing the Middle East's myriad "non-Israeli" conflicts must be established.

SHEIKH VERSUS MULLAH: THE NEW
CENTRAL CONFLICT

Dealing quickly and decisively with the lingering conflicts of the twentieth century, especially the Israeli-Palestinian conflict, is particularly important given the emergence of a new and possibly more dangerous fissure in the region: the battle between Iran and Saudi Arabia for dominance of the Persian Gulf. This rivalry pits two deeply insecure regimes against each other—each with the power to rattle international energy markets, each capable of arming itself with the most sophisticated weaponry on the planet (including nuclear weapons), and each practicing conflicting versions of Islam.

This last point, the Sunni-Shia rivalry, takes the conflict beyond the confines of conventional international competition and into the realm of mysticism, rendering it all the more immune to reasoned mediation. The roots of the Shia-Sunni split date to a seventh-century succession crisis following the death of the Prophet Muhammad. The Shia, representing at most 200 million worldwide out of an estimated 2.3 billion Muslims, are concentrated in Iran, Iraq, Bahrain, and in pockets of minority communities in the bordering states. In the twenty-first century, this schism has taken on a heavily armed, highly ideological form, imposing global economic risks. In Iraq, where a Sunni minority long ruled over the Shiite majority, the US invasion and the democratic elections it imposed turned the tables. Vali Nasr, an Iranian-born scholar and author of *The Shia Revival: How Conflicts within Islam Will Shape the Future*, believes the Iraq War unleashed a new dynamic on the region: "Just as the Iraqi Shiites' rise to power has brought hope to Shiites throughout the Middle East, so has it bred anxiety among the region's Sunnis....The Sunni backlash has begun to spread far beyond Iraq's borders, from Syria to Pakistan, raising the specter of a broader struggle for power between the two groups that could threaten stability in the region. King Abdullah of Jordan has warned that a new 'Shiite crescent' stretching from Beirut to Tehran might cut through the Sunni-dominated Middle East."[32]

Nowhere does the prospect of empowered, angry Shiites inspire as much fear as inside the ruling palaces of the House of Saud. Already concerned about the growing power of Shia Iran, as well as the coolness of formerly close ties with the United States, the Saudis have fears of this "Shiite crescent" partly out of self-interest and partly out of genuine concern about their vulnerability. The unrest in neighboring Bahrain, a Shiite majority island ruled by a Sunni monarchy, was crushed at Saudi Arabia's initiative, with much talk of "Iranian meddling" but precious little evidence. Indeed, a strikingly open investigation of the violence sanctioned by Bahrain's monarch concluded no credible evidence of Iranian involvement exists, even as it chronicled, in lurid detail, the whippings, electrocutions and other torments inflicted on protesters by the island monarchy's security police.[33] To many outsiders, the Bahraini unrest looked less like a religious uprising than a genuine multifaith demand for democracy, much like the movements elsewhere that spring, albeit one tremendously manipulated by regime hardliners. Whatever the facts, because control of two-thirds of the planet's petroleum resources is at stake, neither the United States, the EU, nor the emerging powers of East Asia, including China, will be able to ignore the Iranian-Saudi rivalry.

The United States has long cultivated the Saudi monarchy's fears that an aggressive, unfriendly power might someday overwhelm the relatively weak Gulf Arab states and lay claim to the world's richest oil and gas fields. During the 1990s, America focused on Saddam. With Saddam and his Sunni henchmen toppled, Iran now loomed as the primary threat. These military and economic concerns are valid: the disruption of oil shipments from the Gulf for a few weeks might be enough to plunge the global economy, and particularly the fragile economies in the United States, Europe, and Japan, back toward the precipice of depression. Iran's threat to block the Straits of Hormuz in December 2011, an act betraying the regime's desperation at the prospect of new sanctions, nonetheless underscores this point. The stakes, then, clearly require the United States to remain engaged in the Persian Gulf in some form. What's unclear is how, what the goal should be, and who should foot the bill.

For these reasons, the Obama administration handled the unrest in Bahrain very differently than the earlier uprisings in North Africa. This exposed yet another Western double standard. Though the oil-producing monarchies of the Gulf have not been immune to trouble, Washington decided, with assent from most other Western powers, to back their rulers for the sake of economic (read: energy price) stability.

While a resort to violence by the Egyptian, Tunisian, and even the relatively small oil-producing Libyan regimes was judged intolerable by the United States, the White House never contemplated anything in Bahrain even resembling its call for President Hosni Mubarak's resignation, issued in late February 2011. This caution may yet be born out—the kingdom's willingness to allow a transparent accounting of the violence perpetrated by the regime is unprecedented in the Middle East. Genuine action against those guilty of crimes and longer-term reforms to truly empower the disenfranchised Shias would do more than ten Saudi divisions to keep Iranian influence at bay. That may be wishful thinking.

Without such a surprise, the political lesson for Gulf potentates is a familiar one: oil buys them room to maneuver and moral relativism in the halls of Western power. Yet it has led to rash actions, too. Saudi Arabia and the United Arab Emirates, under the guise of the regional Gulf Cooperation Council, took the fateful step of dispatching troops into Bahrain to help its Sunni monarchy ride out protests by the Shia majority. In the short term, this may buy time for Sheikh Hamad bin Isa Al Khalifa to introduce democratic reforms that save his regime. Yet it has also put Saudi Arabia—and the United States, by extension—on the side of the repressive Sunni monarchy, conversely thrusting Iran into a role it had been unable to claim since the MENA uprisings began: champion of the people.

The Iranian-Saudi rivalry, boiling under the surface for years, now takes on a more dangerous complexion. Iran will certainly step up efforts to radicalize the Shiite minorities in Saudi Arabia's eastern provinces and in neighboring Yemen, where another pro-Saudi Sunni government is on the ropes. The risk of outright war remains slight, as each side has other options. The Saudis can pressure Iran by ensuring oil prices return to pre-crisis levels (below $90 a barrel), making Iran's fields inadequate to meet national expenses (and pleasing Washington, too). Saudi money could find its way to Iran's Green Movement, and the kingdom could cultivate Israeli fears of Iran's nuclear designs.

Iran, in turn, has threatened Gulf shipping lanes, deployed its own intelligence services against Saudi interests abroad, and could infiltrate agents into the eastern provinces to sabotage oil facilities and stir unrest. By intervening overtly in Bahrain, Saudi Arabia further complicated oil market volatility with a centuries-old Islamic schism.

The endless quest for "stability" in the Middle East has led America to ally itself with regimes that it might otherwise have criticized or shunned. This includes the recently toppled autocrats who ruled Egypt and Tunisia, the repressive strongmen in Algeria and Yemen, a host of monarchs from Dubai to Jordan and Morocco, and the intolerant oil kingpins who rule Saudi Arabia. The Arab Spring has finally forced the United States to take a risk on the locals, but not all of them. When peace can be bought without democracy, it seems, Washington's okay with that. Indeed, perhaps the one true generalization about the region's revolutionary season so far is this: the higher the per capita GDP, the less likely a majority of the country's citizens or institutions have been to follow the example of Tunisia's Jasmine Revolution.

There were happy exceptions. Morocco's king submitted to a referendum in which 98 percent of his subjects said they wanted a constitutional monarchy with an elected parliament—something the king has promised to fulfill. Ongoing revolts could eventually oust Syria's Assad, leader of the most brutal of the region's remaining dictatorships. Iran's mullahs could be vulnerable to a new push by reform-minded prodemocracy movements. Israel, too, could wake up and, with help from regional friends and its US ally, make a final, lasting push for peace with the Palestinians.

The likelihood of any of these is still less than 50 percent, however. Even as the Arab Spring rolls on, the dual vetoes wielded by Israel and Saudi Arabia hamstring US policy, preventing Washington from emerging as the inspirational force it represented to an earlier generation of revolutionaries in 1989. In the end, the United States has chosen to sustain—or at least to not challenge—all of these regimes precisely because it distrusted the instincts of those held captive by them. As anyone who has traveled the Middle East will attest, each of these countries—with the possible exception of Israel—contains large populations of underemployed, unhappy youths, providing fertile recruitment ground for Islamic extremists. But extremism had its day in 2001, and it failed, demonstrably, to sweep away the Arab regimes it hated almost as viscerally as the West and Israel. So perhaps Arab society has finally called America's bluff. When the region did erupt in flames, they were largely the flames of liberty. Far from hating our freedoms, they damn well want them, and they want us to get the hell out of their way.

CHAPTER 6

CHINA AND AMERICA: THE PERILS OF CODEPENDENCY

One of the abiding ironies of the controversial US government "rescue" of General Motors (GM) in 2009 is that the postbankruptcy automaker, while still based in Detroit, now earns more revenue from its Chinese affiliate than its native market. Republicans may have focused their fire on the Obama administration's auto industry bailout as a sop to organized labor, but it probably did more for jobs at GM China Group's factories in Shanghai than any United Auto Workers site in North America.

"They're selling a lot more Buicks in China than they are in America, and that's made GM the number one producer in the world's most important emerging market," says George Maglione, a senior auto economist for the consultancy IHS Global Insight. "There is no doubt about it. Your father's Oldsmobile is gone forever, but the Chinese, with some help from Uncle Sam, saved the Buick."[1]

The interdependence that globalization has wrought is far too complicated for zero-sum mathematics about jobs, currency values, and trade deficits. This is particularly true of the most important economic relationship in the world—the one between the United States and China. It would be easy to cast the current economic relationship between the United States and China as a one-way street, benefiting China and undermining workers in the United States even as China's purchases of US Treasuries give it economic leverage over Washington. But this is a simplistic view. In fact, China's dependency on the American market and commercial innovations represents a huge vulnerability for Beijing as it makes its way toward the center of the global stage. Along with its increasing dependence on imported energy, persistent internal unrest, and a susceptibility to bouts of inflation and hoarding, China's *pushmipullyu* relationship with America presents terrible dilemmas for Beijing's communist leadership.

In spite of the alarmist headlines, China's rise as an economic giant, and eventually a military and diplomatic competitor to American power, is taking place under terms the United States can influence and even harness to its own advantage. But the United States, in the three decades since China opened its economy to capitalism and began its breakneck sprint toward world-power status, has failed to develop a coherent strategy to leverage these advantages—particularly in innovation, technology, and intellectual creativity. Such a strategy would require Washington to invest heavily in its own economic and creative strengths, as well as adjust its military posture in the Pacific to accommodate legitimate Chinese interests without sparking accidental conflict. It would also require Washington to insist on greater Chinese participation in international diplomacy and peacekeeping, and prepare American allies in Asia for the realignment of power that looms ahead. It's unfortunate that in the United States, the focus tends to settle narrowly on the negative aspects of the economic relationship, distorting the fact that powerful incentives exist on both sides to see the other prosper.

THE EMPEROR'S CLOTHES

In its dealings with China over the past decade—well before the financial crisis—the United States seemed unaware of its closing window of opportunity to cement a stable, prosperous Pacific Rim as a permanent legacy of fading Pax Americana. A deep freeze enveloped US-China ties after the 1989 Tiananmen Square massacre, a spasm of murderous repression that shut the door for a generation on political liberalization in China. Gradually, isolation gave way to a paternalistic approach as the United States held out "rewards" like most-favored-nation trade status or membership in the World Trade Organization (WTO) as incentives for China to continue opening its economy to competition. As in post-Soviet Eastern Europe, US financiers and economists toured the country to lecture the Chinese about running a market economy responsibly, something Chinese officials suffered politely. All of this made enormous sense early on, when China's home market was largely closed off to foreign products and FDI was limited to stifling joint ventures with state firms. However, the approach lost its effectiveness after China reabsorbed Hong Kong's massive and dynamic banking sector into its economy and after more Chinese trained in US and other foreign universities returned to their homeland. Supercharged by the mix of long-term economic planning, first-class financial acumen, and cheap credit, China's growth accelerated, and it became clear that its emergence as an economic giant would happen no matter what the West thought.

In early 2009, Robert Greifeld, president of the NASDAQ OMX exchange, told me he was taken aback during a recent visit to China at the dismissive attitude of Chinese economic officials. "They basically said, 'Thanks for the advice, but you seem to have your own problems to worry about,'" he said.[2] As the West's great economies remained sluggish and mired in debt, this attitude has spread to other emerging markets. The financial crisis of 2008, writes *Financial Times* columnist Philip Stephens, "was the event that crystallised the new geopolitical order. Hitherto such events had belonged to developing nations—to Latin America or to Asia. This one was made in America. The sacred text of liberal, free-market capitalism known as the Washington Consensus was shredded. As the U.S. and Europe tumbled into recession, it was left to the likes of China, India and Brazil to avert a wider global slump."[3]

The exact shape of the "new geopolitical order," however, remains unclear. Some view the United States and China as rival standard bearers of competing ideologies—democratic market capitalism and repressive state capitalism— bound to clash in the twenty-first century just as fascism, communism, and democracy did in the previous one. But clinging too fervently to this belief risks creating a self-fulfilling prophesy, particularly in a world where the balance of power in Asia and elsewhere is in transition, and where none of the old talking shops, from the United Nations to the Association of Southeast Asian Nations (ASEAN) to the Asia-Pacific Economic Cooperation (APEC), are ready to offer a credible forum for mediating disputes. As previously noted, neither the old G7, the new G20, nor a notional "G2" of the United States and China appears to have sufficient consensus to tackle great transnational issues like climate change, international financial regulations, or nuclear proliferation. While the economic codependence of the United States and China encourages stability in some ways, the new determination of China's leaders to be treated as peers and the wounded defensiveness of the postcrisis United States contain the seeds of disaster if not addressed.

One symptom is a focus on relative minutiae rather than long-term trends. The issues that receive obsessive attention from each side—the undervalued Chinese currency, disputed territorial claims in the South China Sea, and China's gradual modernization of its military—raise the risk of a sudden miscalculation that could have unintended, tragic, and global consequences. What's more, the black-and-white view of this relationship proffered by too many American academics (and happily reproduced in China by nationalists who distrust US motives) obscures the fact that the United States retains the upper hand in many respects, especially militarily and economically. In the case of Buick, for instance, one could argue that these jobs would have remained in the United States had GM not invested in China in the late 1990s by licensing Buick designs and opening manufacturing plants in that country. But such an argument flies in the face of the modern realities of the global economy. Globalization, at this point, is not a choice—it's the air we all breathe. So it would be more accurate to say that Buick would be a museum reference by now had one of America's leading manufacturers not staked its claim in China.

"If Buick hadn't already had a foothold in China, it would have went the way of Hummer, Saturn, Pontiac and Saab in the financial crisis," Maglione says, naming the four brands that GM chose to discontinue or sell off in its bankruptcy fire sale.[4]

Unfortunately, the true extent of America's leverage often gets lost in the sound-bite world of the country's politics. As a result, instead of the focus being on a grand strategy for the next three decades in Sino-American affairs, it is on micro-annoyances that can easily be reduced to campaign slogans or lobbying "fact sheets." The arrival in the US Congress of the Tea Party class of 2010—the first time in generations that a major GOP faction has rivaled the Democrats in protectionist sentiments—has fed this focus on symptoms at the expense of a cure, and its insistence on budget austerity rules out the necessary investments in the country's human capital and innovation infrastructure. This is shortsighted not only for the economic reasons explained in chapter 1, but also because with each passing year, China and other emerging economies whittle away at the remaining advantages of the US economy: innovation, productivity, and entrepreneurial drive.

Washington should be plotting a future based on the awesome strengths of American free society and economic productivity. Instead, it scapegoats China, its chief competitor, for striving to lift its population out of destitution. Since the 2008 financial crisis, the United States has acted like a football team that can only play defense, and that defensive attitude has prevented American politicians, until very recently, from targeting US strategic assets with investments and incentives for private sector research and development (R&D) spending. This reactive crouch creates a dangerous situation for American foreign policy and defense officials, as China's military increasingly rubs elbows with the giant US military and intelligence apparatus in the Pacific.

Case in point is the running dispute over China's currency, the renminbi (RMB), also known as the yuan. The People's Bank of China—the country's central bank—has kept the RMB low in order to maximize the competitiveness of Chinese products. This comes at the expense of the United States and other competitors, particularly China's neighbors in Asia and America's North American Free Trade Agreement (NAFTA) partner, Mexico, which has seen the benefits of its free-trade zone with the United States significantly dented by the emergence of China and other low-cost Asian producers (though rising Chinese wages could reverse this trend over time). For years, critics have pointed out that China's currency is undervalued, and few argue. The dispute pits those who think a strong RMB would make US manufactured goods more competitive globally against those who see it as a relatively small issue in a very complicated relationship. "Some observers mistakenly believe that a marked increase in the exchange value of the Chinese renminbi (RMB) relative to the U.S. dollar would significantly increase manufacturing activity and jobs in the United States," Alan Greenspan, then chairman of the Federal Reserve, told Congress in 2005. "I am aware of no credible evidence that supports such a conclusion."[5]

As already mentioned, the larger problem is not about exchange rates or market access, but "global imbalances"—the fact that China's consumers save at enormous rates and consume little compared with the spend-crazy, credit-addicted West. Getting Chinese consumers engaged in the global economy would do far more to employ American workers than a readjustment of its currency rates. Rather than building a mountainous surplus based on export earnings that it plows into US Treasuries and other investments, China could be recirculating that money domestically and stimulating a consumer boom that would produce a positive effect for every major manufacturing power on earth. Of course, there are enormous structural impediments to this readjustment—for instance, Chinese banks effectively operate as funnels, sucking up much of the savings in Chinese households and transferring them (via bank balance sheets) to the corporate-state sector, underwriting its investments in massive infrastructure and other projects, and keeping consumer spending weak. Reforms to this system, which barely figure in US-China joint communiqués, would mean that more Chinese-made products would stay in China, with fewer dumped cheaply into foreign markets.

"Exclusive focus on the renminbi exchange rate issue is likely to be both ineffective and counter-productive," writes Chinese economist Yiping Huang of Peking University. "Between mid-2005 and mid-2008, the renminbi appreciated by 22 per cent against [the] US dollar and by 16 per cent in real effective terms. But China's external imbalances continued to widen rapidly."[6]

But such subtleties are lost on American legislators. Rather than focusing on ways to maintain and extend the US lead in high-end manufacturing, US politicians have waged a doomed battle to protect manufacturing industries like textiles and furniture that stand no hope of supporting what the American workforce considers a decent life. As a result, in part because of the pressure from US labor unions and in part because of the increasing nativism of the Republican rank and file, Congress has pressured both Greenspan and his replacement, Ben Bernanke, along with a succession of US Treasury secretaries, to make an appreciation of the RMB the featured "task" of recent US financial talks with the Chinese and at G20, APEC, and other international economic gatherings. Granted, the United States has also established an annual bilateral economic summit that attempts to broaden the conversation to such areas as energy and climate change, but with US jobless rates hovering near 9 percent, the pressure to scapegoat isn't letting up anytime soon. The "all eggs in one basket" foolishness of this is clear, and the idea that China will relent given the potential cost to its fragile domestic stability seems unlikely. Even on principle, the US position—presumably, that no nation has the right to control its currency—is simply incorrect. The *Wall Street Journal*, no friend of Chinese economic policy, attempted to refute the US position in a 2010 editorial:

At the core of this argument is a basic misunderstanding of monetary policy. There is no free market in currencies, as there is in wheat or bananas. Currencies trade in global markets, but their supply is controlled by a cartel of central banks, which have a monopoly on money creation. The Federal Reserve controls the global supply of dollars and thus has far more influence over the greenback's value than any other single actor.

A fixed exchange rate is also not some nefarious economic practice rare in human affairs. From the end of World War II through the early 1970s, most global currency rates were fixed under the Bretton-Woods monetary system.... That system fell apart with the U.S.-inspired inflation of the 1970s, and much of the world moved to "floating rates."

But numerous countries continue to peg their currencies to the dollar, and with the establishment of the euro most of Europe decided to move to a fixed-rate system. The reason isn't to get some trade advantage against their neighbors but to gain the economic benefits of stable exchange rates—and in some cases a more stable monetary policy. A stable exchange rate eliminates a major source of uncertainty for investment decisions and trade and capital flows.[7]

FUELING THE FIRE

Indeed, since the financial crisis, the US Federal Reserve has practiced something quite similar, though with even greater global effects. Beginning in late 2008, the Fed began a process known as quantitative easing—QE for short. In order to rescue the US banking system, the Fed began buying "toxic assets" off their balance sheets, amounting to $1.75 trillion in mortgage-backed securities, $175 billion worth of Fannie Mae and Freddie Mac trash, and another $300 billion in long-term US Treasury bonds. After the positive effects of the Obama fiscal stimulus faded in the summer of 2010 and the long-term damage to the economy became clear, the Fed launched QE2, slurping up another $630 billion in US Treasury bonds. This puts the Fed, with approximately $1.6 trillion in US Treasurys, just a bit ahead of China, which holds about $1.2 trillion.[8]

The effects on the US economy, the average person might think, were minimal, except for the decrease in the value of the dollar nominally on currency markets and the increase in the price of gold, on the advice of fund managers and traders like Peter Schiff and Rick Ackerman, who predicted hyperinflation of Weimar German proportions. In fact, inflation has remained fairly tame in the United States, largely due to the gigantic drag on economic activity represented by a nation of three hundred million deleveraging debtors. And in addition to keeping the dollar from rising, which helped make US products cheaper abroad, QE kept US borrowing costs down while devaluing the Treasury bills and other US holdings of creditors like China. Richard Fisher, president of the Federal Reserve Bank of Dallas, opposed the second round of QE in 2010 because he, too, feared inflation. But he also warned of an international backlash if QE continued to water down the value of US bonds held by outside investors. "For the next eight months, the nation's central bank will be monetizing the federal debt," he said in late 2010 as QE2 kicked in.[9]

The more profound effects of QE actually took place outside the United States. Besides diluting the value of the huge Chinese and other Treasury bond portfolios, QE sparked inflation in emerging markets from Brazil to Egypt to China. As the Fed opened the QE spigot, money followed the course of gravity, from the low-interest-rate advanced world to the high interest and growth rates of the emerging markets. It also created a surge of investment into commodities—again, often targeting emerging markets and causing enormous problems. The resulting wave of dollars led Brazil, India, Malaysia, and others to impose currency controls that prevented their economies from being flooded with these "cheap dollars" and the inflation and further appreciation of their currencies that would result. The practice of moving money from low-interest-rate countries to high-rate markets for a quick profit is called the "carry trade," and it has earned US and other investment funds titanic profits ever since QE started. But it has battered many of the countries targeted for investment, whose financial systems simply cannot handle the inundation that QE unleashed. Kevin P. Gallagher, associate professor of international relations at Boston University, describes the effects on emerging economies:

> So you're pulling money out of the United States at a low interest rate, two, three, four percent, parking it somewhere like Brazil, 10.53 percent. That's an amazing, quick markup. Can't get that in the U.S. economy anywhere.... There have been massive inflows of capital to the developing world. It has two effects. One, it raises their currencies, so their exports are more expensive. Brazil's currency's risen by 37 percent since 2008. Their stuff's more expensive out there in the world. So as we are trying

to stimulate our economy [with QE], they can't get many markets around the world because their stuff's too expensive. That's one thing. The other thing…is the fact that this is speculative capital that's going to move in and out of their country and could cause asset bubbles in…their economy. And just as quickly as it comes in, if there's a change in the interest rate in the United States or a little scare in a country, it can pull right out and destabilize their financial system.[10]

For Brazil, India, and China, too, playing defense is a matter of survival. Indeed, like all great powers just emerging from long periods of backwardness, China naturally wants to make the most of its labor cost advantages while they last—something that giants of nineteenth-century American capitalism like David Rockefeller and Andrew Carnegie understood very well. Fair play, which figures high in the rhetoric of contemporary American politicians, featured not at all in the development of American capitalism's march to global dominance. "I can hire one half of the working class to kill the other half," quipped Jay Gould, who ran Union Pacific Railroad like a dictator, using violence to keep down labor costs while manipulating US currency and commodity markets with abandon in the years following the Civil War.

Imagine, now, a China run by a democratically elected government accountable to Chinese voters. Given the likelihood that an appreciation of the RMB would cause mass layoffs as foreign factories switch to other, even cheaper Asian producers like Bangladesh or Vietnam, any government claiming to act in the name of its citizens would resist outside pressure to allow the RMB to appreciate. For political reasons, and because Chinese wages—and thus, the costs of production—have been rising, China has allowed the RMB to rise slightly in recent years, and it may continue to allow small, gradual hikes. If China were a democracy, such a move would be electoral suicide. In the real, authoritarian China, where unrest is one of the few means of expressing real dissent, the Chinese Communist Party (CCP) fears such a course amounts to regime suicide. Whatever its record on growth and poverty amelioration in the past several decades, the CCP believes in nothing above the protection of its monopoly on political power. The fact that 2012 finds the CCP in the run up to a leadership change exacerbates this dynamic. The party's 2012 conference will turn leadership over to the so-called fifth generation of Mao's party, and none of these young strivers are about to undercut Chinese competitiveness before that transition firmly esconces them in power.

Whatever generation, nothing scares the CCP more than the prospect of mass joblessness and labor unrest in its vast, teeming factory cities (indeed, the same prospect gave Carnegie and Rockefeller nightmares in the nineteenth century). The basic deal that the party has made with its citizens trades political rights for steady increases in prosperity. The willingness of Beijing to go to the mat to ensure continued GDP growth of around 8 percent annually—the rate at which most economists believe China can keep raising incomes and forestalling major layoffs and demands by its middle class for more input into the direction of the country—should surprise no one.

Meanwhile, neither the Chinese nor other foreign holders of US Treasuries are under any illusion about the ultimate aim of US policy: a covert devaluing of the US dollar, thus drastically reducing the value of the enormous investment China and other US creditors hold as their shares of the US national debt.

"These foreign creditors have been, so far, willing to finance the U.S. and are actively trying—like China and other emerging markets —to prevent their currencies from appreciating against the U.S. dollar so as to maintain their trade competitiveness," says Nouriel Roubini, the economist who cut his teeth as a US Treasury advisor during the Asian financial crisis of 1997. "They would not happily bend over and accept the massive capital levy on the real value of their dollar assets that inflation and/or dollar depreciation would entail. Thus, the risk that such foreign creditors would pull the plug on the U.S. foreign debt and current account deficit is significant. After all, the U.S. relies on the 'kindness of strangers'—or on a 'balance of financial terror'—to finance its external debt and deficit."[11]

SELF-DEFEATING SELF-DEFENSE

This lack of a "grand strategy" in America's approach to China is also evident in a recent history of minor trade and commercial disputes. Starting in 2005, when China's state oil firm, the China National Offshore Oil Corporation (CNOOC), tried to buy financially strapped California oil producer Unocal, American politicians began to question what constituted an appropriate Chinese investment in the US economy. More recently, a bid by China telecommunications company Huawei Technologies to buy the American firm 3Leaf was dropped under pressure from the US Committee on Foreign Investment in the United States, a Cold War–era body founded to prevent sensitive technology from falling into Soviet bloc hands. In 2007, the same panel outright forbid Huawei to buy an Internet routing company, 3Com, which was ultimately purchased by US giant Hewlett-Packard instead.

There will be times when such actions make sense. Some of China's largest firms remain deeply entangled with the state and China's military. And not all of China's proposed investments rose to the level of political fights—China's Lenovo bought IBM's PC business in 2006, and the huge construction firm China State Construction Engineering Corporation is a major contractor on the reconstruction of the San Francisco Bay Bridge and has won contracts for work on New York City's subway and other large infrastructure projects. But China's FDI in US corporations remains tiny—a paltry $791 million in 2009, compared with the over $43 billion invested in China by American firms that same year.[12] With China's appetite for such investments likely to increase by up to eight times in the next decade, according to a report by the consulting firm Kissinger Associates, the United States would be foolish to continue warding such money off as if it somehow isn't green. "For 30 years, China has grown stronger by opening its door wider to FDI, irrespective of overseas openness. The United States should do the same, or risk Chinese firms setting up plants in Ontario instead of Michigan or Juarez instead of El Paso," the report said.[13] This is particularly foolish behavior given that such investments would help, over time, support US exporters and offset the enormous trade deficit the United States has been running with China for decades, which amounted to $273 billion in China's favor in 2010.[14]

Again, vigilance makes sense, and neither the United States nor other advanced manufacturing nations are under any obligation to turn the other cheek when, for instance, Chinese crime syndicates violate copyrights with abandon. The Motion Picture Association of America, representing one of America's most culturally powerful exports, estimates that Hollywood loses $2.3 billion a year from Chinese piracy. And the urgency increases when technologies potentially applicable to military or strategic industrial advantages are at stake. Beijing makes the most of the appetite that foreign competitors have for its growing market. There may not be much military application to a Buick Regal, but other technologies clearly have been "borrowed," in the preferred phrase of diplomats. Beijing's policy of "indigenous innovation," ostensibly meant to help fund local R&D efforts, is regarded by Western firms as nothing more than a euphemism for reverse engineering and intellectual property theft.

Another insidious practice involves high-value, high-tech products and industrial espionage. Boeing and European aircraft maker Airbus complain— gently, given the size of the market at stake—that Chinese aircraft manufacturers have "borrowed" their designs. Japanese, Swedish, Canadian, and German firms believe that the designs for high-speed railways built recently were purloined during earlier "joint ventures" with the state railroad.[15]

Similarly, the appearance of a Chinese "stealth fighter" in early 2011 during a visit to Beijing by then US defense secretary Robert Gates was embarrassing for political reasons—its maiden flight was six years ahead of Pentagon predictions. But its design clearly suggested the potential for industrial espionage targeting Lockheed, the manufacturer of a strangely similar US warplane, now decades old. The episode no doubt thrilled nationalist-minded officers of the People's Liberation Army, but its deeper implication should trouble them: China is failing to develop its own native technologies.

PLAYING FOR ADVANTAGE

Back in 2007, before the bubble of faith-based US economic growth exploded, the surging vitality of China's smokestack economy was already clear. "China Makes, the World Takes," read the title of a perceptive article in the *Atlantic* magazine, a play on the now sadly inappropriate sign that welcomes motorists to the down-and-out nineteenth-century factory town of Trenton, New Jersey.[16] Like Trenton—and countless other American mill towns that helped bring the Industrial Revolution to the New World—China's great manufacturing complexes now dominate global markets across vast product lines, including appliances, consumer electronics, and consumer durables like sporting goods, clothing, toys, furniture, and textiles.

Yet China lacks something that Trenton and its nineteenth-century peers had in spades: innovators. Charles Roebling, for instance, the son of the man who designed the Brooklyn Bridge, founded Roebling Steel in Trenton and perfected a machine that turned out the huge wire cable that made suspension bridges possible. (He also, incidentally, provided the steel for the first

Slinky, ironically now produced in Taiwan.) While China excels at building and even incrementally improving established product lines like GM's Buicks and countless other Western and Japanese goods manufactured there, it has struggled to innovate. Even in 2010, the year China officially overtook Japan as the world's second largest economy, no Chinese brand could viably be called a household name in any Asian market, let alone in the wider world.[17] The annual global branding study by the market research firm TNS found in 2010 that, while consumer brands from Denmark, Finland, South Korea, and Switzerland make the top 20, no Chinese product or brand appeared in the top 1,000.[18] Eleven of the top 20 brands were American, including giants like Google, McDonald's, Coca-Cola, and Facebook. Four were Japanese (led by Sony [number one], plus Panasonic, Honda, and Canon). Two more (Samsung and LG) hailed from South Korea. The two most famous Chinese inventors of the twentieth century—An Wang, the personal computer pioneer, and Flossie Wong-Staal, a scientist who helped identify the AIDS virus—both made their names in the United States.

Surely, a nation of 1.3 billion will produce brilliant designers, engineers, scientists, and other innovators in this century. Since 2000, for instance, Chinese researchers have created the smokeless cigarette (invented by pharmacist Hon Lik in 2002), a wind turbine driven by magnetic levitation technology (developed by Li Guokun in 2006), and the first quasi-ballistic long-range antiship missile, an invention of great concern to the US Navy (more on this in chapter 7).

Yet, while these are notable achievements, something is retarding China's transition from copycat manufacturer to innovative top dog. The kind of manufacturing that accounts for nearly all of China's export earnings relies on low-cost inputs, including labor, as opposed to the value-adds of quality and technology that underpin an advanced economy's manufacturing sectors, notably in Japan, Germany, and the United States. Annually, those export earnings—essentially the difference between what China pays to import products and what it earns on its exports—have gradually fed the growth of China's best-known sovereign wealth fund, the China Investment Corporation (CIC), and a variety of state companies and policy banks that control the $3.2 trillion war chest of hard currency reserves.[19] It is this money that purchases the sovereign debt of the United States and many other developed economies, along with copper mines in Peru; oil concessions in Angola, Sudan, and Iran; a dominant interest in the Panama Canal Authority; and stakes in US corporations, including a recent bid for a large chunk of Facebook. All of that, to many in the United States particularly, sounds nefarious.

The combination of a nineteenth-century business model and a twenty-first-century pseudo-communist political repression saddles China with disadvantages that make it tremendously vulnerable to small commercial disruptions with not only the United States but also the EU and Japan. This is not just about losing sales for Chinese products in those markets, but losing the designs, technologies, and techniques needed to produce them. The "import/assimilate/reinnovate" model, as economists refer to it, does not foster a climate of original innovation, according to a recent study of US and Chinese competitiveness by the Center for American Progress, a liberal US think tank.[20]

The problem might be solved in the long term by investment in R&D and reforms to China's economic incentives and education system—indeed, Japan suffered from precisely these problems early on in its emergence from the depths of destruction after World War II into a postwar economic powerhouse. But economists also suspect that the centralized nature of China's government will prove a lasting liability, allowing the United States and other advanced economies to maintain their lead in high-tech goods for far longer than might otherwise be the case. While the ability to make clear decisions and adhere to plans decades in advance clearly has some advantages, it also stunts creativity and blunts the incentives a market economy creates for turning patents into viable commercial and technical breakthroughs that respond effectively to evolving consumer demands and complaints.

This underscores a deeper dilemma. China's brute strength in manufacturing is based on the simple, and possibly unsustainable, deal that the Communist Party made with its urban elites—namely, that it will keep incomes rising and leave these urban elites alone to make money as long as they keep their political aspirations to themselves. But as more and more Chinese in the vast, poor interior clamor for their own piece of the pie, wages will rise and demands for safety and environmental codes will erode competitiveness. When this happens and jobless workers get angry, the urban elites may renege on the deal for a greater say in their own government. Even then, the rural millions may not have much patience left.

Ian Bremmer, president of Eurasia Group, a political risk consultancy, told me that he views China as the clear primary rival to America for global power in the twenty-first century, yet also as a state that suffers from contradictions that could potentially be existential. China shares this with other "state capitalist" powers, including Russia, Saudi Arabia, Iran, and—depending on its evolution—Egypt.

> Authoritarian governments everywhere have learned to compete internationally by embracing market-driven capitalism. But if they leave it entirely to market forces to decide winners and losers from economic growth, they risk enabling those who might use that wealth to challenge their political power. Certain that command economies are doomed to fail but fearful that truly free markets will spin beyond their control, authoritarians have invented something new: state capitalism. In this system, governments use various kinds of state-owned companies to manage the exploitation of resources that they consider the state's crown jewels and to create and maintain large numbers of jobs. They use select, privately owned companies to dominate certain economic sectors. They use so-called sovereign wealth funds to invest their extra cash in ways that maximize the state's profits.[21]

But the "state capitalist" model produces profound political paranoia among the elites running the country. China's ruling party, the CCP, at 80 million strong, is no small faction. Yet it still constitutes a tiny, resented elite in a country of 1.3 billion. "Many within the [Chinese Communist P]arty believe it is facing an existential crisis as it prepares for an inevitable eventual economic slowdown, at a time when demands for greater representation for the new urban middle class are growing," Jamil Anderlini, Beijing bureau chief of the *Financial Times*, wrote just before the party celebrated its ninetieth birthday in July 2011.[22]

SMART MANUFACTURING VERSUS SMOKESTACK LIGHTNING

As a recent surge in patents shows, China is by no means doomed to remain a smokestack power. Increasing investment in science, technology, and other innovation sectors, now running at about 1.5 percent of the GDP, puts China at the top of the table among emerging economies in terms of R&D spending, and fourth overall behind only the United States, Japan, and Germany.[23] Put another way, China can claw its way up the value-added food chain and move its companies beyond the goal of building a better, cheaper Buick and into the high-end, high-margin markets for software, aerospace, robotics, and sophisticated engineering currently dominated by the United States, Europe, and Japan. But the progress to date has been almost impossible to measure, and the country's mediocre higher educational system, demographic and political challenges, and corruption suggest that this will be more of a Long March than a Great Leap Forward.

Let's take the problem of demography. China certainly cannot be described as suffering from a shortage of people, but it is suffering from an acute shortage of a certain generation of people, thanks to its enforcement of one-child population control policies since 1979. While some of the slowing of its population growth probably stems from rising prosperity—which usually goes hand in hand with smaller families—the often brutal retaliation against those who flouted this law, including the seizure of children for adoption, has planted a ticking demographic time bomb under the Chinese economy. "China has one of the world's lowest 'dependency ratios,' with roughly three economically active adults for each dependent child or old person," according to the *Economist* magazine in a recent survey on China's demographic problems. "[China] has therefore enjoyed a larger 'demographic dividend' (extra growth as a result of the high ratio of workers to dependents) than its neighbors. But the dividend is near to being cashed out. Between 2000 and 2010, the share of the population under 14—future providers for their parents—slumped from 23 percent to 17 percent. China now has too few young people, not too many. China has around eight people of working age for every person over 65. By 2050 it will have only 2.2. Japan, the oldest country in the world now, has 2.6. China is getting old before it has got rich."[24]

The US figure, according to Census Bureau projections, is 3.7 working people per retiree—and the trend will go gently upward. Indeed, of the countries that will rank as the world's largest economies later in this century, only the United States, Brazil, and Turkey have managed to avoid acute "dependency ratio" problems. For the United States, a relatively high birth rate (compared with other large economies in Europe and Asia) and a much more open approach to immigration have saved it from the worst of the crisis. Germany, France, Britain, and Italy recognize the issue as already contributing to the sovereign debt debacle in the euro zone. For three of the four BRIC economies (Russia, China, and India), severe problems await—all the result of man-made disasters. Besides China's one-child policy, Russia's population has been in a historic decline since the fall of the Soviet Union left its people without adequate government services, with a health crisis, with falling life expectancy, and with rampant corruption. So serious is the decline that President Dmitri Medvedev in 2011 offered free plots of land—one-third of an acre—to any family having a third child.[25] In India, selective abortion of female fetuses—accelerated by the illegal use of mobile ultrasound machines—has led to a male/female imbalance of enormous proportions. A recent study published in the *Lancet*, Britain's leading medical journal, estimates that as few as 806 female births are now registered for every 1,000 boys. China suffers from a similar, though less serious, imbalance, likely due to similar selective abortions. (The social and economic implications of gender imbalance in India could prove to be a major problem and will be discussed in chapter 7.)[26]

Given the extent of the demographic problems facing India and China, the two countries most often portrayed as peer competitors of the United States in the new century, the United States probably doesn't need to worry so much about the retirement of its baby boomers—those born between 1945 and 1964. The Congressional Research Service, in a 2010 report on the issue, conceded that the retirements raise questions about the solvency of the US old-age pension system, Social Security. But unlike the demographic challenges facing China, India, and Russia, which have no obvious solution, the solvency of Social Security is merely a matter of political will: it can be fixed with a mix of tax increases, benefit decreases, and increased immigration to add young, healthy workers to the labor force. As a 2010 report by the Congressional Research Service concluded, without changes to the current system,

the [Social Security] trust fund will be exhausted in 2037 and...an estimated 78% of scheduled annual benefits will be payable with incoming receipts at that time (under the intermediate projections). The primary reason is demographics. Between 2010 and 2030, the number of people aged 65 and older is projected to increase by 76%, while the number of workers supporting the system is projected to increase by 8%. In addition, the trustees project that the system will run cash flow deficits in 2010 and 2011, and again in 2015 and each year thereafter through the end of the 75-year projection period. When current Social Security tax revenues are insufficient to pay benefits and administrative costs, federal securities held by the trust fund are redeemed and Treasury makes up the difference with other receipts. When there are no surplus governmental receipts, policymakers have three options: raise taxes or other income, reduce other spending, or borrow from the public (or a combination of these options).[27]

With over two decades and plenty of incentives to fix the problem, it should be surmountable. For China, however, it could prove destabilizing, both economically and politically. Ideally, economists say, if China's factories suddenly face a shortage of currently abundant working-age adults, wages would rise, savings rates would decline, and consumption would increase—all positive goals for the "global rebalancing" just described. But if these things happen too quickly, steep rises in prices could spark a banking crisis or industrial unrest that would challenge the stability of the whole country.[28]

Again, in the complex relationship between the United States and China (and contrary to the claims of some experts), these challenges are not zero sum; trouble in Shenzhen does not directly equal elation in Akron or Pittsburgh. But these dynamics make nonsense of the theory that China will inevitably roll over the rest of the world. And they represent an opportunity that advanced industrial economies—particularly the United States—cannot afford to miss. The challenge of competing with China toe-to-toe even as it moves up toward the top rungs of the manufacturing ladder can be met, but not by governments mired in deep, radical austerity budgets. Just as Greece cannot hope to restart growth under the terms of austerity plans that prevent any investment in its future productivity, the United States and other advanced economies cannot defend their leads in science and technology if government funding for R&D in those sectors is suddenly slashed. They need a sustained effort by government to incentivize the private sector's R&D efforts and to reward those who take risks to bring new ideas to the market. The United States in particular needs continued outright funding from government sources for the network of laboratories, research universities, and other institutions that make the United States the runaway leader in innovation.

William J. Holstein, an author and journalist who covered China's rise from Maoist backwater to economic power for Businessweek and UPI starting in 1979, argues that the United States can leverage its advantages and take on all comers in global manufacturing. "We can remain ahead of China's emergence," he says. "It is not pre-ordained that America gets blown away in the Asian century."[29]

This is a welcome blast of contrarianism. Sure, Germany, Japan, and other advanced economies continue to run large annual trade surpluses based on export earnings on high-value-added goods and their own relatively small appetite for imports. This has not been true of the United States since the early 1980s, the last time it exported more than it imported. But a number of factors have converged to fuel an export boom for major manufacturers like General Electric, Procter & Gamble, Hewlett-Packard, and others. Recent economic data and changing global trends in labor, energy, and other markets support a longer-term version of Holstein's optimism.

In 2011, the Boston Consulting Group (BCG) reported that, due to a number of changing economic realities—including rising salaries and economic expectations among Chinese workers, new labor, environmental and safety regulations abroad, the higher cost of energy required to ship products halfway around the world, and the US market and the uncertainties of political risk in these places—the cost benefits of producing in Asia no longer automatically outweigh the risks. Indeed, the BCG report predicts a "renaissance for U.S. manufacturing" as labor costs in the United States and China converge around 2015.

"Executives who are planning a new factory in China to make exports for sale in the U.S. should take a hard look at the total costs," says BCG's Harold L. Sirkin, an author of the report. "They're increasingly likely to get a good wage deal and substantial incentives in the U.S., so the cost advantage of China might not be large enough to bother—and that's before taking into account the added expense, time, and complexity of logistics."[30]

Anecdotally, the effects can be seen in new plants created in the United States and in some instances in which plants set up abroad a generation ago to leverage lower labor costs have relocated back to America—dubbed "backshoring" or "reshoring" in market parlance. GE, two years after announcing it would move production of energy-efficient refrigerators abroad, reversed itself in January 2011 and decided on a $93 million upgrade to its plant in Bloomington, Indiana, saving over seven hundred jobs. The company did the same thing earlier in Louisville, Kentucky, investing $80 million in modernizations for a water heater facility rather than moving its four hundred jobs overseas. GE competitor Whirlpool, another big appliance manufacturer, already has several factories in Mexico, and its South Korean rivals make some of their cooking products there. But after months of study, Whirlpool decided in mid-2010 to spend $120 million on a new plant in Cleveland, with a net gain of one hundred and fifty jobs once it's up and running. Although labor costs would be lower in Mexico, Whirlpool found lots of reasons to stay in the Cleveland area. It already had a trained workforce there and wouldn't need to pay severance costs. Freight costs would be lower since most of the plant's products are sold in the United States.

This trend goes beyond "consumer durables," too. Caterpillar is building a $120 million plant to make giant earthmovers in Victoria, Texas, including some models that were previously built in Japan and shipped back to North American customers. The Japan plant is now free to devote more capacity to the booming Asian market. Dow Chemical, the cash register company NCR, Sauder Woodworking, lock maker Master Lock, and the machine tool firm GF AgieCharmilles have all brought overseas production back to the US market in the past three years.

If the main factors in these decisions were labor costs and the weak dollar, the victories would be Pyrrhic. "Inputs"—energy, transportation, raw materials, and other production costs—will fluctuate. But, as Holstein and others have argued, the decisive advantages include innovative management and production techniques, savings on transportation costs, lower political risk and corruption, and the productivity and relatively high skill levels of the American workforce. An added benefit is the effect that China's gargantuan manufacturing sector is having on other world currencies. As China buys coal, oil, wood, minerals, and other resources, the commodities boom inflates the currencies of countries that also compete with US products, including Canada, Australia, South Africa, Brazil, and Russia.

These factors have driven advances by US manufacturing across the board. A sector-by-sector analysis of manufactured products on sale in the United States in 2011 concluded that American manufacturers are either competitive or hold an advantage in 94 percent of all goods sold in the United States, which the authors of this analysis contend is up from 91 percent just two years ago. That difference—just three percentage points—means billions in profits and tens of thousands of jobs in the world's largest consumer market. It also means that moving production offshore no longer makes economic sense for the vast majority of companies producing for the US domestic market. It is important to understand that the results pertain to goods produced for consumption in North America, not for export, where lower prices and added transportation costs change the math considerably. But the study, by management consulting firm Booz & Company and the University of Michigan's Tauber Institute for

Global Operations, divided manufactured products sold in the United States into four segments.[31] In industries like aerospace, medical equipment, chemicals, and food and beverages, the study says, the United States can produce products that compete or dominate the competition in the domestic American market. But production for the US sale of low "value added" products, including textiles, furniture, toys, and some components of electronics and computers, simply won't pay.

With regard to the 6 percent of goods considered impossible to produce profitably in the United States, the study blamed a relentless pursuit of cheap labor in places such as Vietnam and Sri Lanka. This helps explain, for instance, why the once-thriving furniture and textile mills of the American south have fallen on hard times.

For another 41 percent of products, including automobiles and some luxury goods, the value added from manufacturing is "on the bubble," meaning production could stay in the United States or go abroad, depending on a company's manufacturing skills. Here advanced techniques and efficient management are crucial to making production lines in the United States profitable.

THE PERILS OF PARALYSIS

Of course, having an advantage and pressing it home are two different things. For years, Germany, Japan, and other advanced manufacturing economies have managed to run large annual trade surpluses by harnessing these factors: innovation; flexible production based on innovative designs; high-value-added products; and long-tenured, high-skilled workforces. With its scale and openness, the United States could outdo all comers if they struck the right balance between light regulation and investment. Germany and Japan, for instance, incentivize university-level degrees and postgraduate degrees in science as a matter of government policy; they also run extensive secondary vocational training schools. The United States has no such national programs.

With job creation a national priority, Democratic politicians have warmed to the innovation theme, but the term *investment* is parroted as "stimulus" by the latest class of GOP lawmakers, particularly in the Republican held House. Obama has tried to build support for such programs across party lines by teaming with the CEOs of two of America's most successful export manufacturers, Boeing and GE.[32] "The assumption made by many that the United States could transition from a technology-based, export-oriented economic powerhouse to a services-led, consumption-based economy without any serious loss of jobs, prosperity or prestige was fundamentally wrong," wrote GE's chairman and CEO, Jeffrey Immelt, in a *Washington Post* op-ed written as part of this effort. "GE sells more than 96 percent of its products to the private sector, where America's future must be built. But government can help business invest in our shared future. A sound and competitive tax system and a partnership between business and government on education and innovation in areas where America can lead, such as clean energy, are essential to sustainable growth."[33]

In Washington's current climate, this relatively anodyne prescription has met significant opposition. Said GOP House majority leader Eric Cantor, "When he talks about investing...when we hear invest, to me that means more spending."[34] You can bet that when China's central planners hear short-term talk like that, they breathe a little easier.

The carefully balanced interrelationship has, so far, worked out to both sides' advantage. For every job lost in the United States, China's repressive overlords must contend with another citizen whose expectations have risen beyond subsistence levels. It may be that the clash of ideologies is forestalled by a slow, smooth democratization as a result of these very expectations. This was the reality that Mikhail Gorbachev faced in 1987: central planning, even the supercharged state capitalist variety, simply cannot tap the creative genius of a great nation. The Chinese political class studies the events that led to the collapse of the Soviet Union the way the United States studies the Great Depression. China's ruling party is determined to avoid Gorbachev's mistakes, but as recent US economic history shows, such determination is not immune to outside forces.

The US economy, with its potent, creative corporate sector; transparent bureaucracy; world-beating universities; and highly skilled labor force, does not have to bow down in surrender to China. It can compete and adjust to the arrival of China and to the billion-odd other middle-income workers being added to the global economy in other emerging-market countries by stretching its lead in high-end, knowledge-based commerce. The true danger for the United States does not lie in predatory Asia sweatshops. Instead, this danger lies in bumbling, for political reasons, into an overtly hostile stance that puts the world's two most powerful nations on course for a war so terrible that no nation, regardless of its choice of economic or political models, will survive it.

CHAPTER 7

THE NOT-SO-PACIFIC RIM

"L'Angleterre est une nation de boutiquiers," Napoleon famously said of France's primary military rival, England, dismissing them as "a nation of shopkeepers." Of course, he lived to regret it. Today, his description captures what all nations hope for in their rivals, especially large neighboring ones— that they would be focused on the domestic, obsessed with commerce rather than the military sciences, and determined to prosper rather than conquer.

Is China a "nation of shopkeepers"? A billion and a half Indians, Japanese, South Koreans, Vietnamese, Filipinos, and countless smaller nations, including a dwindling, insecure tribe of about five million far-eastern Russians, sure hope so.

Beijing wants to project the goal of commercial—not territorial—gains, as set forth in its official policy of a "peaceful rise, peaceful development" in Asia. "China has quickly enhanced its comprehensive national strength and international status by adhering to peaceful development," writes Chinese political commentator Zheng Xiwen for the *Guangming Daily*. The piece channels the voice of the Communist Party's powerful Central Committee, which publishes the paper. Zheng, like the party that pays him, argues that foreigners should calm down about China's military spending and determination to enforce its territorial claims in the South China Sea. After all, war would be a distraction from China's business plan. "At present, China is at a crucial period in its reform and opening up, and problems should be avoided whenever possible. A war may put China at risk of losing rare development opportunities and momentum for growth."[1]

Why would China kill—or even rattle—the goose that lays the golden egg? The question is worth dwelling upon for a moment. China is thriving, and though its territorial disputes with neighboring states make headlines and the unresolved issues of Taiwan and the Korean peninsula still loom ominously above Asia's prosperity, the incentives seem to argue for a "peaceful rise." The Buick-loving cadres of China's ruling party have invested so much in the US economy, and are making so much money in the lopsided trading relationship with it, that only a grave miscalculation by one of these giants could possibly lead to open warfare. Neither side, we can safely assume, is busy plotting Pearl Harbor–like treachery against the other.

But mistakes do happen. The war in Iraq and the global financial crisis are only the most recent reminders. As China grows, the outriders of its newfound strength and ambition increasingly rub elbows with American power. They also rub up against the interests of many nations in the Pacific Rim that rely on the United States to maintain the region's balance of power. Trade between China and all of these nations is brisk, yet they have all recently begun thinking seriously about how long China's rise will remain peaceful. Taiwan remains a "renegade province" in Beijing's eyes, though the tensions have subsided in recent years. Territorial disputes have flared with Japan, South Korea, and the Philippines in the past two years over tracts of the East and South China Seas. Along its Himalayan border with India, too, China has grown more assertive. Meanwhile, China's peculiar and still-close ties with the unpredictable North Korea stoke these fears about its own long-term motives. So, too, does a military modernization program that has upgraded every facet of China's armed forces over the past decade. China will commission its first aircraft carrier in 2012, and it has shown that it can shoot down satellites with lasers. Its progress in developing antisatellite and antiship weapons makes it harder for the United States to project power in the region and, thus, to "have the back" of its Asian allies. Among China's neighbors and in the halls of power in Washington, those disinclined to believe in the "peaceful rise" are amassing this evidence to argue that China is bent on challenging US power in Asia.

THERE GOES THE NEIGHBORHOOD?

Not everyone in the region has reacted fearfully. "There is a case to be made that China's maritime military advances are partly intended to safeguard its legitimate interests as a major seaborne trading and energy-importing nation," writes Rory Medcalf, an Australian security expert and former diplomat. "I am broadly in accord with the argument that China's military modernization is, in substantial part, the understandable behavior of a great power with a fast-expanding economy and wide international interests."[2] If so, its behavior since late 2009, at the very least, raises real questions about China's understanding of how its actions are viewed abroad. The series of spats with its smaller neighbors drove many of them to increase defense spending and renew ties with the US

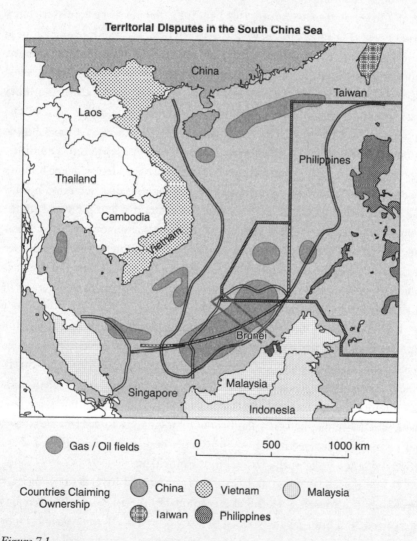

Figure 7.1
Source: *South China Sea, Analysis Briefs, U.S. Energy Information Agency, March 2008,* accessed
December 6, 2011, *http://www.eia.gov/countries/regions-topics.cfm?fips=SCS*

military. To the Singaporean author and strategist Kishore Mahbubani, this just proves that Beijing is like any other power—including the United States: "They make short- term mistakes, but in the long term they correct course very quickly. And that's the strength that they have....On the South China Sea, they made some statements. They got people very upset. And then they sensed that the mood was getting angry, and I think they quietly, in their own way, would lower the temperature on those areas."[3]

Whether China's new assertiveness is indeed a mistake or the foreshadowing of a more aggressive future, this handful of incidents certainly stirred a hornet's nest. The most serious, a clash between Japanese warships and Chinese fishing vessels in the East China Sea, ended in humiliation for the Japanese. Both countries claim a small group of islets near Okinawa, and during naval operations in that area in September 2010, the Japanese took a Chinese fishing boat captain into custody for ramming two Japanese coastal patrol vessels. The captain, held for two weeks, was ultimately released. However, it was Chinese economic muscle flexing, not military power, that forced Japan into a humiliating climbdown in spite of the fact that the Japanese had video evidence backing their version of the event. China responded to the captain's detention by cutting off exports to Japan of rare earths, a product mined and produced almost exclusively by China and used widely by Japanese manufacturers in automobile, solar, and electronics factories. Japan was the dominant importer of rare earths, and China no doubt hurt itself economically with the ban. But the incident confirmed that Beijing is willing to act against its economic interests in cases where its national will is challenged.

While there has never been love lost between China and its old foe, the timing was particularly poignant for Japan. Chinese media never miss a chance to note that their economy officially overtook Japan's in 2010 as the world's second largest.[4] But Japan also rediscovered the value of the US-Japan military alliance. Not coincidentally, Japan's Liberal Democratic Party government, which campaigned on a platform of removing US forces from Okinawa and pursuing Asian security ties with China and others, has shelved these proposals in the wake of the East China Sea incident.

While tensions calmed and Japan was confronted by cruel new distractions after the March 2011 Tohoku earthquake, the island dispute remains unresolved, and Sino-Japanese ties have grown brittle. Another serious Sino-Japanese incident could cause major regional problems, quite possibly spurring rearmament in Japan at a time when recession, earthquakes, tsunamis, and melting nuclear reactors should take priority. Another lasting effect is this: Japan and China suspended an agreement to jointly develop part of the East China Sea's natural gas reserves, estimated by CNOOC at 1.7 trillion cubic feet, plus up to eighteen million barrels of oil, suggesting that one or the other may now attempt to move ahead unilaterally.

This is just one of a half dozen disputes stoked by China since the extent of America's economic troubles became clear during the global financial crisis. Regional defense officials believe the timing, too, to be poignant. High in the Himalayas, a dispute over territory that sparked a Sino-Indian war in 1962 has flared anew, and the two giant neighbors back opposing political interests in Nepal. In North Korea, China appears to have concluded that a nuclear-armed Kim dynasty is more favorable to its interests than an implosion of the Stalinist state that creates refugees out of its twenty-three million inmates. Beijing backed the military junta in Myanmar and Cambodia's dictatorial strongman, Hun Sen; Beijing is also widely regarded as the source of ballistic missile and various nuclear weapons technologies for Pakistan. And it has continually intimidated its smaller neighbors in the South China Sea, where naval standoffs with Vietnam, South Korea, the Philippines, and Malaysia could easily escalate to violence. China insists that it will enforce its somewhat fanciful claim of "indisputable sovereignty" over the entire body of the South China Sea, extending hundreds of miles beyond its mainland borders or any internationally recognized maritime boundary. With oil and gas reserves thought to lurk beneath those waters, the stakes will rise as China's economy grows ever more thirsty for growth-sustaining energy sources. US Secretary of State Hillary Clinton declared in 2010 the US interest in "freedom of navigation, open access to Asia's maritime commons and respect for international law in the South China Sea," a statement taken as a challenge by China and an offer of protection by its worried neighbors.[5]

GULLIVER'S FOOTPRINTS

Behind these disputes lurk the large American garrisons on Japan and in South Korea, along with the US Navy's Seventh Fleet, the primary guarantor of America's long-standing promise to defend Taiwan if China ever attempts to take the island by force. With two aircraft carriers on station, three more nearby with their surface and submarine escorts, plus several amphibious task forces and their US Marine assault groups, the Seventh Fleet represents the largest forward-deployed military force on earth. The fleet's headquarters at Yokosuka, Japan, is complemented by American airfields, bases, and port facilities across the region, from Australia to Okinawa, Seoul to Singapore, and Guam in the central Pacific to the tiny island of Diego Garcia located 1,780 miles south of Sri Lanka in the middle of the Indian Ocean. Added late in 2011: a new U.S. Marine Corps deployment to Darwin, at the northern tip of Australia. "The United States is a Pacific power, and we are here to stay," President Obama told the Australian parliament in a speech announcing the new basing agreement. "Indeed, we are already modernizing America's defense posture across the Asia Pacific. It will be more broadly distributed—maintaining our strong presence in Japan and the Korean Peninsula, while enhancing our presence in Southeast Asia. Our posture will be more flexible—with new capabilities to ensure that our forces can operate freely. And our posture will be more sustainable, by helping allies and partners build their capacity, with more training and exercises."[6]

These forces symbolize America's larger strategic commitment to the region to maintain the balance of power. All of this might, originally conceived to fight Japan in World War II and adapted to deter the Soviet Pacific Fleet in the Cold War, now focuses primarily on China and its unpredictable ally, North Korea. For years, the mere presence of this awesome American force imposed a kind of stability, preventing rational watchfulness among smaller powers from turning into paranoia and an arms race. The Japanese in particular, but also the South Koreans, Indonesians, Australians, and even the Filipinos, have looked to US power to provide the same kind of security umbrella for them that Europeans have come to expect from NATO. It also gave Taiwan the security it needed to concentrate on economic matters rather than devoting all of its energies to warding off Chinese attempts to absorb it forcefully.

But the balance of power in the region is clearly shifting, and America's allies with it. Until recently, this was driven only by the economic heft of China, which has gone from a relatively small trade partner with many of the region's economies to the dominant one. China now ranks as the number one trade partner of South Korea, Japan, Australia, and even India, a regional rival that until 2002 had almost no trade with Beijing. All but India had, until recently, counted America as their best customer.[7] Yet in the capitals of America's closest Asian allies, and even in some countries loath to publicly admit a dependence on US power, the hedging of bets is well along by now. Consider the clear signs of a strategic rethink among these countries:

- In Seoul, the capital of a nation that hosts twenty-seven thousand US troops and arguably would not exist except for the 1950–1953 war that cost the lives of fifty thousand American troops, a recent attack by North Korea on South Korean civilians had the nation's diplomats looking eagerly toward China's capital. Beijing has leverage over the communist north, rather than Washington, which is loath to add an outright conflict with the nuclear-armed North to all of its other troubles. In the end, China's interests in stability and fear of refugees resonates with South Koreans.

- In Japan, taboos that prevented a real debate on the country's military power and the American presence have fallen away. In 2009, Japanese voters put the Democratic Party of Japan (DPJ) in power, led by Prime Minister Naoto Kan—the first Japanese leader since World War II to publicly question whether his country's alignment with the United States is a permanent state of affairs. One of the DPJ's first decisions was to make an early bet on a regional hedge against America's sliding influence in Asia in the form of an East Asian community that would involve Japan, China, South Korea, and other countries in an all-Asian security pact. Kan's government lasted until September 2011, and in that time, events intervened to force the DPJ to back away from these vows. The government similarly softened a vow to eject US Marines from their bases in Okinawa after American aid to victims of the Tohoku earthquake shed new light on the value of having big friends. Yet the debate invigorated Japan's domestic foes of the still-sizeable US military presence in Japan—indeed, it legitimized the question and sparked a significant review of Japan's military posture that stresses Japan's need to be more self-reliant.

- In Australia, a serious debate rages about the increasing dependence of the country's economy on China. While exports of raw materials have fueled a boom in Australia, think tanks and war colleges debate whether Australia should move closer to India, Japan, and Indonesia in anticipation of the United States' diminishing ability to maintain the regional status quo. Australia and Japan signed a mutual defense treaty in 2007. The new US base in Darwin notwithstanding, the clear opinion of Australian defense officials is that, as a government white paper put it as far back as 2000, "the trilateral relationship between China, Japan and India will define the East Asian strategic framework."[8]

- In India, the United States miscalculated the desire of Indian officials for a tight strategic relationship, entering two aging warplanes, the Lockheed Martin F-16IN and Boeing's F/A-18 Super Hornet, into India's competition for a future national fighter aircraft. The F-22 and F-35, the frontline US warplanes being offered to Australia, Britain, and Israel, were ruled out by Washington. India, perceiving a snub, rejected the US airframes in the first round of the competition, leaving France's Rafale and the Eurofighter, built by a European consortium, to duke it out for primacy and billions in business.

But the truly stunning turnabout is Taiwan. Technically, China and Taiwan have been engulfed in a civil war since 1949, when the Nationalists of the Kuomintang (KMT) fled the mainland for what was then called Formosa. The Chinese regard Taiwan, which the KMT ruled as a military dictatorship into the 1980s, as a renegade province. But Taiwan has thrived economically, and even after the United States switched its diplomatic recognition from Taiwan to Beijing in 1979 as part of the rapprochement negotiated by former secretary of state Henry Kissinger, the United States has ensured that the island's military remains well equipped and that China is under no illusion about US military involvement were it to attempt an invasion. Indeed, as late as March 2005, Taiwan appeared bent on declaring independence, and China responded with a law authorizing the use of force if the island dared to try. US carriers routinely hovered nearby as a sign of support. A RAND Corporation report for the US military from 2007 concluded that "Taiwan's status is unlikely to be decided any time soon" and that the status quo would probably persist for another generation, "however strategically uncomfortable that may be for leaders in Washington, Beijing, and Taipei."[9]

IF YOU CAN'T BEAT 'EM...

But the global economic crisis, combined with China's increasing heft and local calculations among Taiwanese voters, has changed things enormously. In June 2008, as the US economy came unglued and American forces remained mired in Iraq and Afghanistan, Taiwan's voters rejected another term for the proindependence Democratic Progressive Party. Instead, they elected a man who campaigned for closer economic ties to the mainland, Ma Ying-jeou of the KMT, who as president has proceeded to hedge dependence on American power.

Unlike the situation in the Middle East, where Israel continues to make policy as though American power remains undiminished, Taiwan has chosen to remove some eggs from the US basket. "President Ma has made important breakthroughs in cross-Strait reconciliation, as well as in broadening and deepening the synergistic nexus between China and Taiwan," writes Fu S. Mei, an Asia defense analyst for a conservative US think tank, the Jamestown Foundation. "The next step for Beijing going forward is formal political dialogue, which Chinese authorities have been applying increasing pressure for the Ma administration to start. Taipei has been trying hard to stall as long as possible, because issues of sovereignty are politically sensitive in Taiwan. Moreover, perhaps Mr. Ma realizes that he has yet to assemble the bargaining chips he would need at the peace talks table."[10]

From the view of Jamestown and most other American security organizations, those bargaining chips must include a new round of weapons purchases to bolster Taiwan's diminishing technological lead over its giant would-be dance partner. Along those lines, the Obama administration sold Taiwan air defense missiles and upgraded communications equipment for its F-16 fighters and other arms in January 2010, a $6 billion deal that prompted China to suspend all military ties with the United States—a high-stakes game given the importance of mutual understanding as China's navy and other forces increasingly come in contact with the Seventh Fleet. A lobbying campaign for a second sale raged through the summer of 2011, presenting an enormous dilemma for the United States. "The effort to satisfy both parties is extremely difficult and will likely fail," wrote Ted Galen Carpenter, a military expert at the Cato Institute.[11]

Admiral Mike Mullen, chairman of the US Joint Chiefs of Staff, voiced concern over offending China yet again after returning from a July 2011 visit in which he rode in a Chinese submarine and watched People's Liberation Army counterterrorism exercises. It was the first US high-level exchange with China's military since the 2010 arms sale, which resulted in a complete freeze on US-China military relations. With American allies brushing uncomfortably close to China's military, this self-imposed blackout carries real risk—akin to trusting the most important relationship in the world to the young commanders of minor Chinese, Japanese, Vietnamese, and Filipino warships rubbing elbows in Asia's coastal waters. By the time of Mullen's goodwill trip, which followed a similar trip to the United States by China's military chief of staff, Taiwan had requested a second, more controversial arms sale: the delivery of an upgraded version of the F-16 warplane that the island's air force first purchased in 1992. The older aircraft, Taiwan argued, risked being outclassed by the latest models built in China. Obama chose to split the difference—rejecting the sale of more-advanced aircraft but agreeing to supply "upgrade kits" for the older warplanes' avionics and weapons systems. In Taiwan, the decision confirmed the new reality: the United States would risk only so much today on behalf of a promise made when Jimmy Carter was president in 1979.

The Taiwan decision raised the usual accusations of appeasement, particularly from the largely Republican congressional delegation representing the F-16's production lines in Texas. But the uproar remained local. Beijing chose not to freeze military ties this time, apparently satisfied at the compromise. In Washington, the voices who once asked, "Who lost China?" had passed from the scene. In the Pentagon, tempered by a decade of overreaching, reality prevailed. As Mullen explained in a *New York Times* op-ed after his China visit, the United States must place coexistence with China above other concerns. "I understand the concerns of those who feel that any cooperation benefits China more than the United States. I just don't agree. This relationship is too important to manage through blind suspicion and mistrust. We've tried that. It doesn't work. I'm not suggesting we look the other way on serious issues, that we abandon healthy skepticism, or that we change our military's focus on the region. But we need to keep communication open and work hard to improve each interaction."[12]

Even before the F-16 decision, Taiwan had hedged its bets. It has pumped money into a domestic arms industry as sophisticated as anything on the mainland, though it cannot hope to match the scale of Beijing's buildup. More importantly, in June 2010, Ma's government inked the landmark China-Taiwan free-trade agreement, officially opening commercial links and charting a path to future political negotiations.[13] The deal lifted over five hundred tariffs on trade between them. It also opened Taiwan's private enterprises to Chinese investment for the first time. While Taiwan has continued to limit the stakes China can purchase, no one can be sure how much of the investment that actually pours into Taiwan each year already contains Chinese money, channeled via foreign investment banks. An influx of tourists from the mainland—another result of the newly warmed ties—has also bolstered Taiwan's economy.

This is not to say that sentiment for reunification is strong in Taiwan. Many Taiwanese have personally experienced life under their own dictatorship and harbor a sophisticated view, through access to Chinese media and their own tenacious journalistic outlets, of the downside of life across the Taiwan Strait. Mainland Chinese were deeply impressed by the conduct of Taiwan's January 2012 elections, which gave Ma a second term. Ma's slogan, No Unification, No Independence, has allowed diplomats on both sides to explore the kind of halfway house the British negotiated with Beijing in 1979 when they agreed to hand back Hong Kong. That may not appeal to many Taiwanese: the lack of democratic guarantees in Hong Kong after China assumed control in 2004 belied the popular idea that, in absorbing a freewheeling democratic society, China itself would somehow be democratized. But many among China's elite believe Taiwan could, indeed, be the host that changes everything.

Britain's mistake was not in trying for a negotiated solution, but rather in waiting too long. By 1979, when talks began under Margaret Thatcher, Britain had sunk to second-tier military and economic status and had no real ability to project power into Asia. The United States, as the guarantor of the democratic freedoms Taiwan had struggled to fashion since the end of the KMT dictatorship in the 1980s, should be seeking to move this cross-straits process forward now, while the Seventh Fleet still rules the Pacific and the US economy still ranks at the top of the heap. If the stalemate lasts beyond another decade, the question will not be what guarantees the United States can extract for Taiwan in a peaceful reunification, but rather how Taiwan would like to be digested—quickly and violently, or voluntarily, under economic and political duress.

ENTER THE "CARRIER KILLER"

The jitters affecting the arc of US-supported governments along the Pacific Rim have multiple sources—from North Korea's nuclear program to the territorial disputes of the South China Sea to long-term calculations about America's ability to sustain its huge military footprint in the region. But 2011 added a new fear that has US Navy strategists equally concerned: deployment of a new Chinese ballistic antiship missile capable of striking warships as far as twelve hundred miles offshore.

As with China's stealth fighter prototype, US intelligence had long known that China was trying to develop such a "sea denial" weapon but was caught off guard by the speed with which it was deployed. Admiral Robert Willard, commander of the US Pacific Command, told reporters in December 2010 that the DF-21D had reached initial operational capability, and China's top commander, General Chen, claimed in April 2011 that the missile had a range of nearly seventeen hundred miles.[14] If the range is even half of that, the carrier strike forces of the US Seventh Fleet have a serious problem.[15]

For China, which cannot hope to match the might of the US Navy's carrier strike forces anytime soon, keeping the American armada so far offshore that it cannot strike at the Chinese mainland has been a goal for decades. The arrival of the new missile, technically the DF-21D but dubbed the "carrier killer" by US Navy analysts, fundamentally changes long-held assumptions about how a US-Chinese clash over Taiwan or any number of other fraught scenarios would play out.

The US Navy understands this better than anyone. The range of un-refueled carrier-based aircraft is approximately 735 miles—well within range of China's ballistic antiship defenses. In an article in a Navy scholarly journal entitled "The Twilight of the $uperfluous Carrier," two Pentagon strategists contend that this new reality should force a major rethink of US naval construction plans and Pacific strategy. In effect, they write, putting a nuclear aircraft carrier like the new *Gerald R. Ford* and its crew of five thousand in range of such weapons simply will not be an acceptable risk—or a credible deterrent—in the twenty-first century.

Factors both internal and external are hastening the carrier's curtain call. Competitors abroad have focused their attention on the United States' ability to go anywhere on the global maritime commons and strike targets ashore with pinpoint accuracy. That focus has resulted in the development of a series of sensors and weapons that combine range and strike profiles to deny carrier strike groups the access necessary to launch squadrons of aircraft against shore installations.

... [A] series of poor acquisition decisions, beginning with the mismanagement and ultimate cancellation of the A-12 Avenger as the replacement aircraft for the A-6 Intruder deep-strike aircraft, have exacerbated the challenge to carrier efficacy. The resulting reduction in the combat-effective range of the carrier air wing from 1,050 to 500 nautical miles forces the carrier to operate closer to enemy shores even as anti-access systems would logically force the carrier farther seaward....[The president] would need to be facing a gravely extreme scenario to commit this sort of strategic asset, with a crew of 5,000 men and women. The *Gerald R. Ford* is just the first of her class. She should also be the last.[16]

CHAPTER 8

INDIA, BRAZIL, AND THE NEW AMERICAN DREAM TEAM

After decades of leading grand coalitions against one "-ism" after another—monarchist absolutism in World War I, fascism in World War II, communism during the Cold War, and terrorism after 9/11—it's not surprising that America is dazed and confused by the complexity confronting it today. None of the "victories" won over the past century were absolute—some semblance of all the aforementioned "-isms" survive somewhere in the world, and while the phrase *war on terror* has fallen out of favor, the battle on that "-ism," too, rages on.

But these fights against sweeping and easily characterized "evils" obscure the urgent need for a deeper, subtler strategy. For most of the twentieth century, American policy makers pursued a grand strategy that sought to spread the ethos of capitalism—and if those countries also chose their leaders democratically, so much the better. As many writers have noted, the collapse of the last great tangible threat to market capitalism—the Soviet Union—and China's defection from Marxist economic principles basically got the job done; most of the goals of America's grand strategy were achieved. Then the drift began, and the illusion of omnipotence set in to devastating effect.

Lacking a great, overarching strategy—due in part to America's own hardy denial, as well as the transitional nature of the times—the United States has fallen back on an often-contradictory mixture of old habits and bad instincts. Some specific policies—for instance, emphasizing the inherent instability of authoritarian states and avoiding precipitous withdrawals from Iraq and Afghanistan—work for both the short- and long-term good of the world. But just as in America's stewardship of its domestic economy, its cultivation of friends and allies abroad will require short-term sacrifices and significant flexibility aimed at winning the long game for itself and keeping the liberal market economic model from going the way of its Marxist nemeses.

The global financial crisis, which highlighted the resiliency and growth rates of emerging economic powers like China, India, Brazil, Turkey, Indonesia, and others, also sent a message to Washington policy makers that its own traditional allies were suffering stagnation or decline even more profound than its own. The financial travails of the euro zone, in spite of Germany's potent economy, will doom the EU to decades of brutal infighting over pension reforms and sovereign deleveraging, and in the worst-case scenario, even cause it to break up. Japan, already laid low by the bursting of its economic bubble in the early 1990s, shows no signs of recovering its 1980s vigor, and the burden of reconstruction after the 2011 earthquake-tsunami-nuclear crisis will certainly prevent it from breaking out again anytime soon. Indeed, of the traditional American allies, only Canada, Australia, and Norway appear to be emerging relatively unscathed from the financial disaster of 2007-2009, and then only because they are resource-rich economies—"commodity plays," in the parlance of the markets—exporting an increasing amount of raw material and energy to China.

THE SANDLOT DOCTRINE

How has the United States responded to these dynamics? After two decades of acting as though American hegemony was a permanent state of affairs, America has struggled to adjust to reality. Instead, like a kid picking a team for sandlot baseball, the United States has been sizing up the potential value of new allies with an eye to augmenting its existing bench. This is a poor strategy for an outdated game, but the United States appears intent on pressing forward under the old rules, mistakenly anticipating a global competition in which it will lead a defense of democracy, capitalism, and other concerns consistent with American (and thus, humanity's) interests. Judging from the recent public statements and policy moves of US leaders, diplomats, and corporate executives, the desired cocaptains for this American Dream Team are India and Brazil.

On paper, this approach has a lot to recommend it. Brazil and India, the legitimately democratic half of the BRICs, each dominate the economic and military affairs of their regions—South America and South Asia. Economically, they have as many differences as similarities, but their dynamic growth rates, large labor forces, improving educational levels and infrastructure, and relative openness to FDI put them, alone among the world's other emerging economies, in the same category as China.

A thumbnail profile of the two economies gives the lie to easy assumptions: that India's growth is driven by software firms and "offshored" call centers, or that Brazil's centers mostly around the raw material riches of the Amazon. These factors, to be sure, helped vault each from the seemingly hopeless depths of the old Third World into hotbeds of investment and growth. But their economic development over the past decade and the paths that they have plotted going forward aim to navigate the difficult "middle income" challenge of pulling vast numbers of deeply impoverished, ill-educated, and often discontent masses into the middle and lower middle class.

India's challenge, in both political and numerical terms, is far greater. Good, then, that it has shown a much more aggressive posture on reforming its labor laws. Until recently, these laws have prevented the development of medium and large firms necessary to employ the population of about seven hundred million rural workers currently tied to subsistence-level jobs in agriculture, mining, and other preindustrial pursuits. Morgan Stanley, the investment bank, expects that India's economy will grow faster than any other large economy over the next quarter century—at 8 to 10 percent (versus about 7 to 8 percent for China). "We believe India's growth will accelerate to a sustainable 9-10% by 2013-15, after an average of 7.3% over the past 10 years," wrote Morgan Stanley economists Chetan Ahya and Tanvee Gupta in a recent report comparing the two economies.[1] Furthermore, India's much younger workforce should help it continue to outpace China's growth rates going forward, with a much higher percentage of the population actually in the active labor force to support the elderly.

"We believe that, by 2012, India and China will likely achieve similar growth rates of closer to 9 [percent of the GDP annually] and from 2013-15 India will start outpacing China's GDP growth notably. The demographic trend is likely to diverge in the two countries. China is expected to reach an inflexion point in its age-dependency ratio around 2015."[2] Combined with continuing reforms to open India's economy to FDI, a very high rate of reinvestment in

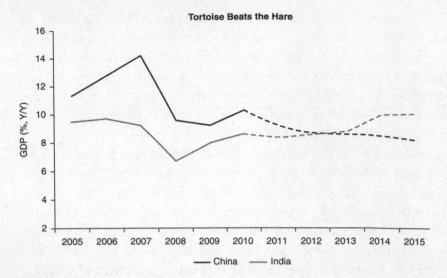

Figure 8.1
Source: National Bureau of Statistics, India Ministry of Statistics, Roubini Global Economics
Forecasts

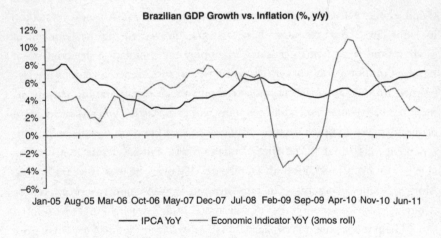

Figure 8.2   "ICPA" = Brazil's Inflation Consumer Price Index; "Economic Indica-
tor" = Brazil Central Bank index
Source: Haver/Roubini, Global Economics, http://www.roubini.com/analysis/165606.php

infrastructure, and a surge in spending on education and basic research, India's
economy could well surpass both China's and the United States' in the second
half of the twenty-first century as the world's largest.

Brazil, in both scale and intensity, is in a slightly different league. This
stems partly from the cautious nature of Brazilian economic reforms, which

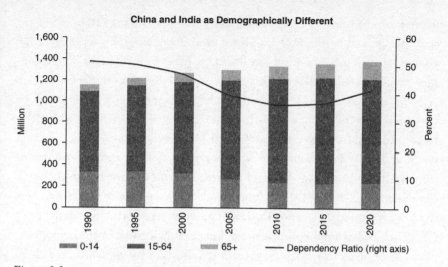

Figure 8.3a
Source: US Census Bureau/Roubini Global Economics

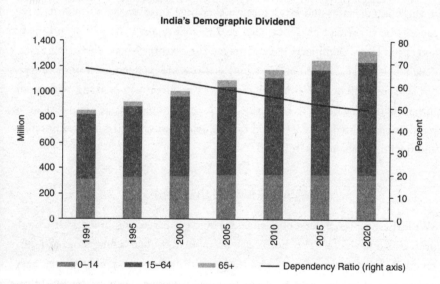

Figure 8.3b
Source: US Census Bureau/Roubini Global Economics

have left large and important elements of the economy in state hands, including some of its most successful international brands—the mining giant Vale, the aircraft manufacturer Embraer, and, of course, its oil monopoly, Petrobras. With a population of 193 million, Brazil contains only as many people as a medium-sized Indian state. The average Brazilian, largely as a result, is far better off: the GDP per head is $10,816, ranking it fifty-sixth in the world. The figure for India is barely a sixth as high at $1,265—a ranking of 138 out of 185 countries ranked by the IMF.[3] This excuses, to some extent, its lower GDP growth rate of 4 to 4.5 percent. But Brazil has other problems that, if not managed properly, could lead it to falter in its climb to global prominence.

The country remains highly dependent on commodity exports, which would not be a bad thing except that commodity prices have been volatile in recent years and the percentage of Brazil's export earnings that depend on China and other East Asian economies has risen to the point where a downturn in Asia could do great damage in Brazil. Even more worrying, the boom in commodities—combined with China's undervalued currency and the successive waves of cheap dollars flowing into economies like Brazil's due to the Fed's QE policies—has fired up inflation and made Brazilian labor uncompetitive. This has caused a worrying dip in Brazil's industrial sector, which as a share of the country's economy, fell to its lowest point in a half century in 2009 at 15.5 percent. "Many in Brazil are concerned that loose monetary conditions in the United States and large foreign exchange interventions in China have caused the [Brazilian currency, the] real to soar against the dollar and yuan, and cheap Chinese imports have damaged the country's manufacturing base," concluded a 2011 Council on Foreign Relations independent task force report. "Brazil's inefficient and complex regulatory environment—along with poor infrastructure, inadequate education, high and complex taxes, and rigid labor requirements—make it costly and difficult to commercialize new technology and start new businesses in Brazil."[4]

VALUES AND VISIONS

While these represent huge challenges for both countries, combined with growth prospects and the fact that both have accumulated huge reserves of hard currency, they also represent opportunities for the nations of the old G7, who have the technological knowledge and experience in navigating these tricky transitions, having done so only a generation or two ago themselves. US, Japanese, and European companies have rushed into both markets, and—regulatory and cultural frustrations notwithstanding—partnerships like those struck by GE or Japan's Nippon Steel in Brazil or Credit Suisse or Cisco in India can do more than years of old-fashioned development aid to foster economic success.

While the economic case for closer cooperation between the old G7 powers and these two emerging giants is obvious, American policy makers are even more excited about the political and social instincts that theoretically make India and Brazil natural potential allies. Like the United States and its older allies, these giant multiethnic states embrace the idea that the sometimes-chaotic political freedoms of democracy are necessary to nurturing economic creativity and helpful as a safety valve in keeping social peace. Constitutionally, they respect religious and ethnic differences and have enshrined a flexible sense of what it is to be a Brazilian or an Indian. Both are home to leading global industrial brands and have sent hundreds of thousands of immigrants to economic success in the United States and Europe. While Brazil renounced nuclear weapons in the 1980s after secretly pursuing them, it will soon join India and six others as the only nations operating nuclear-powered attack submarines.

Most importantly, from Washington's perspective, both Brazil and India have demonstrated a serious desire to begin exercising their huge potential influence beyond their local neighborhoods. Brazil and India aspire to join Washington and four other permanent members of the UN Security Council. They both operate aircraft carriers and will likely build more in the future. Each, like the United States, takes an active role in international peacekeeping, and they are both continent-sized yet still present an open face to the wider world, which is typical of maritime powers—unlike the insular Chinese and Russians. In short, when Captain America glances down the bench at the aging, apathetic, and atrophied remnants of the team that "won" the Cold War, the need for new blood is painfully clear, and Brazil and India seem like the solution.

Yet the United States, again, has run into a familiar problem—one that tends to dog many of its larger initiatives overseas. For every commonality just mentioned, there are equally compelling economic, political, and histori-cal reasons why neither India nor Brazil—nor other super middleweights in the emerging powers—would want to tie itself into anything that could be construed as an "anti-China" alliance with America. Unlike disputes between China and Japan, Taiwan, South Korea, and the countries of Southeast Asia, disputes between Beijing and the largest emerging powers, if they exist at all, are easily overshadowed by the ebb and flow of trade and investment with China. Even India, which has a genuine history of antagonism with China—the 1962 border war, lingering territorial issues, and geopolitical concerns about Chinese influence in its backyard—prefers not to place too strong a bet on a strategic alliance with America at this stage. "Is it in India's interest to join the West in thwarting the rise of China?" asked Kishore Mahbubani, a Singaporean author and strategist, in a recent lecture. "I presume that the answer is no. There is a simple rule of geo-politics. In any three-way contest of power, the best position to occupy is the middle-position."[5]

A MESSAGE TO INDIA

"The middle" is a familiar place for India, which managed to stay "non-aligned" during the Cold War, yet caught between China and Pakistan in the Himalayas, and the United States and Soviet Union in the long-running ideological warfare of the late twentieth century. Even its initial breakout as a global force in economics had something of the middle man about it, as call centers, accounting units, and other American corporate back-office functions moved to Bangalore and other Indian cities starting in the 1990s, sparking a backlash about offshoring US jobs to "Asian sweatshops."

But India's potential as something more than a place to write software cheaply had long tantalized American foreign policy thinkers, particularly those who believed that the longer-term "fight" of the twenty-first century would pit democracies against authoritarian states. In 2000, one such person, Condoleezza Rice, was serving as a campaign advisor to GOP candidate George W. Bush. Rice, who in spite of her youth had played a significant role in the Reagan and Bush Sr. administrations during the final years of the Cold War, wrote a piece in *Foreign Affairs* magazine that year in which she laid out the future administration's approach to foreign affairs. As a period piece, it makes fascinating reading: neither the word Afghanistan nor Al Qaeda appears within, though Russia does thirty-six times; NATO, eight; and Milosevic, three. Nonetheless, Rice also signaled a new interest in India—then still under US economic sanctions for its 1998 nuclear tests— that would blossom into a full-blown courtship during her time in office. The United States, she wrote, "should pay closer attention to India's role in the [Asian] regional balance. There is a strong tendency conceptually to connect India with Pakistan and to think only of Kashmir or the nuclear competition between the two states. But India is an element in China's calculation, and it should be in America's, too. India is not a great power yet, but it has the potential to emerge as one."[6]

This is fairly tame stuff—yet barely a year later, with the Trade Center towers and the Pentagon in flames, Rice led the Bush administration's charge to lift the sanctions on both India and Pakistan, as Washington lined up support and airspace for its counterpunch in Afghanistan. The sanctions, President Bush said on September 23, 2001, with typical bluntness, are "not in the national security interests of the United States."[7]

The happiness in India was palpable, but it would be short-lived. Desperately concerned that its rival, Pakistan, would use the upcoming war to forge closer ties to Washington, India offered access to its air bases and its own rich intelligence on the Taliban and their Pakistani allies in the first days after the attacks—an unprecedented gesture given the history of suspicion that had characterized US-India relations since the latter's independence in 1947. But the Bush administration decided that Pakistan, which had fought alongside the United States against the Soviets in Afghanistan two decades before, had to be the priority in spite of Pakistan's own close ties to the Taliban. This was a historic miscalculation—Pakistan arguably has proven to be as much of a problem as an advantage—and a decision that may have thrown away the best chance the United States would ever have to conclude an actual military alliance with the world's largest democracy.

CLOSE, BUT NO CIGAR

The decision to decline India's offer and place America's bets on Pakistan's General Pervez Musharraf reconfirmed Indian suspicions that America could never really grow into a reliable strategic ally. As billions of dollars in weapons and high-tech intelligence capabilities poured into the hands of its enemy, Pakistan, Indian intelligence watched helplessly as much of that aid was diverted from its intended purpose of rooting Taliban and Al Qaeda cells from their redoubts in Pakistan's Frontier Provinces and directed instead to a buildup against India. Of course, the Bush administration had good reasons to try and leverage help from Pakistan, though clearly throughout the war in Afghanistan, Pakistan's intelligence services and some elements of the army continued to sympathize with and support the Taliban, which they had nurtured as a means of keeping Afghanistan in the pro-Pakistan camp during that country's long civil war. Regardless, India complained frequently about the military aid diversions, as well as the activities of Pakistan's venal intelligence agency, Inter-Services Intelligence (ISI), which continued to train and even direct Islamic militants for infiltration and terrorist attacks against India (like the one in November 2008 that killed 164 people in Mumbai). In hindsight, US general Stanley McChrystal, who led the Afghan war from 2008 to

2010 and helped write the counterinsurgency strategy of the US Army, concedes that Pakistan will never be the ally America needed to win outright in Afghanistan.[8]

While the 2001 decision on Pakistan probably destroyed the nascent "pro-American" lobby inside India's military and foreign policy establishment, India still saw value in cooperating with the United States on Afghanistan. India is as determined to prevent a pro-Pakistani regime from emerging in Kabul as Pakistan is intent upon creating one. Over the years, India has fed a stream of intelligence information to Washington describing continuing ISI links to Al Qaeda and Taliban insurgent groups. Hot on the heels of 9/11, the ISI evacuated hundreds of Taliban commanders and other "assets" to safety—the so-called airlift of evil.[9] This intelligence also included information on the murderous Haqqani network, which has killed dozens of American and NATO troops and has been blamed for kidnappings, suicide bombings, and beheadings of Afghan and foreign civilians.[10] This intelligence, confirmed by US sources, was highly inconvenient; however, the US decision to place its eggs in the Pakistani basket left it little recourse once the war was under way. It took nearly a decade before US officials finally concluded that they would make little progress in the fight against Al Qaeda and the Taliban until Pakistan's ISI, and even its military, were cut out of the loop. The decision to do just that for the operation that killed Osama bin Laden is dramatic evidence of this fact, to both Washington and New Delhi's deep dismay.

From the start, the Bush administration apparently recognized that India, not Pakistan, would be the more valuable regional partner when the dust of Afghanistan settled. The Bush administration fought hard to balance its increasing dependence on the unreliable, corrupt Pakistani regime with largesse toward India. In July 2005, in the most dramatic example of this effort, President Bush and Indian prime minister Manmohan Singh signed an agreement trading US assistance in India's civilian nuclear industry for expanded US-India cooperation in energy and satellite technology. While still not ratified by India's raucous parliament, the deal provides a relatively minor opening for American technology companies in India's civilian nuclear sector, and it requires India, which has never signed the Nuclear Non-Proliferation Treaty, to at least allow inspections of its civilian facilities by the International Atomic Energy Agency (IAEA) and to announce a moratorium on nuclear weapons tests. But the deal failed to satisfy nuclear arms control experts because India still avoided signing the treaty, meaning its military nuclear program remains outside international scrutiny. At the same time, the two sides initialed agreements on joint military cooperation—in particular a pledge to work toward "interoperability"—military jargon for the ability, like the United States and Britain, to put their forces together on a battlefield with a reasonable certainty that they will kill more of the enemy than themselves.[11] (This is not a given when allied troops mingle with the US military.)

While the value of the nuclear deal and other logistical arrangements might be questionable, Washington's motives were crystal clear. "The United States is trying to cement its relationship with the world's largest democracy in order to counterbalance China," Charles Ferguson, president of the Federation of American Scientists, said of the nuclear deal.[12] India's powerful Communist Party agrees—and if the deal isn't ratified, it likely will be because the Indian Left sees it as part of a plan to trick India into leading an American-designed containment ring around China. Meanwhile, the logistical deal, which also would have permitted the transfer of highly sensitive intelligence and communications technology, was still not signed as of late 2011. India argued it would compromise their own systems, another sign that the Indians prefer to keep Washington at arm's length.

FLYING HIGH?

Like any competent suitor, the United States is nothing if not persistent, remaining aflame with passion for India in spite of signs that the efforts may be backfiring. With both the nuclear deal and military technology agreements in limbo, the United States hoped that it might be able to nurture the relationship through the back door: by becoming India's most important source of high-tech armaments. The United States has sold a series of weapons systems to India since 2001, including deals for C-130 transport aircraft in 2008 and Boeing long-range maritime patrol jets in 2009. But nothing says "love" at the strategic level like a high-performance warplane, and here the United States thought it finally would set its hook.

In 2010, the Indian Air Force, still equipped primarily with Soviet-era warplanes well into the twenty-first century, began a competition—potentially worth $11 billion to the winning manufacturer—to purchase a fighter aircraft that would be the mainstay of India's air defenses for the next few decades. The United States had hoped to have stronger military-to-military ties established by this point but still felt confident that it could offer the best overall package—weapons system, servicing contract, and all the added "benefits" that come along with being a top-end client of the US military establishment. Besides food and energy, the thinking goes, nothing binds a country to another like a dependency on major weapons systems, and India's own dependency on post-Soviet Russian gear had begun to look like a major problem. With Pakistan already flying old but very serviceable versions of the F-16, vintage about 1982, India wanted a guaranteed advantage.

The aircraft competing for this prize included two American jets, both proven in combat time and again. The Boeing F/A-18[13] and the Lockheed Martin F-16[14]—the latter a much more advanced model than those flown by Pakistan—were thought to have an advantage over the Russian and European rivals in the competition, given Washington's assiduous wooing of India. The United States decided not to offer the F-22, its top-of-the-line air combat warplane, or the new F-35, which will be sold to Australia, Britain, and other close US allies. Still, Boeing and Lockheed Martin swaggered into the competition, accustomed as they were to winning in these military beauty contests. Yet, in a jolt to U.S. pride, both warplanes were rejected in the first round on "technical grounds." India's air chiefs preferred the French Rafale and the pan-European Eurofighter Typhoon, which will duke it out for the 126-aircraft deal—and the influence over India's military that Washington so coveted. (Also rejected were the Swedish Saab Gripen and Russia's MiG-35.) Bruce Riedel, a South Asia expert who advised the Clinton and both of the Bush presidencies, saw geopolitical strategy rather than avionics at work. "There is a belief that in a crisis situation, particularly if it was an India-Pakistan crisis, the U.S. could pull the plug on parts, munitions, aircraft—precisely at the moment you need them most," he said. "Memories are deep in this part of the world,"[15] he told the *Washington Post*.

At the Pentagon, the cold slap in the face administered by India's military brought some belated clarity. In November, 2011, the Defense Department issued an ad hoc report to Congress on "U.S.-India Security Cooperation" which, without fanfare, reversed the decision to withhold the F-35.[16] Too little, too late, from New Delhi's point of view, though India's generals certainly made their point: the next time a U.S. trade envoy thrusts forward with a complaint about Indian call centers stealing American jobs, the F-35 episode will provide a reasonable Indian parry.

The US wooing will continue, of course. President Obama thrilled his hosts in November 2010 by throwing his weight behind India's bid for permanent status on the US Security Council. His chief diplomat, Hillary Clinton, stressed common values in a visit to the booming city of Chennai in August 2011. "India's leadership has the potential to positively shape the future of the Asia-Pacific," she said. "We think that America and India share a fundamentally similar vision for the future of this region."[17] All of this, again, is absolutely correct. But India has other fish—closer to its own borders—in the frying pan.

ENTER THE RED TEAM

The founding meeting of the Shanghai Five—now known as the Shanghai Cooperation Organization (SCO)—drew little notice in 1996 amid an American presidential election (Clinton vs. Dole), the Olympics in Atlanta, and the dispatch of forty thousand American-led peacekeepers to end the violence in Bosnia-Herzegovina. To those in the West who even knew of its existence, the SCO, which linked China, Russia, Kazakhstan, Tajikistan, and Kyrgyzstan, seemed more like a support group for ailing former communists than a serious global player. "The Scared Commie Organization," a senior US diplomat in London quipped to me at the time, back when I was the US affairs analyst at the BBC.[18] "It can't be easy to have spent your whole life preaching central planning, only to find out that capitalism is what people really wanted all along."

The SCO persisted in spite of such views, holding annual summits that regularly complained about America's high-handedness, adding Uzbekistan as a member in 2001 (thus, the name change) and talking about cross border cooperation in combating terrorism and drug trafficking and improving infrastructure. In 2006, however, the SCO invited Iran, India, Pakistan, and Mongolia to attend the annual event as observers, and suddenly eyebrows rose in Washington. Kazakh president Nursultan Nazarbayev, the summit host that year, bragged that "the leaders of the states sitting at this negotiation table are representatives of half of humanity."[19] Since then, the group has held joint military exercises, joined together to condemn a planned US antimissile shield in Eastern Europe, demanded a new voice for the world's emerging economies in the IMF, preached a phasing out of the US dollar as the world's reserve currency, and is currently considering Iran's application for full membership.

"We now clearly see the defectiveness of the monopoly in world finance and the policy of economic selfishness," Vladimir Putin told his fellow SCO leaders in 2007. "To solve the current problem Russia will take part in changing the global financial structure so that it will be able to guarantee stability and prosperity in the world and to ensure progress."[20]

For India, granted SCO "observer" status in 2006, attending these summits has provided a useful opportunity for high-level talks with China and, in private settings, its rival, Pakistan. The SCO would dearly like India to join up, which would add considerable heft to its influence. But India knows that the SCO poses a dilemma. With China pressing old territorial claims in the Himalayas and standing as the primary supporter of Pakistan's claim on the disputed Indian-ruled sections of Kashmir, it is hardly clear that the Chinese-dominated SCO has India's interests in mind. Nor does India always agree with the stridently worded criticisms of the United States and Europe that have become a regular feature of SCO joint communiqués. In fact, until recently, India had decided that observer status was enough.

"If the historic purpose of NATO was to 'keep the Germans down, the Americans in and the Russians out', then SCO is at least minimally united around the motto of 'keeping the Americans out,'" writes Professor Sreeram Chaulia, a security expert at the Jindal School of International Affairs in India. "India's strategic establishment is contradictorily keen on keeping the Americans in Afghanistan for as long as possible, believing that a US withdrawal would throw open the doors to renewed Pakistani (and indirectly Chinese) hegemony in a geostrategic lynchpin."[21]

This may have changed in 2009, when the United States publicly committed to withdrawing from Afghanistan by 2014. Those in India who had argued that the United States would prevent a new Taliban state in Afghanistan and prevent the Pakistani use of terrorism in pressing its claims on Kashmir lost significant capital as a result. India, hedging like everyone else, officially put in for SCO membership in June 2011. Again, it had good reasons beyond a fear of growing too close to America—for one thing, India is keen to press the case for a new oil pipeline across Central Asia to deliver energy to its hungry economy. But, in an echo of Turkish foreign minister Ahmet Davutoglu's point, in an age of social networks, if the country's population opposes the government's foreign policy, it is unsustainable. Despite all their commonalities—and the dreams of linking the world's largest democracy with its most powerful one—the idea of a United States and India as *jugalbandi*, the Hindi word for "entwined twins," fights against nearly a century of misunderstanding and a cultural and economic chasm that is difficult to understand without going to India.

Harish Khare, former media advisor to India's prime minister and editor of the *Hindu*, one of India's most influential newspapers, points out that the urbane India that Americans seem to see is barely a fifth of the nation. The rural population—*mofussil*, or "up-country" nationalists, as he calls them—makes up most of India's billion souls. They remain strongly anti-American "for the simple reason that the 'American dream' has no relevance for 700 million Indians who struggle everyday with deprivations and discomforts. In small and medium towns like Sitapur, Moradabad, Ambala, Kota, Kozhikode, and Dharwad, the U.S. remains a distant country that can only wish ill for this nation. The *mofussil* nationalist has not been given any reason to revise his traditional view that suspects Washington of resenting our rise as a great power."[22]

Some three hundred million others, India's urban middle classes, have concluded quite differently. They wield more power, but as a democracy, they must face India's complex realities, too. For this reason more than any other, India is likely to seek a position in "the middle," avoiding arguments between China and America that are not directly relevant to them in the hope that it can solve its own complex ethnic and economic challenges while the two other elephants lock tusks. China, which has been building a line of naval bases in the Indian Ocean, could change this situation if it does not tread carefully. Already, India's war colleges turn out reams of analysis of the "string of pearls," the Chinese bases, airfields, and ports that run from its southern-most island of Hainan through Myanmar, Bangladesh, Sri Lanka, and Pakistan to Somalia. China, importing most of its energy from the Persian Gulf and Africa, has good reason to protect shipping lanes. But this means Chinese warships transiting India's sea lanes, too, and with both constructing more modern, capable navies, "mistakes" will be harder to avoid. But Indian analysts insist that it would take something more than a naval incident to drive India into a real alliance with the United States. "Residual skepticism of the U.S. in India runs deep," writes Shashank Joshi, an Indian fellow at the Royal United Services Institute in London. "India's interest is in hedging, not outright balancing. In the longer-term, that will lead it to proceed with great caution in using naval assets east of Singapore."[23]

PUTTING THE *B* IN BRIC

If the United States is resented for taking too much for granted its relationship with India, that same approach seems to suit the Brazilians just fine. When it comes to the great giant of the north, Brazil prefers to stay off the radar. "Being the source of American attention raises expectations in Washington that Brazil will work as a 'responsible stakeholder' according to some arbitrary criteria of what 'responsible' means, or it turns Brazil into a target of U.S. pressure when interests don't coincide," writes Matias Spektor at Rio de Janeiro's Center for International Relations. "As a result, there is a consensus among Brazilians that a policy of 'ducking'—hiding your head underwater when the hegemonic eagle is around—has served them well."[24]

If so, the ducking came to an abrupt end in May 2010, when Brazil and Turkey announced that they had concluded a deal on Iran's nuclear weapons program that they believed would prevent Iran from building a nuclear weapon while forestalling threatened US or Israeli preemptive military action.[25] After a press conference with a smiling Iranian president Mahmoud Ahmadinejad, Brazil's president at the time, Luiz Inacio Lula da Silva, learned that the United States was furious with the deal. A week prior, he had received a letter from President Obama explaining the US position and why Washington was unwilling to take Iran's word on the complex question of uranium enrichment: "Throughout this process, instead of building confidence Iran has undermined confidence in the way it has approached this opportunity. That is why I question whether Iran is prepared to engage Brazil in good faith, and why I cautioned you during our meeting. To begin a constructive diplomatic process, Iran has to convey to the IAEA a constructive commitment to engagement through official channels—something it has failed to do."[26]

For Obama, this was tough talk, and US officials rejected the Brazilian-Turkish initiative. Lula, exasperated, said on Brazilian television afterward, "Why doesn't Obama call Ahmadinejad? Or Sarkozy, or Angela Merkel or Gordon Brown?" naming the French, German, and British leaders also involved in the Iran nuclear talks. "People aren't talking."[27]

Brazil's decision to step onto the international stage, following the Turkish lead, caught Washington by surprise. In fact, as we now know, Brazil has for years been quietly evolving into something quite more complicated than the vast, bikini-clad, rain forest–clearing, developing nation of yesteryear. Old-style geographical tallies of its importance are outstripped by economic figures now, but they still remain impressive. Brazil is the fifth-largest country by landmass, controlling 18 percent of the world's fresh water in the Amazon basin, and its rain forest produces 20 percent of the world's oxygen. It will be a top-ten producer of oil by the end of the decade, will move up in economic rankings from eighth to fifth largest, and will jump even further up the wealth chart in terms of per capita income. But geopolitically, it had always been a quiet giant, which is why Lula's Iran initiative struck an American nerve.

"The unease is palpable," writes Celso Amorim, Lula's foreign minister at the time. The Iran deal, he said, "caused some discomfort in Washington, DC. The agreement obliged the U.S. government to explain, not always convincingly, its reasons for refusing an agreement that met all the points in President Obama's letter to President Lula less than three weeks before."[28]

Brazil, in fact, began wresting control of the region's economic and diplomatic agenda well before the Obama administration took office. Emboldened by its achievement of financial stability after decades of boom-to-bust cycles, and finding itself suddenly on the world stage in climate-change talks due to the Amazon's huge importance to the planet's environmental health, a country that had been a reliably pro-American voice in world affairs began—politely—to let Washington know that its priorities were not always in lockstep with Latin American views.

Iran aside, however, Brazil's ability to remain on good terms with often diametrically opposed players echoes Turkey's "no problems" approach to its own neighborhood. Problems, of course, abound—but like Turkey, Brazil appears intent on playing the regional voice of reason, whether the issue involved is global, like Iran's proliferation, or regional, like the tension between Venezuelan president Hugo Chavez and the pro-American government of Colombia. Brazil intervened diplomatically in 2008 to head off a possible clash between Colombia and Venezuela over alleged support by Chavez for left-wing guerrilla movements inside Colombia. Lula, always sensitive to the appeal of Chavez's left-wing populism for Brazil's poor, tolerated the Venezuelan's bluster and angered Colombia by publicly criticizing a deal that would have allowed US troops to be based in the country. In the end, Brazil got what it wanted—cooler heads in its neighborhood; a new, less bellicose leader in Colombia who dropped the plan for a US military base; and the gradual but steady discrediting of Chavez as his policies faltered, leaving Venezuela as the latest state where misuse of oil riches retard and corrupt the political system.

Lula, during his tenure, regularly managed such tightrope walks. For instance, he played a starring role at several of the annual World Economic Forum talks between global capitalism's most important officials, bankers, and investors one year, only to perform an about-face the following year, snubbing Davos and hosting instead an anti-Davos "protest summit" with Chavez and other left-wing regional figures. It was the kind of move that exasperated Washington but kept Lula's base among Brazil's working poor loyally in his thrall.

Even as he toyed with populist politics abroad, however, both Lula and the woman who succeeded him as president in 2010, Dilma Rousseff, have appointed well-respected centrists to key economic posts, including Brazil's finance ministry and central bank. Even as Lula occasionally railed against the Washington Consensus, the 1989 template for austere IMF and World Bank "economic reform" so widely reviled in Latin America, his macroeconomic policy makers have paid homage to it by sticking at least to the spirit, if not the letter, of its ten-point plan that discouraged large budget deficits and called for market liberalizations, inflation-fighting interest rate policies, and lighter regulations.

Again, Brazil's healthy growth rates allowed Lula to have it both ways: from the outside, his pro-growth policies encouraged foreign investment. From within, he implemented well-regarded social welfare policies, including Bolsa Familia, which trades social services and funding for pledges like keeping children in school longer, and Fome Zero, a nutritional program that eliminated a majority of Brazil's malnutrition in the first decade of this century.

Some worry that Rousseff may face difficulties going forward as she attempts to push further reforms of the economy at a time when inflation is causing real problems in Brazil. Lula's "have it both ways" approach may come back to bite them. Rather than raising interest rates to battle inflation, said Mark Weisbrot, an economist at the Center for Economic and Policy Research in Washington, "the central bank has met its inflation target over the last seven years through a continual real appreciation of Brazil's currency. This has consequences, and needs to be understood." In effect, he said, Brazil's industrial sector—a vital part of its plan to keep moving up the economic food chain—is being eaten away by policies that make Brazilian factories uncompetitive.

"Brazil is projected to have a $100 billion trade deficit in manufactured goods this year, up from $71 billion last year," said Weisbrot. "This is partly the result of an overvalued currency, which has appreciated by 46 percent since

the beginning of 2009."[29] This will put Brazil on a collision course economically with the United States, where the Fed has indicated that it may be forced
to again unleash again unleash a torrent of QE—which, again, encourages
investment banks to borrow at near-zero rates in the United States and invest
in high-interest-rate countries like Brazil. The situation will be much the same
in Europe, where the crisis over sovereign debt inside the euro zone will force
the European Central Bank to lower its own rates and, quite possibly, go on a
bond-buying spree to save countries like Greece, Ireland, Portugal, and Spain
from default. This, too, increases the pool of capital circling the globe, looking
for high-yield places like Brazil to land.

FROM MONROE TO LULA

If macroeconomic policy bedevils efforts by Europe and the United States to
keep Brazil "on side" in global affairs, Brazil's very slow maturation as a traditional great power poses another dilemma. While its troops have a long record
of joining international humanitarian actions under the UN flag, including a
leadership role in the Haiti mission during the late 1990s, Brazil's troops have
not been in combat since the last year of World War II, when they sent an
infantry brigade to join Allied forces in Europe.

President Rousseff, too, seems as an unlikely champion of a military
buildup. Four decades ago, the Brazilian military dictatorship tortured her
when she was a young guerrilla fighting their rule. Yet, starting under Lula
and slowly accelerating, Brazil has significantly expanded its military power—
particularly its naval power. This will change the dynamics of the southern
Atlantic significantly, creating a true Brazilian zone of influence extending deep
into the ocean above the oil riches recently discovered there. But it also means
that, for the United States and Europe, accustomed to dictating events on the
high seas—particularly in the Atlantic—some important facts will change,
especially with regard to the long-running Falklands/Malvinas dispute.

Imagine, for a moment, a British admiral's nightmare scenario: in the
not-too-distant future, a nearly bankrupt Argentine government invades
the oil-rich Falkland Islands. For the second time in half a century, Las
Malvinas—the islands of Latin America regarded as a stolen piece of
Argentina—spark a war meant to divert public attention from the Argentine
government's economic failings.

With twenty-first century budget cuts biting hard, the British, at the moment, have no aircraft carrier. Argentina retired its own carrier in the late 1960s. Yet, unlike 1982 when Britain's prime minister Margaret Thatcher dispatched a flotilla to retake the islands the last time Argentina seized them, this time the South Atlantic is anything but empty. It's home to a Brazilian carrier, the *São Paulo*, along with a fleet of nuclear-powered attack submarines being built in partnership with Argentina.

In effect, these weapons give Brazil the ability to impose an updated version of the Monroe Doctrine on regional waters. Call it the "Lula Doctrine." With its new confidence and military ambition, Brazil is a vocal advocate of Argentina's claim on Las Malvinas. While few can imagine Britain and Brazil ever coming to blows, signs of a very different reality for Britain are starting to take shape.

Brazil's 2009 decision to build a fleet of five nuclear attack subs took Western military experts by surprise. Expected to start entering service in 2016, the submarines promise to dramatically alter the balance of power in the South Atlantic. Lula, who led the push for the nuclear sub program, said before leaving office that the subs were "a necessity for a country that not only has the maritime coast that we have but also has the petroleum riches that were recently discovered in the deep sea pre-salt layer."[30]

The last time this scenario played out, Britain won the day and the United States backed its European ally—even privately offering to lend it one of America's huge aircraft carriers (an offer turned down because of the complexities of operating one on such short notice). Back in 1982, when the Argentine junta led by General Leopoldo Galtieri invaded the islands, Britain mustered a small but viable fleet of aircraft carriers, submarines, and surface ships to support a Royal Marine landing force that retook the islands. The retaking of the Falklands became emblematic of the determination of then prime minister Margaret Thatcher that the once-mighty British military not sink to third-class status. Yet it also left a deep scar on the Latin American psyche. Brazil and other Latin American countries backed Argentina during the war but had little real ability to help militarily. In particular, the region never forgot the single most deadly action of the war: the sinking of the Argentine cruiser *General Belgrano*, a hulking relic of World War II, by a British nuclear attack submarine, killing 323 sailors.

Until recently, experts regarded the Falkland Islands as an unlikely place for further trouble. But the discovery of oil in the North Falklands Basin in

2007 changed this. As a result of Argentina's near-perpetual state of bankruptcy and Brazil's new assertiveness on the world stage, sensitivities over the disputed islands have risen. In January 2011, for instance, Brazil refused a small British warship, HMS *Clyde*, permission to dock in Rio de Janeiro. Neighboring Uruguay turned away the British destroyer HMS *Gloucester* in 2010. In Britain, meanwhile, the commander of the 1982 Falklands fleet, Admiral Sir John Woodward, published an op-ed in June warning that current defense cuts likely would leave the Falklands helpless in the face of a new Argentine invasion, leading to political pressure to reinforce the British garrison.

But Brazil's submarines change the naval balance of power in the region even more dramatically than Britain's own defense woes. British strategists worry that Brazil may now demand that foreign powers simply steer clear of its backyard as the United States did in the nineteenth and twentieth centuries. Brazilian officials have been careful not to portray the subs as a response to any outside threat as they continue to support Argentina's Malvinas claim in international bodies. Gentle giant or not, Brazil's backyard will have to be respected.

COUNTING YOUR CHICKENS

For the powers of Europe and North America, this is just another example of the subtle but very real changes sweeping across the planet. For Europe, economic cooperation and genuine talks on some kind of cooperative future for old colonies like the Falklands are the only hope for avoiding sudden, jarring crises. For the United States and its European allies, the simplistic notion that Brazil and India can be enlisted in a kind of global version of NATO—a "Concert of Democracies," as former GOP presidential candidate and Arizona Senator John McCain proposed—simply ignores realities.[31] So, too, does the American elite's more recent prescriptions: In the autumn of 2011, The Aspen Institute and the Council on Foreign Relations issued a joint study group report on U.S.-India relations that concluded a close partnership, even if difficult, was inevitable. Getting way ahead of themselves, the report's authors seem to relish the day when India's military might can fill a role once reserved for America's NATO allies. "India's growing national capabilities give it ever greater tools to pursue its national interests to the benefit of the United States. India has the world's third largest army, fourth largest air force, and fifth largest navy. All of these services are modernizing, and the Indian air force and

Indian navy have world-class technical resources, and its army is seeking more of them. Moreover, *unlike some longtime US partners* [emphasis added], India has demonstrated that it possesses not only a professional military force, but also a willingness to suffer substantial military hardship and loss in order to defend Indian national interests."[32]

But cultural differences and historical suspicions remain serious impediments to the multi-player trade that American foreign policy thinkers would like to make. What's more, there are genuine conflicts of interest between the three around issues far weightier than Las Malvinas—global currency rates; climate change policy; Brazil's continuing ties with Iran; its increasing reliance on trade with China; and for India, the futile alliance Washington clings to with Pakistan. As Parag Khanna, the geostrategist and author, notes, it will be very dangerous for the United States to continue to assume that countries like Brazil or India—or any of the other democratically ruled middleweight powers like Indonesia, Turkey, or Mexico—will fall over themselves to play the kind of role in the twenty-first century that Britain played in the latter part of the twentieth century. "The U.S. now must face a world in which its power is declining, in which it is just one of several competing brands," he says. "You can see that in how often America must go it alone, militarily or economically, whether it wants to or not. In that sense, the world is really becoming not anti-American but simply non-American."[33]

Non-American may be a good way for average Americans to think about these issues. Too often in the past, the assumption—sometimes correct—has been that all countries seeking to engage the United States were also seeking to somehow become Americans. While this may have been true to some extent in war-ravaged Europe, for various Third World countries in the Cold War, and for some of the newly independent countries of the former Soviet bloc, it never really applied to India, Brazil, or countless other larger countries that managed to steer a relatively neutral path through the Cold War. To expect, after all those decades, that any of these nations would simply fall in line behind the leadership of a declining United States—particularly after the geopolitical and economic mistakes it has made in of the past decade—is worse than wishful thinking. It is collective national denial.

CHAPTER 9

EUROPE: PIIGS, CANARIES, AND BEARS—OH MY!

For all the disastrous miscalculations of American policy, foreign and domestic, in recent years, the citizens of the United States need only look across the Atlantic for a bit of solace. At a time when growth is accelerating elsewhere, Europe is aging to the point of economic atrophy, and in spite of a last hurrah in Libya recently, it has given up on its military muscle, too. Politically, it's haunted by the rival specters of Islamic radicalism and a violent right-wing backlash against the continent's growing Muslim minority. The EU appears increasingly incapable of agreeing on fundamental issues, from fiscal and monetary policy to whether or not Turkey should become a member. In all, the "European Superpower," the dream of Europe's left for decades, is looking extremely mortal these days.

All grand projects face challenges, and the creation of a continent-wide, polyglot super state out of Europe's diverse and tribal nations is grander than most. But even its harshest critics could hardly have imagined the problems it faces today. If the American superpower has grievously injured itself with reckless foreign policy moves and a "see no evil" approach to its financial system, its European cousin was brought low by the bloat that comes with an indiscriminate expansion of the central state on the national level, and its own borders transnationally. As the EU took in new members one gulp after another, going from a club of six to today's twenty-seven, they ingested kryptonite in the form of small nations like Greece, Portugal, and Ireland, all incapable of competing in the global economy yet allowed to borrow in international markets as though they were as productive and stolid as a German state—for a while at least.

In Europe's continental core—the so-called euro zone of 17 countries that ditched their own national currencies in favor of the euro—the decision to allow poorly run or overly leveraged countries into the club looks disastrous, even suicidal, in retrospect. Like a character in a cautionary tale, Europe has been brought low not by revolution, famine, or war but rather by gluttony and indigestion.

A TASTE FOR PORK

The EU began in 1958 as a relatively narrow effort—the European Coal and Steel Community—to help the postwar western European economies of France, Italy, Belgium, the Netherlands, Luxembourg, and West Germany get back on their feet. By the millennium, it had grown into a club of 15 nations, with a half dozen others, including large economies like Turkey and Poland, waiting at the door. Today there are 27 member nations, after a binge over the last decade that added most of the economies of Central and Eastern Europe, as well as the islands of Cyprus and Malta. Over the years, internal debates raged over the propriety of these expansions, which brought low-wage, struggling economies into the fold, inevitably transferring money from richer, established members to the less affluent newbies. But by 2000, a conventional wisdom had set in, seemingly borne out by experiences with countries like Ireland (which joined in 1973), Greece (in 1982), and Spain and Portugal (in 1986), all of which seemed to have prospered and raised their game after joining. Supporters argued that by shackling these nations to the powerhouse economies of the EU core and forcing them to adopt certain fiscal and regulatory reforms, they could be dragged into the top tier of the world's advanced economies, thus expanding the EU's own economic might.

In fact, the chains linking these four nations—collectively derided as the PIGS today—worked in precisely the opposite way. In the winter of 2010, it came out that tiny Greece was effectively bankrupt and—worse—had cooked its books, hiding billions in debt (including defense spending spurred by its historic paranoia about Turkey). The debacle of Greece—an inept political elite and economy completely incapable of producing the kind of growth and serious reform that would allow it to pay its debts to international lenders and bond holders—sent a shudder through the Rube Goldberg machine that is the EU system. The shackles meant to drag Greece up to euro zone standards were instead dragging its EU partners toward the economic abyss.

At this juncture, in early 2010, the "European Project" was still quite viable. The Greek economy simply was not large enough—even with debts equaling 142 percent of the economy's output in the GDP—to bring the mighty EU to its knees. It would have been justified in expelling Greece, though that was never seriously considered. At the very least, the EU should have insisted that Greece go into default—effectively acknowledging that Greece was bankrupt—which would have imposed short-term losses on its creditors but prevented a larger crisis. For a variety of reasons, however, EU leaders instead decided that they could bluff their way through the crisis and avoid an embarrassing "first world" default. This myopic response was a catastrophe, not just for Greece but for Europe as a whole, and it proved beyond a doubt that for all the talk of European unity, when push comes to shove, national priorities and tribal prerogatives still take precedence.

Germany and France, along with the smaller but economically solid euro zone economies of the Netherlands and Finland, refused to allow Greece to submit to the forces of gravity and default on its debts—an ugly option, to be sure, but one that, if handled carefully, could have paved the way out of the crisis and prevented its spread to other weak euro zone economies. By early 2010, a range of economists and other experts, including Edward Hugh, the historian Niall Ferguson, economists Nouriel Roubini and Kenneth S. Rogoff, saw the edge of yet another cliff approaching. The virus, this time around, would originate in the "old world," but as in 2006, the globalized nature of finance made it almost certain that it would quickly spread across oceans, mountain ranges, or polar ice caps to infect the new.

Roubini who cut his teeth on the Asian financial crisis of the late 1990s as a Clinton administration economic advisor, declared in June 2010 that Greece was toast and that the insistence of European politicians that they could manage its insolvency quietly amounted to a systemic risk to the global economy. "An orderly default of Greece's debt is achievable and desirable for the debtor

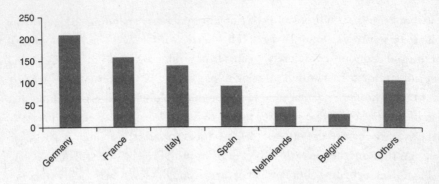

Figure 9.1   Contributions to PIIGS Bailouts (as of September 2011)
Source: European Financial Stability Facility/Roubini Global Economics

and its creditors. If Europe wants to avoid a deepening crisis, it is unavoidable, too," Roubini wrote.[1]

In a harrowing repeat of 2006, when many of the same experts realized that the "creativity" of the US financial sector, combined with its lack of regulation, was a ticking time bomb, Roubini and others who argued for action were ignored, even denigrated.[2]

If prickly European pride played its part—many had, after all, spent the previous few years smugly mocking America for the mess it had made of the global economy—the cozy realities of power and profit inside the "single market" created by the euro also served to stay the hand of those who might intervene. The corporate sectors of the so-called EZ core—the prosperous and relatively prudent economies of Germany, the Netherlands, Luxembourg, and, to a lesser extent, France—had thrived selling wares to their less competitive euro zone brethren. Local firms in countries like Portugal, Greece, Ireland and elsewhere fell on hard times or were snapped up at bargain prices as the economies of scale available to giants like German engineering titan Siemens, the Dutch electronics firm Phillips, or France's supermarket giant Carrefour, vaulted them into dominant market positions. The same held true in the banking sector. After all, the wizards of BNP Paribas, Commerzbank, and Barclays reckoned, if these people are paid in euros, and their governments are part of the euro zone, their credit is good: an "A" rating even!

Indeed, true to form, the three global ratings agencies dropped the ball once more, failing to warn about vast mountains of accumulating debt in the so-called PIGS until financial markets pointed it out for them by demanding higher interest rates when these nations needed to roll over their bonds. The EU's financial officials, according to type, blamed foreigners (since Fitch, Moodys, and S&P, by and large, are American creations) and creation of a new European ratings agency. Helmut Reisen, a top economist at the Organization of Economic Cooperation and Development (OECD), responded to this myopia with outrage. "[Y]ou do not destroy a mirror merely because it tells you that you are ugly. You should, however, discard a mirror that is blind and has nourished illusions for too long." The real problem, he pointed out, was unchanged from the run-up to the 2008 Lehman collapse: the main source of ratings agency revenues is the very banks, governments, and other entities they are rating. Investors, not borrowers, should be bearing the costs of the analysis that goes into assessing the risk of a given product.[3]

Such reforms have failed to appear on either side of the Atlantic. Nonetheless, by early 2010, it was too late for Europe and its banks. Among those who loaded up on Greek debt—in effect, lent Athens money by purchasing galleys full of Greek government bonds—German and French banks suffered most and are by far the most exposed to a Greek default (French banks are owed about $90 billion, German banks about $57 billion).[4]

In effect, BNP Paribas, Deutsche Bank, Dresner, and the other titans of continental banking played the same role in the Greek crisis that fly-by-night mortgage brokers did in the American one. Loans were made to a nearly indigent borrower because the returns looked so attractive, regardless of the risks involved—and a blithe assumption that, as euro zone sovereign governments, their debt ultimately was backed up by the power of the German economy. In practice, there is no real evidence that the risks even truly registered within these banks or that any serious study of how default in even a small economy like Greece could feasibly bring the whole edifice of European finance down. As in America, where banks assumed that the federal government would back its real estate shell game forever, in Europe bankers viewed a loan to an A-rated EU sovereign—which is where Moody's pegged Greece as late as 2009—as practically risk-free. In truth, Greek debt is as toxic as the mortgage-backed securities that gutted Lehman Brothers in 2008. Thanks to European bankers, Europe's political leaders, who distribute billions a year in aid and other largesse to help the emerging economies of the world, suddenly faced a new class of nation-state among them: a submerging economy.

FAILURE TO STAUNCH

Rather than lancing this Olympian boil when even the ratings agencies took notice in 2010, the decision of the Germans and French to bluff their way out has prolonged and deepened the crisis. In mid-2010, euro zone leaders created a European stability fund that, together with loans from the IMF, slowed Greece's slide toward bankruptcy—for about a week. The timidity proved to be a tremendous error. The rescue fund—at just €45 billion (about $64 billion)—was too small to fool international markets or to effectively stabilize Greece, which was now so debt burdened that international markets were demanding interest rates as high as credit cards to purchase Greek bonds—the source of an increasing portion of the Greek government's operating budget in recent years. But the multibillion-dollar rescue was plenty large enough to infuriate taxpayers in the carefully managed northern European economies at the idea of their hard-earned euros going south to "bail out lazy, profligate Greeks," as the British economist Charles K. Rowley put it.[5]

The European Central Bank, led by Jean-Claude Trichet, made things even worse by raising interest rates, compounding an earlier error committed just as the global economy crashed in 2009. (The bank reversed course in November 2011, the day Italian Mario Draghi took Trichet's place as ECB president—again, a day late, many euros short). Under Trichet and at the insistence of the euro zone's largest player, Germany, the ECB insisted on policies aimed at curbing inflation, even though deflation posed the much larger risk. This reflects a historical bias aimed at avoiding a repeat of the hyperinflation that helped send Germany into the hands of Adolf Hitler. But raising interest rates, of course, strengthened the euro in international markets, making it that much harder—impossible, really—for Greece to ever hope to restructure itself into a competitive economy, given its debt burden and its very rigid labor and laws.

Worst of all, the failure to deal with the fire ravaging Greece invited an even wider disaster: contagion. Before 2010 was over, the flames had spread to other weaker economies—and "PIGS" became "PIIGS" with Italy, the world's eighth-largest economy, thrown into the mix. A kind of domino effect took hold, starting with Ireland, rattled by the burst of a property bubble that made the American version look tame. The EU and IMF bailed out Ireland to the tune of $120 billion in November, demanding harsh austerity conditions in exchange. The reaper, prodded by international bond investors driving up the

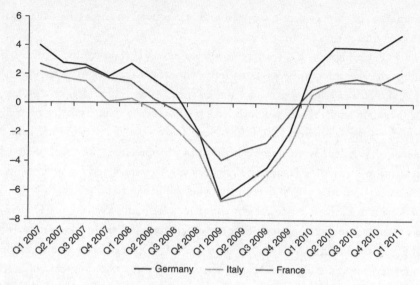

Figure 9.2   Italy Lagging Behind Germans, French (GDP Growth)

cost of borrowing for all these governments, took longer to reach Portugal, but the EU-IMF tandem coughed up another $78 billion to save it in May 2011. By the end of the summer, the European Central Bank was defending even larger European economies from disaster—intervening to purchase $6.5 billion worth of Spanish and Italian government bonds to temper their rising borrowing costs. In the end, Greece and Ireland can be rescued, and Spain, perhaps, can be sandbagged and the damage limited. But if Italy, a G7 nation and a founding member of the EU, were to default, international markets would likely seize up even more seriously than they did when Lehman bit the dust.

Much of this, sadly, could have been prevented if the "transnational" spirit of Europe had really taken hold. Daniel Gros, the director of the Centre for European Policy Studies in Brussels, calls the actions of Germany and France—the ultimate drivers of euro zone policies—suicidal.

"Canaries were kept in coal mines because they die faster than humans when exposed to dangerous gases," Gros wrote in his widely read blog, *VoxEU*, in August 2011. "When the birds stopped singing, wise miners knew that it was time to gear up the emergency procedures. Greece, as it turns out, was the Eurozone's canary. The canary was resuscitated and a small rescue mechanism was set up to revive a further canary or two—but beyond that the warning was ignored. The miners kept on working. They convinced themselves that this was the canary's problem."[6]

The breakup of the euro zone now seems a very real possibility—meaning either the ejection of the weaker nations (who would then relaunch the drachmas, punts, and escudos that once underpinned their economies) or a pullout by Germany and France, who are fed up with the constant transfer of their wealth to the "periphery." One European bank—the Belgian-French lender Dexia—has failed. More ominously, some of Europe's most powerful financial institutions, including Deutsche Bank, Societe Generale, and Commerzbank, are so exposed to a Greek default that they will require hundreds of billions of dollars from their respective governments to remain solvent. For EU members who never signed up for the common currency—Britain especially—the plight of the PIIGS is a lesson not soon forgotten. The creation of a common currency without a common fiscal policy turned out to be the worst of both worlds, subjecting strong economies to contagion from weaker members, and trapping the weak economies in a union with stronger, more competitive states that will not allow them to devalue or inflate their way out of debt. When push came to shove, Germany, France, and other strong euro zone economies looked after their own interests—and voters—first.

THE SICK MAN *IS* EUROPE

Even if the euro zone does survive, its fiscal problems, exacerbated by a population that will soon be, on average, older than all others in the developed world except Japan, will accelerate its retreat from world affairs. Once a dominant force from the Pacific to the Middle East and Africa, Europe is fast becoming incapable of dealing with the political and security challenges even in its own neighborhood.

A host of forces is turning the aging of Europe from a demographic phenomenon into an economic and political time bomb. Productivity—the fuel of economic growth in the competitive global economy—has disappeared from some of Europe's economies, particularly those in the southern tier along the Mediterranean. This exacerbates the frustrations in northern Europe, which has held its own in terms of productivity.

Longer life expectancy, better health care, and drastically slower birth rates have driven up the average age. Relatively early retirement ages, generous social spending, and an inability in most countries to reconcile national culture

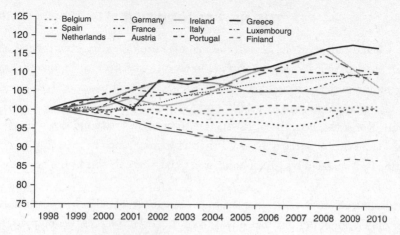

Figure 9.3 Intra-EU Labor Costs
Note: ULCs are computed as the ratio between compensation per employee and real GDP per employed person
Source: European Commission

with the energizing effects of immigration foreshadow the crisis to come. Studies suggest that by 2050, the age of the average European will climb from about 37 today to around 54, while at the same time, the ratio of active workers to retirees will drop to two to one from the current four to one.[7] Even after the "reforms" imposed by the EU-IMF austerity rescues, for instance, Greece's retirement age was only raised to 60. The law raising the retirement age from 60 to 62 in France in 2010 brought hundreds of thousands of protestors into the streets (though it did ultimately pass). Elsewhere in Europe it is different: Britain's age will soon rise to 68, and Germany and Spain are targeting 67. Still, the demographic arithmetic puts Europe on a steep downward trajectory in terms of economic output at precisely the moment when the EU's largest economies—Italy, Britain, France, and Germany—will be overtaken by those of the BRICs and the rest of the emerging world. Germany has managed to retain its awesome export industry—still the second largest in the world after China—in the face of competition from Asia and other lower-cost regions by concentrating on the high end of the manufacturing scale: complex engineering (Siemens, ThyssenKrupp, Henkel), chemicals (Sigma-Aldrich, BASF), automobiles (BMW, Mercedez Benz, Porsche), and design (Bosch, Braun). This may be replicable in the United States, where a huge domestic market and culture of innovation can be counted on to keep US factories relevant at the high end. But elsewhere in Europe, the picture is grim.

THE NEW SECOND TIER

France and Italy, both leaders in the manufacture of luxury goods, have seen their share of global trade deteriorate in recent years. In France, manufacturing only represents 16 percent of the GDP, compared to around 30 percent in Germany. While France still ranks fifth in the world as an exporter, South Korea, Mexico, India, Russia, and others are breathing down its neck. President Nicolas Sarkozy has said that he wants France to expand manufacturing by 25 percent by 2015, but he hasn't said where he thinks the buyers will be found.[8]

Italy faces an even steeper decline—Brazil surpassed it last year, bumping the G7 founding member down from the seventh largest economy in the world, with India, Russia, and South Korea likely to push it from the top ten by decade's end. In terms of exports, Italy's life's blood, South Korea and the Netherlands nudged it from sixth to eighth in 2010, an even starker measure of its sclerosis.

Italians had better get used to it: their manufacturing sector, which revived strongly after World War II, has been a major loser since the end of the Cold War. A handful of the great names remain linchpins of the Italian economy: Pirelli, Fiat, Parmalat, Ferrari, and Ducati—all leading global brands. But Italy, more than any economy in Europe, is desperately dependent on exports to fuel GDP growth. Over the past decade, growth has barely registered 1 percent and has been negative for two consecutive years, with the IMF predicting more of the same for 2011. Italy accounted for about 5 percent of all global trade in 1990; today, that figure is 2.9 percent, and it is falling fast.[9]

If anything, the story for Britain is even darker, though its more flexible labor markets and a history of government experimentation provide a window of hope. Though Britain was once the world's dominant trade powerhouse, its manufacturing sector has shriveled to a shadow of its former self. In 1965, it still held a 7 percent share of global trade, but by 2010, that figure had dwindled to 2.7 percent, a testament to a near-complete collapse of infrastructure investment during the 1960s and 1970s, exacerbated by the abandonment of heavy industry during the Thatcher years in favor of the service sector, particularly finance.

The importance of London as a global market center echoes throughout the British economy, which is tremendously dependent on The City of London, as the financial district is known, and the fees, bonuses, and salaries it generates. Damaged almost as badly as Wall Street during the 2008–2009 financial crisis, London remains in the doldrums, shrunken in both size and reputation and facing new restrictions on its activities that have some major international banks currently based there considering moving trading operations to Switzerland. (Nomura, HSBC, and UBS have already started booking trades through Zurich, a potential loss of billions in tax revenue for Her Majesty's treasury.) The shrinking of Britain's banking sector could actually have a positive effect over time, potentially giving the economy a more stable foundation. An overreliance on finance, a legacy of the go-go Thatcher years, partly explains Britain's current dire straits; while it does not quite nose around with the PIIGS, the British economy has shrunk by more than four percentage points since its peak in early 2008, largely because of a terrible slump in British banking. The questionable government policies described earlier have strangled economic growth in the name of taming the country's addition to deficit spending. Even with Prime Minister David Cameron's budget-slashing fiscal policies, the original expectation was for Britain's national debt to reach 70 percent by 2015 before beginning to shrink. In late November 2011, Cameron revised that radically, admitting that Britain faced a decade of austerity to reach that target, with debt now reaching 78 percent before starting downward. The news ignited labor unrest not seen since the 1970s, with the OECD and other independent analysts warning that household incomes would tumble precipitously (by an average of about $4,000 over the next three years and, overall, the British economy would shrink by 15 percent as a result of the austerity by 2015, when a new election would be due. Even some Tories began to worry about the course they had plotted.[10]

If Britain is to revive its fortunes and reverse the growth of its national debt, it must do more than shrink its banking sector; it must also grow other industries, particularly manufacturing. George Osborne, Cameron's Chancellor of the Exchequer, conceded as much with a rare plan to spend a bit of money on infrastructure, research, and enterprise zones. While a start, it hardly amounts to the Manhattan Project. The logical alternative route—as in the United States—involves meaningful short term stimulus of as much as 3 percent of annual GDP, followed by a more sustainable plan for budgetary austerity.

Oddly, while Britain's postwar governments have plenty to answer for in terms of growth-killing industrial policy, funding useful (both economically and commercially) R&D efforts once counted as a British strength. Today, outside the pharmaceutical industry and oil—where British firms like GlaxoSmithKline and AstraZeneca or BP and Royal Dutch Shell (which is half British) rank among the world's best—bright spots are few and far between (they include aeronautics giant BAE Systems and Harland and Wolff, the Belfast shipyard that built the Titanic and other great vessels and has tapped a lucrative new market in offshore wind and tidal energy farms).

But the larger story of recent British industry is a story of decline and deindustrialization on a massive scale. The once great names have passed into history or been acquired by foreign competitors. Rolls-Royce was acquired by Germany's BMW. In perhaps the ultimate symbol of how tables have turned, Tata Motors, which is based in Britain's former colony, India, snapped up the company that makes storied Jaguars and Land Rovers in 2008. Tellingly, these products improved—both in quality and market share—after the foreigners took over.

Manufacturing now accounts for only 12 percent of the GDP—the lowest percentage of any of the world's ten largest economies and down from 20 percent at the turn of the twenty-first century. To his credit, Cameron has made "rebalancing" Britain's economy a goal of his government. But besides a lot of talk about creating an innovation economy and cheerleading for the creation of a British version of Silicon Valley, his policies have had mostly negative effects. Draconian budget cuts still threaten to tip Britain back into a recession (GDP growth in 2011—as of October, at least—amounted to less than 1 percent). The battered banking sector, as in the United States, has raked in profits by borrowing from the Bank of England at record-low interest rates and investing in high-interest-rate emerging markets. But from 2009 to 2011, they failed miserably at what they are supposed to do: lend to the small and medium-sized businesses that are the engines of future growth and incubators of innovation. Britain's banking regulators, unlike those in the United States, have taken steps to correct this. Without the access to greater pools of private investment—from "angel" investors, private equity groups, hedge funds, and other sources—that help US firms weather this problem, even a conservative government had no choice but to step in. A February 2011 deal between regulators and the five largest British banks, called Project Merlin, put limits on executive pay and bonuses and forced the banks to pledge to lend £190 billion ($308 billion) in 2011.

PAX GERMANICA

Much of Europe's future development as a global player will be determined by the continent's lone star economic performer, Germany, and its relationship with its EU partners on the one hand and the most powerful of its neighbors, Russia, on the other. Current trends suggest that the era of European influence in the world is coming to a quick end. If the economic engine of Europe is sputtering—and even Germany's vaunted export economy slowed to a crawl by the middle of 2011—then its political and military heft is seizing up. This reflects not only a relative decline in power, as in America, but also a real decline of French ambition and the exhaustion of British capabilities by the foolish Iraq War and sustained, deeply unpopular deployment in Afghanistan. More important in the long term, though, is that it also reflects the deliberate policies of Germany, which increasingly sees its interests (and, thus, those of Europe as a whole) in standing aloof from the world's trouble spots—especially American-led campaigns in far-off lands.

On paper, the decline of Europe's "hard power" over the past decade is arresting, and it will only accelerate as Europe's taxpayers demand, even more forcefully than their American cousins, that national wealth be directed at domestic problems rather than foreign entanglements. Measures of military might went out of vogue in Europe about the time the American armed forces became the most important element of the continent's security in 1945. But the extent of their demilitarization is still shocking. The 26 European members of the NATO alliance field only one real aircraft carrier between them: the French *Charles de Gaulle*. China, by the end of the decade, will have at least three, as will India. Britain fields 190 combat aircraft, which is fewer than the US Coast Guard. The German military's 22 helicopters would fail to meet the demands of a midsized oil company, and reforms aimed at ending Germany's draft—a long-overdue modernization—will nonetheless decrease the size of its armed forces from about 251,000 today to 185,00 by 2015. Only about 7,000 of them are deployable abroad (and about 5,000 are—in Afghanistan—though under rules that prevent most offensive operations).

IHS Jane's, a defense analysis firm, says the defense budgets of Europe's NATO members—already infuriatingly low to American defense secretaries—are set to decline another 2.9 percent by 2015.[11] Ten years ago, NATO's European members made up half of the alliances' spending; today, according to NATO figures, they account for barely 25 percent. Anders Fogh Rasmussen, a former Danish prime minister who now holds NATO's top civilian post, fears that the United States will eventually detach from Europe as a result, choosing to forge alliances with the emerging powers of Asia and Latin America and leaving Europe to fend for itself. "This increasing economic gap may also lead to an increasing technology gap which will almost hamper the inter-operability between our forces. The Americans provide…still more advanced military assets and equipment; the Europeans are lagging behind. And eventually it will be difficult to co-operate even if you had the political will to co-operate because of the technological gap."

The Libyan mission, on its surface, might seem to contradict these concerns. But in reality, France and Britain, by far the most capable of Europe's military powers, strained to the breaking point just to sustain a relatively limited bombing campaign against a disorganized, ragtag foe. Without the initial US effort, which took out much of Colonel Muammar Qaddafi's antiaircraft and radar capabilities, the air campaign would have been impossible. Even after that, President Obama's insistence that Europe assume the operation lead—a useful baby step in calling the 60-year bluff of NATO's European military capabilities—was really only a symbolic precedent. While the United States did not dominate the air strikes, it had to repeatedly resupply its European partners with smart munitions and other high-tech weapons; otherwise, NATO air forces simply would not have been able to risk operations in areas populated by civilians. Wrote Steven Erlanger in the *New York Times*,

> Libya has been a war in which some of the Atlantic alliance's mightiest members did not participate, or did not participate with combat aircraft, like Spain, Turkey and Sweden. It has been a war where the Danes and Norwegians did an extraordinary number of the combat sorties, given their size. Their planes and pilots became exhausted, as the French finally pulled back their sole nuclear-powered aircraft carrier for overdue repairs and Italy withdrew its aircraft carrier to save money. Only eight of the 28 allies engaged in combat, and most ran out of ammunition, having to buy, at cost, ammunition stockpiled by the United States. Germany refused to take part, even in setting up a no-fly zone.[12]

Such talk leaves Europeans cold—particularly the Germans. From the German perspective, Europe is threatened by no outside power. Besides, with some forty-two thousand American troops still based on the continent—most of them in Germany—why waste precious national treasure on the tools of war? In an article entitled "Hands Off Our Shackles, Please" that appeared in *Der Spiegel*, Germany's most influential news magazine, German security analyst Constanze Stelzenmueller wrote that Germans appear content to let others do the hard work of defending their freedoms.

> The United States has a national security strategy. The United Kingdom and France have one. Even the European Union has one. What Germany has is a White Paper issued by the Ministry of Defense and thus a programmatic void at the national level.... Obviously, it is a problem for our allies when we are unable or unwilling (or both) to supply military clout to joint operations. And when we do decide to contribute military force, we place it under geographical and legal caveats which substantially restrict its efficacy. Lastly, the handicaps we so compulsively impose on ourselves make us politically vulnerable to the demands our allies make. Still, the core problem of our value as an ally is one of political will. Among NATO members the Germans are seen as passive, reactive, and inclined to block or put a brake on things: in short, the Germans are the new French.[13]

IT'S OVER "OVER THERE"

One vital difference between today's Germany and the prickly Gaullists is this: French president Charles de Gaulle, in 1966, demanded that US troops be "removed from French soil" (which prompted US secretary of state Dean Rusk to answer, "Even the ones buried in it?"). Germany, on the other hand, shows no sign of discomfort at being essentially an occupied power some six and a half decades after the death of Hitler. Given the posture of the United States in recent decades, it is hard to blame them. For all the ritual complaining in Washington about the Europeans "not pulling their weight," the Americans have made up for it and then some with troops, air wings, naval fleets, and a vast European military infrastructure that gave little hint that Johnny wanted to come marching home.

From the balconies of the Edelweiss Lodge and Resort in the Bavarian town of Garmisch-Partenkirchen, American soldiers and their families survey the same jagged peaks that formed the backdrop of Hitler's infamous retreat at nearby Berchtesgaden. The commanding heights of the Zugspitze, site of the 1936 Winter Olympic Games, tower over the town, forming part of the border between Germany and the even-more-imposing mastiffs of Austria's Salzburg region to the south.

Built at a cost of $80 million, the Edelweiss opened in 2004 to offer American military personnel and their families a subsidized vacation spot—one of five such spots around the planet—when they are on leave. Given the pace of deployments over the past decade to Iraq and Afghanistan, the rest is well deserved. Yet the resort, with its spas and restaurants and guided Alpine excursions, also stands as a powerful reminder that, some 15 years after the fall of the Berlin Wall, the US military was still building infrastructure on the territory of the united Germany as if it had no intention of ever leaving. Today, in Germany alone, 51 US military bases, large and small, still remain. These bases—ranging from the huge army tank base at Schweinfurt to the incongruously located headquarters of US Africa Command—are no longer geared toward the defense of western Europe from Warsaw Pact armored divisions; rather, they serve as depots, logistics bases, training facilities, and like Edelweiss, R&R spots for America's global gendarme.

Sixty-seven years since American troops first set foot on German soil, the scale of the American presence in a nation that, by any standards, is fully capable of defending itself has finally become an issue. Surprisingly, though, save for a few critics on the fringe, it is not the Germans who are complaining.

"The widely held sentiment among Tea Party Patriot members is that every item in the budget, including military spending and foreign aid, must be on the table," Mark Meckler, cofounder of the Tea Party Patriots, said during the blistering debt ceiling talks in the summer of 2011.[14] This opinion is widely shared by the newest members of the GOP's congressional ranks and has long been gospel for dovish liberal Democrats. But even the rock-ribbed are falling in line, including the 2012 GOP presidential candidates to a man.

"In our current budget environment, we must cut spending, particularly where we can find efficiencies, such as reducing overseas military basing. By streamlining and downsizing our excessive force structure in Europe, we will save billions in military construction, operations and maintenance and family support costs," said Texas senator Kay Bailey Hutchison, no "bring the troops home" liberal. "In addition to saving billions in taxpayer dollars as well as improving troop readiness, thousands of jobs will be brought back to the United States."[15]

Anger about "freeloading" Europeans, a sentiment that neither acknowledges their contributions in Libya, Iraq, and Afghanistan nor the titanic challenge of the euro zone's sovereign debt crisis, has been building for years. For lawmakers like Hutchison, who until recently never saw a defense authorization bill she didn't love (and try to expand), the fiscal crisis at home makes this an irresistible bandwagon to join. (It doesn't hurt that one of the units coming "home," the US Army's 1st Armored Division, will be creating those "thousands of jobs" near its headquarters at Fort Bliss, Texas, in the senator's home state.)

Cynicism aside, the financial case for a major drawdown of US troops is powerful. According to a 2011 study by the Institute for Policy Studies, it costs the United States $250 billion a year to maintain its forward-deployed military forces. About $100 billion of that gigantic annual sum—representing over a third of annual US defense spending—represents the costs of the slowly diminishing Iraq and Afghan wars. But another large chunk—as much as $100 billion annually—goes to fund American forces in rich countries like Germany. "Most soldiers are stationed in high-wage countries, such as Germany and Japan. Payments from host countries for the presence of U.S. troops could result in a net benefit to the United States," the study notes. "However, these payments are minor. Total direct contributions from allies amounted to just over $4 billion, with another $4 billion in 'indirect contributions,' according to the last available information. Moreover, 78% of direct contributions come from one country, Japan," and these contributions are diminishing fast. "Other countries make little to no direct contribution to the U.S. bases."[16]

Over the past several decades, leaders in Germany and many other European countries hosting US forces, including Spain, Italy, Belgium, Portugal, and even Britain, increasingly face an angry public when American leaders choose to go to war. Outside the early days of the Afghan campaign—which fell under the article 5 mutual defense clause of the NATO treaty—actions in Somalia and Iraq (both in 1991 and 2003) and the involvement of German-based facilities in "extraordinary renditions" led to massive antiwar demonstrations in European cities. And yet none of Europe's major political parties include a demand that American forces, whose presence on the continent dates to June 6, 1944 (i.e., D-Day), should pack up and leave. Why?

"Frankly, why should they want us to leave?" asks Stephen Sestanovich, a Russia and Eurasia expert at the Council on Foreign Relations. "With the

British slashing their defense budgets, really only Turkey and France continue to make serious investments in military forces. For the rest, the postwar American subsidy of all their defense and deterrence needs has been so complete that the very concept of 'national security' has disappeared. As long as the U.S. stations tens of thousands of troops in Europe, nothing is going to change."[17]

Indeed, in spite of the wars in Bosnia and Kosovo during the 1990s, the Russian-Georgian war of 2008, and the continuing tensions between Europe and its Muslim citizens, Europeans simply do not feel that armed conflict is a realistic threat to their security. If anything, experts say, as a result of the experience of Bosnia, which saw the initial European intervention bailed out in humiliation by the United States, and then the unpopular Iraq and Afghan wars, Europe will be less inclined than ever to pitch in for its own defense.

"Europeans now embrace the whole Venus versus Mars thing unreservedly," says Nick Childs, defense and security correspondent for the BBC. "Let the Yanks play warrior—we've got soft power, goes the argument."[18]

Britain and France remain determined to play as large a global political role as their diminishing economic vitality can afford, but both are cutting defense spending significantly. More importantly, the continent's true heavyweight, Germany, has developed a worldview at odds with Washington, nurturing the pacifist streak instilled by the occupying powers after World War II and, to US dismay, applying it more broadly than ever. Its vocal resistance to the Iraq War marked an especially sharp turning point. Since then, German support for US policies cannot be taken for granted. In 2011 alone, Germany joined China, Russia, and others in abstaining in the UN Security Council's vote on NATO's intervention in Libya; it has also joined the world's other export giant, China, in opposing US-led efforts to tackle global imbalances. And for the first time ever, Germany supported a Security Council resolution deeming Israel's settlement construction and occupation of the West Bank illegal, and demanding their immediate halt. Heather A. Conley, an expert on Germany at the Center for Strategic and International Studies in Washington, sees this fissure only growing.

The American foreign and security policy glue that held Europe and the transatlantic community together during the Cold War and immediate post–Cold War era is no longer an effective adhesive. Today we are bearing witness to the first tentative policy steps by Germany without Europe and the United States. German leaders believe that militarily the United States will continue to be Europe's military default power for the next ten years as Germany grows increasingly reliant on U.S. security guarantees as it reduces its own military expenditures. On critical international economic issues, however, Germany will be more willing to challenge U.S.-led global economic policy prescriptions over the coming years as Germans firmly believe that the United States is headed in the wrong direction by not investing in or focusing on the "correct" policy priorities: energy security, climate change, budget austerity, and regulating financial markets appropriately.[19]

But Germany—and the "Europe" it has seen as its salvation ever since the fall of the Third Reich—has a surprise coming. With US forces looking for the exit in Iraq and Afghanistan, and in an era when the national debt has replaced Al Qaeda as the great enemy in many American minds, Europe's free ride on security issues is coming to an abrupt end. US defense dollars will be pinched and keeping up with challenges in Asia and the Middle East—not least the growing power and sophistication of the Chinese military—will be the obvious priorities for the United States. The luxury of maintaining multiple combat brigades in Europe—or luxury hotels to rest them—while the Europeans themselves slash military spending further cannot survive. Unless the struggling EU wants to be pushed around by Moscow, it will have to do something more to pick up the slack.

A STEPPE BACKWARD

Lurking just to the east is Russia. Insecurity, always a hallmark of the Russian character, has manifested itself in new and potentially dangerous ways since the collapse of the Soviet Union. Russia's hostility to the notion of NATO membership for either Ukraine or Georgia sparked a small war (with Georgia in 2008) that bolstered ethnic Russian separatists in the enclaves of Abkhazia and South Ossetia, effectively shrinking Georgia's national territory by a quarter. Kremlin interference in Ukraine, meanwhile, has turned that large country's political system into a miasma of intrigues between pro-Western reformers and pro-Moscow revanchists. In 2007, the Kremlin engaged in an international publicity stunt by sending a submarine to plant a tiny Russian flag in the seabed at the North Pole, effectively claiming the top of the world for the

Kremlin's oil concerns. This spurred Canada to begin construction of two Arctic military bases and to organize exercises with two other Arctic powers, the United States and Denmark.

Back in Europe, meanwhile, Russia has backed other separatist claims in tiny Moldova, to the east of Romania, and has alarmed Polish and Baltic states with a series of provocative military exercises in recent years. In 2009, Russia held military exercises based on a ridiculous scenario: a "rising" of ethnic Poles in western Belarus (a territory that had been part of pre-1939 Poland) followed by invasions of Russia by Lithuanian and Polish elite troops. The Polish government was so concerned that its foreign minister at the time, Radek Sikorski, asked Washington to station troops on Polish territory "if you can still afford it."[20] Instead, NATO agreed to take turns flying air patrols over the Baltic states.

As the century unfolds, Russia will be a diplomatic headache for Americans; for Europeans, it may be a bully or—worse—a resurgent threat. "In theory, the Europeans should be responding to U.S. force cuts by studying... whether they need to augment their forces to replace the departing U.S. ones," says Tomas Valasek, director of foreign policy and defense studies at the Centre for European Reform. "But the opposite is likely to happen: without U.S. pressure, many European governments will feel freer than ever to reduce military spending and forces. This may yet turn out to be the most significant and corrosive legacy of current U.S. budgets cuts for allied security."[21]

Recent events suggest that Moscow feels it has bested NATO twice now in the past two years: first, by going to war with Georgia and shrugging off Western condemnation, and next, by convincing the United States to back down over construction of a major antimissile defense system in Poland and the Czech Republic. Far from discouraging future bouts of chauvinism, these "victories" for Russian nationalism are likely to encourage the Kremlin to continue testing its limits. Russia's short-term goal is a tacit recognition that NATO expansion is over. In the medium term, Russia would like to use its earnings from oil and gas exports—much of which is sold to the EU—to rebuild its military, confirming its already well-known willingness to use the EU's growing dependence on Russian energy resources to neutralize its diplomatic clout on human rights and security issues. Meanwhile, Russia's defense expenditures have climbed dramatically since their post–Cold War nadir, which is strangely unremarked upon in Western Europe. In 2001, Russia spent $28 billion on its military—not nearly enough to maintain the deteriorating

Soviet-era force it inherited. By 2010, however, that figure had more than doubled, with Russia spending more than any other European country on its military ($59 billion, precisely what Britain and France spent that year— before both ordered sharp cuts). Relations are relatively good at the moment between Europe's largest nations, though Russia and Britain have jousted over allegations that Moscow sent a hit squad to London to kill a KGB defector and critic of Putin, Alexander Litvinenko, who was poisoned with polonium. But diverging growth rates and Russia's own desire to reassert itself in the world after a humiliating period (Vladimir Putin called the Soviet Union's collapse "the greatest geopolitical catastrophe of the twentieth century") suggest that Europe will need to maintain some credible defense capabilities.[22] Nature abhors a vacuum, after all, and few creatures will range as far to fill it as a bear.

THE BRIC-BEAR

The inclusion of Russia in the now-ubiquitous BRIC acronym, coined by Morgan Stanley analyst Jim O'Neill, was perhaps the greatest propaganda victory for Moscow since it convinced the world that the Nazis, rather than its own troops, had murdered over twenty-one thousand captured Polish military officers in the Katyn Forest in 1941. Unlike for China, India, or Brazil, for instance, Russia's future prominence appears to hinge not on its vast potential as a manufacturer, the expansion of its middle class, or the reputation of its products, but rather almost completely on three commodities: oil, gas, and nuclear weapons.

Ian Bremmer, the president of the political risk consultancy Eurasia Group, dismisses Russia as "a commodity play."[23] Beyond its oil and gas, and some diamonds, Russia's veneer of good governance has little to support it. It still makes excellent warplanes and tanks, though they're a step behind top Western competitors. It talks a good game in international forums and has consistently punched above its brittle-boned weight in geopolitical disputes with the United States. But rule of law—at least in the eyes of many international investors—simply does not exist.

A tranche of WikiLeaked US diplomatic cables provided a rare glimpse at the depths of this problem. High officials, the US diplomats charged, engaged in money laundering, narcotics trafficking, and the collection of protection payments from gangsters that they quickly stashed in offshore bank accounts in Switzerland, the Cayman Islands, and Cyprus. Bribery alone, classified US intelligence sources estimate, accounted for $300 billion annually. Russia, of course, denied it all, and Vladimir Putin complained in an interview with CNN's Larry King about cables that depicted him as Batman and his youthful protégé, Russian president Dmitri Medvedev, as Robin. But the US cables only reinforced what other international sources have said for years. In 2011, Russia ranks one hundred and fifty-fourth out of 178 nations in Transparency International's annual corruption index. That's 20 rungs lower than Nigeria!

The roster of international oil companies that have been strong-armed out of their concessions in Russia, after state-owned firms have bled technology and investment from them, is significant: Chevron, France's Total, Shell, and most recently BP, which thought it had locked up a history deal with one of the Kremlin's favorites, Rosneft, to exploit vast oil fields in the Russian Arctic. Instead, the Byzantine workings of Russia's state oil firms landed BP in court, facing billions of dollars in lawsuits filed by some of the most connected billionaires in Russia. Russian police then raided BP's offices in Moscow, seizing documents on behalf of the plaintiffs. In the late summer of 2011, ExxonMobil displaced BP, with its chairman, the hard-charging Texan Rex Tillerson, beaming beside Putin at the signing ceremony. Putin, too, was smiling. After all, in the deal's fine print was the prize he probably cared about most: a pledge to share hydraulic fracturing technology—"fracking," as it's known in the industry—a controversial but effective method of extracting gas from deep subterranean formations pioneered in the United States.

Russia, by some measures, surpassed Saudi Arabia as the world's largest producer of oil in 2011 and has the largest reserves of natural gas on the planet, along with the second-largest reserves of coal. In spite of this natural inheritance, its economy has problems. The scientific infrastructure that gave the United States a run for its money in nuclear armaments, outer space, and general military power during the Cold War suffers from chronic underinvestment and a brain drain. Infrastructure remains badly underdeveloped—so much so that a publicity stunt by Putin in 2010, aimed at encouraging the development of a national highway system and bolstering Russia's auto industry, backfired badly when it emerged that the Russian-built Lada Kalina model he was driving on the trans-Siberian road trip had to be repeatedly replaced by spares from a car carrier that trailed him on the spine-jarring ride.

Beyond corruption and a crumbling infrastructure, the true challenge to Russia's future prosperity lies in demographics. A combination of massive emigration, plummeting post-Soviet life expectancy, and negative birth rates make Russia an incredible shrinking giant—a fact that should disqualify it from true BRIC status. Russia's Federal State Statistics Service has tracked what it calls the "natural decline of the population" ever since 1992, when the Soviet Union collapsed.[24] In the worst years, 1993 to 2006, Russia's population dropped by more than 700,000 annually, though that has slowed somewhat more recently (2010's figure was 239,468 and 2011's looks to be roughly similar). The improvement in the rate of decline suggests that this could level off, but it also masks an important fact: many of Russia's most creative and talented minds are long gone. The range, just to name a few who came to the United States, is telling: Sergey Brin, cofounder of Google; physicist Alexei Abrikosov; art dealer Serge Sorokko; and tennis star Maria Sharapova. They joined a historical roster of luminaries who fled Russian or Soviet tyranny over the years, including helicopter pioneer Igor Sikorsky, composer Igor Stravinsky, choreographer George Balanchine, and pioneering mechanical engineer Stephen Timoshenko. Such losses cannot be quantified, but the US National Science Foundation tried this simple metric: as of 2002, about 30 percent of Microsoft products had been designed by Russian émigré programmers. Similarly, the National Bureau of Economic Research, the preeminent US clearinghouse for economic studies, views the post-Soviet brain drain of scientific talent as a warning about the long-term effects of the collapse of research grants and other support for intellectual pursuits on a major scientific power.

The lower population-loss figures of recent years have some experts recanting earlier apocalyptic predictions about Russia's population collapse. But the optimists, as always in Russia, remain a minority. Dmitry Oreshkin, a Russian political analyst, argued that Russia is on the verge of a new surge in emigration as the first post-Soviet generation grows disillusioned. "It's basically just those who in the 1990's, because of their youth and innate optimism, believed that freedom would finally come and Russia would become a normal country," he wrote in *Novaya gazeta*, a Moscow newspaper that still speaks its mind (and has had four of its journalists murdered since 2004). "The Putin decade sobered them up. You can't get anything if you [sic] father is not a KGB colonel, a member of [Putin's party] United Russia, or an employee of [state-owned energy giant] Gazprom."[25] Add Russia's bellicose bullying of smaller neighbors (e.g., Georgia in 2008) and its intolerant approach to organized domestic dissent, and it's hard to see why anyone views Russia as a player with stamina in this century. The second half of the twenty-first century is a long way off.

Given current trends, the three million Russians living on the vast, sparsely populated hinterland of the country's Pacific coast and bordered by eighty million overcrowded Chinese and North Koreans could well have names that are not written in Cyrillic by 2050. What, realistically, could Moscow do to prevent it, short of nuclear war with the emerging behemoth, China? All in all, Russia seems more slick than BRIC.

Mikhail Khodorkovsky, one-time chairman of the Russian oil giant Yukos and, as of 2004, Russia's richest man, now sits in a Siberian prison convicted of fraud and embezzlement. His sentence runs through 2019. Many, including international human rights groups, view his 2003 arrest and the subsequent trial and takeover of his company as politically motivated—he had been a rare public critic of Putin's campaign to roll back dissent rights in the country. While the Russian oligarch may well have engaged in illegal shortcuts to build his fortune, he was electrifying on the eve of his sentencing in 2010, when he spoke in court one last time, expressing sentiments shared by many of the reformers who toppled the Soviet Union decades ago but which few dare express publicly today:

> [I] hope that Russia will yet become a modern country with a developed civil society. A society free from the arbitrariness of bureaucrats, free from corruption, free from injustice and lawlessness. It is clear that this could not happen by itself and in one day. But to pretend that we are developing when we are in actual fact standing still, or slipping backwards, even if it is under a cloak of a noble conservatism, is no longer possible, and simply dangerous for the country. It is impossible to reconcile oneself to the fact that people who call themselves patriots are so desperately resisting any change that will limit their access to the feeding trough, or their ability to get away with anything.[26]

The four great trends on the European continent of the next decade will create precisely the vacuum that Europeans worked for centuries (usually unsuccessfully) to prevent. They are the diminishing power of the old economic and military establishments of western Europe; the withdrawal of all but a token number of American military forces; the determined insistence of Germany that Europe concentrate on its core problems and steer a more neutral, middle course in global politics; and the cash-fired ambitions of a Russian state struggling with criminality and nursing a historic grievance over the humiliating collapse of the Soviet empire. Though the United States has failed to initiate the necessary but difficult conversation with its allies in Asia and the Middle East over its own diminishing role in their security affairs, Washington has been blunt and insistent with Europe. But Europe has embraced denial of these dangers as earnestly as it ignored the peril posed by Greece to its economic vitality. Sometimes, all a friend can really do is hope for the best.

CHAPTER 10

IN THE GAME, OR
IN DENIAL?

There is no time to lose. Neither the government nor the economy can live beyond its means year after year. The room for maneuver, to live on borrowed money or time, does not exist any more.[1]

This quote might have come from any number of crisis-plagued European, Japanese, or American politicians today who would most likely, but not necessarily, be a figure on the political right. Indeed, the current Democratic president, Barack Obama, has expressed this opinion, as have leaders from left to right, from the socialist former Spanish prime minister, Jose Luis Rodriguez Zapatero, to conservative German chancellor Angela Merkel. Yet these words came not from the debates of contemporary Washington or Brussels. Rather, this ominous warning came from an Indian finance minister, Manmohan Singh, in 1991. Singh, an eventual prime minister, went before his parliament that year and issued a clarion call for fundamentally changing the way India operated. At the time, India was in severe economic straits—it was a deeply backward economic laggard awakening to the fact that its elites had favored the wrong side of the Cold War and modeled their economy on the failed concept of self-reliant socialism. The country was mired in the so-called Hindu rate of growth—that is, growth too low to keep up with the rapid expansion of India's population. This was a life-or-death moment for the world's most populous democracy, and India rose to the cause. With a political scene that makes the two-party American system look like child's play, Singh and his adherents fought entrenched interests—including a powerful communist party, an establishment that still associated capitalism with the bitter centuries of colonial rule, and a military skeptical of change—and turned India into a dynamic giant that, last year, outgrew China. The reforms he sparked have their flaws and remain incomplete, but by calibrating these changes to economic reality and the ability of Indian society to absorb them, Singh and reformers who followed literally changed the world—slowly, deliberately, and without destroying India's character or strangling growth and throwing its economy into the abyss. In 1991, India was broke and appealing to the IMF for a $1.8 billion bailout. Just two decades later, it is the tenth-largest economy in the world and will almost certainly overtake Canada and Italy in the next two years on its way toward the top of the global rankings.

While India two decades ago may be a poor analogy for the complex and gigantic (if sputtering) American economy today, the lesson lies not in the particulars of industrial production, technological breakthroughs, trade, or finance but rather in politics. India mustered the political will to admit decades of error, making changes to its approach to commerce and government that broke outdated taboos, undermined old power centers, and transformed the lives of hundreds of millions. It remains a poor country in many ways, but the poverty once associated with India—the wrenching, famine-stalked, epidemic-prone India of old—died that day in July 1991. Over the next 20 years, its New Economic Policy would produce growth averaging 6.6 percent annually, unleash entrepreneurs, and create new industrial and service industry giants like Tata Motors, Infosys, and Sun Pharmaceutical.

Compared with the challenges facing Singh's India, America's challenges look very surmountable. No one will starve or die of dysentery; food riots will not rock Kansas City or Buffalo (though, as Occupy Wall Street demonstrated in the autumn of 2011, and the Tea Party in the autumn of 2008, determined citizens can creatively remind society of unfinished business). But the American rate of growth—growth that allows parents at least the dream that their kids will do better—is very much at issue. Another self-induced round of economic insanity—draconian spending cuts that gut the good along with the bad programs of the federal government, or simplistic tax code reforms (*nein, nein, nein*, I say!) that accelerate the middle class's slip downward in relation to the wealthy—could lower America's potential GDP growth rate permanently, ceding the future to larger, hungrier rivals.

Has the United States learned the lessons of the past decade or will denial prevail? Much, both inside and outside of its borders, rides on the answer to that question. Troubles elsewhere can, through economic contagion, have global impact. But only the United States is wired geopolitically into the framework of regional stability in almost every corner of the globe. Denial afflicts Europe, too, as euro zone political leaders face a kind of high noon over the flaws in the union's fiscal architecture. A round of major sovereign defaults involving, say, Greece, then Spain, then Italy will devastate financial markets, collapse some major European banks, and hurt all emerging market economies that rely on Europe for trade and foreign direct investment with Europe. Similarly, Japan's inability to break free of the insular, cozy banking practices that deflated its soaring prosperity two decades ago will have consequences not only in Japan itself in the form of continued stagnation, but also around Asia as China, South Korea, and other players snap up opportunities that might have fallen to a better-governed Japan.

But neither Europe nor Japan underpins anything globally in the long run other than their own brands, trade relationships, and living standards. The long-term decline of Europe and Japan certainly has strategic significance in that these weakened powers could eventually tempt a more aggressive approach to regional issues by Russia or China. And, as ailing European banks retreat from their traditional dominance of emerging markets, growth globally will slow. But ultimately US and, more likely, BRIC money will fill the vacuum. Indeed, Erika Michele Karp, managing director of investment research at the Swiss bank UBS, believes Europe's pain may be America's gain in this respect. "The Europeans were there first, in former colonies where French, British, Dutch or Spanish banks have deep roots. As they rebuild their balance sheets or disappear, it could be an opportunity for US banks to get in these fast growing markets at just the right moment."[2]

America's decline, on the other hand, contains no real silver linings. Over the medium term—over the next decade or so—every citizen on the planet has a real stake in the outcome of the current struggle within the United States to adopt rational economic and national security policies. Regardless of your nationality, in spite of the fact that past American actions may have harmed or angered you profoundly, the United States alone can ensure that the journey from the millennial world of American dominance to the fast approaching multipolar future proceeds smoothly, without constant economic crises, widespread unrest, climactic disruptions, and major wars.

The signs that America will right itself remain mixed. Wars are being wound down, and the country's staggering debts—driven home by the bracing but well-deserved 2011 downgrade of its sovereign credit rating by S&P—are the central topic of contemporary US political conversation: all that is good. Yet at the same time, revisionists blame the government for the recent financial crisis. This is akin to blaming the neutral Swedes or pacifist Swiss for not preventing World War II. The US government's primary failing in the crisis was in buying into and then incentivizing the doctrine of radical financial deregulation. It deserves deep disdain for allowing the private sector to run amok—for pulling the sentries from the walls defending American democracy, in the oft-cited words of Aaron Sorkin's 1992 film, *A Few Good Men*.[3] But that still leaves government as the patsy, not the perpetrator. Like the toothless League of Nations during the 1930s, the US government shirked its duty to halt the slide to disaster. But it was Hitler, not the League or the British and French who appeased *Der Fuehrer* at Munich, who invaded Poland.

Can Americans handle the truth? Amazingly, ideological puritanism, the very evil that led to the 2008-2009 financial crisis, continues to stalk the United States. In recent congressional debates on fiscal policy—particularly the bruising and inane debt ceiling fiasco in the summer of 2011 that led to the S&P downgrade—the world watched in amazement as dogma, ignorance, and outright lies threatened what has been history's most successful experiment in self-government. As a Washington-based reporter early in my career, with the stakes far lower than they are today, I saw firsthand the tunnel vision that envelops the American capital when party-line instincts take hold. Today, however, with the trajectory of US national growth threatened and foreign economic rivals growing rapidly, profound damage will stem from delay, and irreversible damage from basing decisions on ideology rather than fact.

And yet it persists: One side in Washington wants to cut taxes and spending primarily because its core constituents value tax cuts over government services. The other side wants to do precisely the opposite for the sake of pandering to its own supporters. As the 2012 presidential campaign picks up steam, both sides dress their Machiavellian prescriptions in the garments of economics, supply side or Keynesian. The fact is, among the very few American legislators who understand anything about the intersection of politics and economics, there is a keen awareness that this crisis has arrived at a perilous moment just as the Democrats and Republicans start pandering to the extreme fringes that make up the lion's share of presidential primary voters. At some point, one hopes, the rival captains of this lifeboat—Congress and the Executive—will stop bashing each other with the oars, start filling the holes that are letting in the sea, and get back to rowing.

In any other context, the recent behavior of Washington's political class would be deemed highly unpatriotic—akin to fiddling while Rome burns. But in the modern United States, outrageous behavior is shrugged off during the ever-expanding election cycle as part of the theater of politics, where pleasing "the base" is deemed the paramount concern. Among major economies, the United States is not the most profligate debtor on the planet just yet—that title goes to Japan. But turning Japanese cannot be ruled out if politics continues to block progress on a medium-term plan for debt reduction that will avoid producing a short-term economic heart attack.

What is clear is that with both parties pandering to their respective base, the risk is high that global markets will unleash a punishing, irreversible verdict on the competence of American economic leadership that would ruin millions of American lives, precipitate a new crisis in global market capitalism, and grease the skids of American decline.

Ever since the mid-1990s, when easy credit became the primary fuel for consumption-led growth in the United States, leaders of both US parties have charted a course of blinkered denial. This inability to face the true state of the country's relative power and economic health was repeatedly sanctified by US voters. We now know that as the twentieth century gave way to the twenty-first, a credit bubble was prodded to life by the embrace of fundamentalist market economics that totally ignored the lessons of past crises. This unleashed the financial services sector to follow its "creative genius" and encouraged less savvy people to treat their homes, credit cards, and even 401(k) plans like piggy banks. We've seen how that turned out. Twelve years ago, at the turn of the twenty first century, the inflation adjusted per capital income in the United States stood at $28,293. The figure for 2010 was $26,487—a loss of 6.8 percent of income.[4]

Much has been written about the bursting of the mortgage finance bubble and the global effects that followed. Yet there was a second, primarily psychological bubble inflating America's self-regard to the point where all prior restraints on its global activities were assumed to be obsolete. This view was encouraged by the steroid-driven economy, the natural optimism and trusting nature of Americans, and the vacuum created by the collapse of the United States' former rival, the Soviet Union. The constant drumbeat of political nonsense about the "exceptional nature" of the United States was supercharged by the 9/11 attacks and exacerbated by Bush administration politicians who took advantage of that trauma to advance their own partisan agenda.

If those bent on denying these problems represent one obstacle to assessing America's true situation, those eager to pen the country's eulogy symbolize the other. As usual, the reality lies in between the extremes. America's days of overwhelming global dominance have indeed passed, and its future prosperity has been compromised by financial cynicism. But the United States remains, and will remain for some time, the world's most powerful nation. As the German political commentator Josef Joffe puts it, China notwithstanding, the United States will be the world's "default power" for decades to come.[5] If that sounds a bit less sexy than "superpower" or not as awesome as "hegemon," so be it. The United States squandered any sympathy it might otherwise have expected from the rest of the world with its abysmal record in the first decade of the century. And who knows—Americans may just find that they enjoy hanging up the superpower cape and spending a bit more time rambling around their continent-sized homeland.

Comparisons with the past are of limited value in all this, especially overused analogies to the decline of the British, French, Spanish, Dutch, or Roman empires of yesteryear. But some similarities do exist. For instance, as with Britannia's long retreat from global dominance in the early twentieth century, the pullback of American power in our time will expose, for the first time in decades, parts of the geopolitical shoreline that American might, political will, and diplomatic influence have heretofore sheltered. In some regions, this portends a true reordering of the global status quo—a stability almost entirely engineered and sustained at great cost by the United States since the end of World War II, primarily on behalf of its own interests and those of its allies. Postwar American power has sustained a roughly consistent status quo across great areas of the planet, to both the benefit and sometimes the detriment of large swaths of humanity. Revolutions, wars, technological innovation, and social upheaval have disturbed and upended parts of this status quo, with countries defecting from a broadly pro-American line (Iran, Nicaragua, Eritrea, and Venezuela) and others moving in the other direction (India, Egypt, Brazil, and the countries of Central and Eastern Europe).

It has become common wisdom in some places that the period between the fall of the Berlin Wall and 9/11 represented a transition. In fact, the violent train of events sparked by 9/11 merely disturbed the larger transition. By any measure, the most profound development of the past three decades had nothing to do with war, Islam, color revolutions, or even financial incompetence. The great, defining change that continues to drive global events is the addition of three billion or more people to global capitalism's labor force since the vanquishing of communism. It took these billions half a generation to gear up, but today, no one in North America, Europe, or Japan can afford to ignore the competition.

The "victory" of the Cold War caused a rapacious bubble of self-regard to begin swelling within the collective American cranium, a skull so apparently thick that even a near depression and a credit downgrade fail to penetrate it. The disastrous deregulation of its financial industry—a philosophy it strong-armed onto its allies, too—very nearly destroyed global capitalism. Europe, smugly critical of America's troubles, meanwhile began to dig its own sovereign grave by putting politics over economic gravity, ignoring basic issues of currency management, credit, and accounting.

What, then, must be done? Effective action will require ideological flexibility and a casting off of political dogma rooted in a bygone era—the American Century.

From an economic standpoint, the Keynesians are less wrong than their opponents. For similar reasons, Democrats currently come closer to a rational diagnosis of America's problems than the GOP. In Europe and Japan, advocates for a looser monetary policy and tighter fiscal controls—roughly defined as European federalists—appear far more determined to face reality than their opponents. The trouble in Europe is that their opponents include just about every national leader in the EU, not to mention the majority of the electorates of the wealthier counties.

Geopolitically, the United States must launch a serious effort to design new security arrangements that will cushion the impact of diminishing American power.

As this book has tried to explain, the webs of influence and complex arteries and capillaries that constitute global economic relations defy simple prescriptions. Black and white solutions will work no better in this crisis than they did after 9/11. But some broad rules and specific policy approaches should be considered in order to prevent worst-case scenarios while the world remains in transition from the America-centric age to the peer-to-peer future.

- **A reorientation of US international security priorities away from "stability" and toward "managed transition."** The United States continues to approach the world with the assumption that, in the end, Washington's rule is law and that a world ordered to benefit the United States will, by definition, benefit humanity. Those days, an era of the unipolar world never entirely accepted by the rest of the planet, are over. American policy—grand strategy as the think tank set would term it—should stress the unique capabilities that the United States retains diplomatically and militarily to convene the summits, forums, and alliances necessary to build resilient relationships between emerging regional powers who ceded regional security to various fleets and divisions of the US military. This strategy will require bilateral guarantees in some parts of the world, multilateral organizations in others, and mutual defense treaties in others. While in some cases old-fashioned guarantees like the one that prevents a war between North and South Korea may be exceptions, in most cases the United States should take the role of "architect" literally, helping regional powers design a system that will function without the United States as a full member. This approach not only makes political sense in the sovereignty-sensitive world of Asia, but also maintains a maximum degree of flexibility for the United States to deploy its own resources as needed around the world.

- **Tough love for US allies.** American security guarantees take many forms—some (NATO, South Korea, Taiwan, Japan) explicit and others (Israel, Ukraine, Saudi Arabia, Australia, Mexico) more implicit for historical and diplomatic reasons. While America stood like a colossus astride the planet, opaque promises had their advantages. In today's world of WikiLeaks, conspiracy theories, and diminished respect for American power, transparency should prevail. If not, US allies may discover too late that they have a paper tiger on their side, and the United States may find itself faced with awful dilemmas as nations that formulated their own national security policies based on blanket assurances from Washington stumble into conflicts that America can neither prevent nor afford to fight. The United States should take the lead in encouraging an end to such diplomatic anachronisms as Japan's constitutional prohibition on spending more than 1 percent of its GDP on defense, Israel's "no comment" nuclear arsenal, or the long-running imbalance in US-European NATO defense spending. In a similar vein, Washington should end the foolish economic embargo of Cuba, which at this point is about the only proof the Castro brothers can point to of their relevance to the modern world. US defense commitments should be in treaty form and debated in Congress. NATO commitments should be borne according to the relative GDP of the member state, and those who failed to spend a mutually agreed percentage of their GDP on defense should be suspended from membership. Allies like South Korea and Japan should pay far more of the costs associated with the US military presence on their soil or, if they see fit, eject American troops and defend themselves. Taiwan and Israel, perhaps the two nations whose destinies are most tied to American power, should be told that American economic, military, and political support will rise and fall according to their commitment to negotiating an end to the destabilizing hostilities that persist with their neighbors.

- **A "controlled burn" fiscal policy for America.** By far the most serious short-term challenge facing the world involves the need to restore what Keynesians call "aggregate demand" in the developed world—especially in the United States—without resorting to policies that cause the collapse of sovereign credit ratings and default or a new, even larger bubble built on credit, "cheap money" from the US Federal Reserve, or sloppy stimulus plans that rely solely on tax cuts. As in most (though not all) such debates, the right solution lies between the ideological poles of America's two parties. The Right is right about one thing: disaster looms if a business-as-usual attitude toward government borrowing and spending persists. But the American economy is not merely stagnant: it is damaged and struggling to adapt to global change. A spark is needed—think of it as a controlled burn: a two- to three-year program of national investment that consumes the most precious national resource America has, credit, in order to create a firebreak that allows long-term economic fixes to succeed. This must be accompanied by a binding reform and austerity plan that would kick in only after two consecutive years of GDP growth in excess of 2.5 percent, a realistic rate that suggests a return to potential, and a fall in unemployment to below 7.5 percent—close to the "new normal" structural rate wrought by the 2008 crisis. Politics looms as the primary challenge: the United States needs to emerge from the 2012 election with a leader who holds a mandate to impose a serious plan for reducing government spending commitments after short-term efforts to reignite consumer demand. Only then can a well-designed austerity plan begin the crawl back to fiscal health without the risk of snagging one of the many economic trip wires that America's decades of profligacy buried in the road ahead.

- **A serious examination of US income distribution.** Quite contrary to the dogma of the US Right, the past quarter of a century has visited a disaster upon the US middle class. Even as productivity and corporate profits soared, income stagnated and job security all but disappeared. A clever shell game based on deregulating the lending industry and securitizing the loans that middle-class Americans took out on their most important investment—their homes—masked this erosion for nearly a generation. The idea that all of society would benefit from tax rates structured to maximize net income for the top 5 percent of Americans was decisively disproven when the carefully engineered housing bubble burst. The clang of this wake-up call continues to ring four years later, but American policy makers apparently prefer hitting the snooze button to waking up. The housing crisis, and it is a crisis, must be solved by forcing US banks (including government entities Fannie Mae and Freddie Mac) to absorb the losses that their recklessness enabled. No stimulus would be more powerful than unburdening American households and resetting loans according to actual values rather than those set by deeply corrupt mortgage-lending syndicates in the first decade of the twenty-first century. The alternative—inaction—will doom most US housing values to a continued decline in most US metropolitan areas for another half decade, retarding the broader economy's growth, too. On the political front, cries of "class warfare" emanating from right-wing commentators every time these dire facts are pointed out need to be seen for the absurdity they are. Calls for higher taxes on the rich are not tax warfare but merely a skirmish. The war has been underway since 1970, and the super rich have enjoyed an amazing string of victories. Time for a counter-offensive.
- **An aggressive move to restore ratings credibility.** The two economic mega-crises of the twenty-first century, the 2008-2009 Great Recession and Europe's sovereign debt debacle, offered ample warning that the bridge ahead was out. As noted in chapter 9, intellectual

arrogance led established financial institutions and economic policy-makers to ignore the human harbingers of these disasters, too—economists like Nassim Taleb and Roubini, regulators like Brooksley Born ahead of the subprime meltdown, Roubini again and his fellow dismal scientists Bernard Connolly and Kenneth S. Rogoff, in the run-up to the euro zone mess. Central bankers and politicians wore ideological blinders; investment professionals happily drank any Kool Aid that would keep capital flowing. But the three global ratings agencies, Moodys, Fitch and S&P, have no such excuse—except that their business model predetermined their incompetence. These agencies should be forbidden from accepting money from market makers—banks and brokerage houses or issuers of debt—and instead charge investors for the privilege of having a professional assessment of the risks entailed in any given transaction. Dissidents within these agencies would be empowered, and investors would ask questions when noted experts from the outside raised issues. This change would eliminate a serious conflict of interest and a serious "false positive" in the global economy. After all, in many ways, a faulty condom is worse than no condom at all.

- **A "Gloves Off" Approach with Financial Sector:** The reforms of banking regulation and securities law in the United States and Europe have been uncoordinated and, while sometimes useful, often blunted and sidestepped by the financial industry. Amazingly, the market for over-the-counter derivatives—the SIVs (structured investment vehicles), MBSs (mortgage-backed securities), and CDSs (credit default swaps) that dragged the world toward the abyss in 2008—remains almost entirely unregulated. Thirteen years after Brooksley Born, then-chairwoman of the Commodities Futures Trading Commission, warned that this market concealed a ticking time bomb, and four years since it detonated, trillions of dollars' worth of transactions that tie American banks to their counterparties around the world remain opaque.[6] Similarly, efforts to reimpose the Glass-Steagal separations of commercial and investment banking also, by and large, failed, as described in chapter 2. This, for now, appears to be the state of play—American democracy, entangled in the political complexities of legislative wrangling, has chosen to cross its fingers rather than put up its dukes. But the US administration can still do a great deal of good by simply rediscovering its stomach for prosecution. The Justice Department in the United States should pursue broad charges against those who led America's leading investment banks and other financial institutions to the brink of collapse in 2008. Focusing on fraudulent claims about the performance of complex securitized financial products—products sold as AAA risks—should be possible, particularly if the Justice Department employs the RICO (Racketeer Influenced and Corrupt Organizations) statutes that helped bring the US mafia down to size two decades ago. Astoundingly, when Goldman Sachs was found to have sold subprime mortgage products that it specifically designed to fail—in part so that a major client, Paulson & Company, could be against it—the government accepted a 2010 settlement offer rather than continue with a criminal case. The settlement was a record $550 million. That's a rounding error on Paulson's balance sheet (though they had a miserable 2010, it must be said, as karma apparently has finally taken a hand).[7] But pursuing such cases to their legal end, even if the prosecution somehow failed, would restore credibility to US regulators and ultimately have a much more profound effect on the financial sector. Instead, the government sent a message that, yes, it may pursue charges in egregious cases, but the option to pay it off will remain.

- **Tax Reform in the United States that Sparks a "Releveraging" of the US Corporate Sector:** Two sectors of the US economy must continue to deleverage—government and individual households. However, cash mountains in excess of three trillion dollars molder away in the accounts of US corporations, which, due to political uncertainties and their memory of the short-term credit seizure that occurred in 2008, are keeping it out of circulation. At least some of the payroll tax breaks proposed by Roubini and I (described in chapter 2) appear likely to survive into the presidential election year. But the real goal should be a macro-reform of the US tax code. Tax reform proposals currently under debate propose simplification of the code, the closing of loopholes that often leave corporations and investment professionals paying little or no taxes, and (more controversially) a return to progressive rates that reverse decades of losses by middle-class families. All this makes sense. But by providing a tax holiday to corporations who invest their current war chests in the two to three years before a new tax code can go into effect would coax that money back into the economy, creating jobs, output, and a stimulus funded entirely by the private sector. Even I'll raise a cup of tea to that!

- **Federalism and exit doors in Europe.** The EU risks collapse if its leaders fail to create a "fiscal union" that enables economic policy makers to enforce minimum requirements on borrowing, government spending, and other factors among its members. Imagine the United States with 50 different labor markets and 50 separate standards on retirement age, Social Security, bank reserve requirements, and state government spending. Within Europe's euro zone, this situation, along with some political shenanigans and (in the case of Greece) fraud, has created an economic time bomb. A currency without a fiscal mechanism for enforcing basic standards is like a revolution without a leader—it soon begins consuming itself. A European finance ministry able to issue bonds, enforce fiscal discipline, and, ultimately, recommend the ejection of euro zone members that cannot meet basic standards is the way to defuse this bomb. A European Central Bank prepared to be the Fed of Europe—the lender of last resort should systemic risks loom—will contain future crises.

- **Restructuring America's Military:** In the foreseeable future, the powerful US armed forces will remain dominant. In spite of some significant restructuring in the late 1990s that moved it away from the force structures and doctrines of the Cold War, the anomalous wars that followed 9/11 proved to be a double-edged sword, tilting spending priorities toward a kind of ground warfare the United States should strive to avoid at all costs in the future. Over the next decade, defense will claim approximately $600 billion less of the US federal budget than it would have if current levels and programs persisted. This, and the winding down of the Iraq and Afghan wars, offers an opportunity for radical reform. Naval and air capabilities should take priority, with a renewed focus on reducing personnel demands through automation. The Army should be reduced both in global footprint and overall size, exiting from Europe and ceding its post-Afghanistan operations in the Middle East to an expanded Marine Corps. Spending should also favor more intensive training of the Army's reserve units, where pay should be kept at levels that make reserve service attractive across the US socioeconomic spectrum. The Navy should cease construction of the Ford-class aircraft carriers and its purchase of the carrier-borne version of the F-35 Lighting II warplanes. The Navy should shift its emphasis to the development of smaller platforms that house pilotless drones of much greater range than the current 730-mile reach of the F-35. Aggressive efforts to pursue deeper cuts in the US and former Soviet nuclear arsenals should be made, with a new emphasis on engaging second-tier players, particularly China, India, and Pakistan, in global talks. Spending on missile defense systems should be made contingent on actual capabilities, and the myriad agencies currently involved in separate initiatives, including US Space Command, Air Force Global Strike Command, the National Missile Defense Agency, and the United States Army Space and Missile Command merged into a single, cost-effective US Missile Command. The Air Force, like the Navy, should begin to phase out piloted combat aircraft and consider early retirement, in particular, of strategic bombers and deep strike aircraft. As ground capabilities go, the Army should continue the phaseout of its remaining heavy armor in favor of lighter, more deployable forces, with special emphasis on special operations capabilities. The Marine Corps should retain its current structure, though operating its own air arm probably is not sustainable going forward.

- **Avoiding War with China:** While China and India likely will rise and ultimately displace Britain, France, and Russia as the world's most capable "second-tier" military powers, the idea of China as a "peer competitor" of US forces simply is as unrealistic as the dream of drafting India as a partner in making the world safe for democracy. The United States, as the more mature military and diplomatic player, can take steps to ensure China does not assume the label "enemy" in the American psyche. With the exception of forces aimed at Taiwan, China's blueprint stresses "area denial," disruptive defense tactics, cyber warfare, and old-fashioned nuclear deterrence (thus its relatively small nuclear arsenal). Prudence and human nature mean both nations will continue building capabilities aimed at countering the other, but US-China military ties must be taken to a new level and walled off from routine frictions of trade, currency, and geopolitical matters. Additionally, US foreign policy should raise pressure on China to deploy its forces to international peacekeeping missions and to work with US and other military forces in Asia to create a joint Pacific Rim rapid response capability to deal with natural disasters. China should also be drawn into a broader dialogue on nuclear disarmament, ballistic missile technology controls, and talks aimed at controlling the weaponization of space—something both have enormous stakes in preventing.

- **Extracting the United States from unilateral responsibility for Middle Eastern stability:** The United States should inform Israel and Egypt, whose large gifts of American military aid annually are roughly proportional, that such funds will diminish in real terms over the next decade until phased out altogether, though economic aid might shrink less quickly, depending on developments in post-revolutionary Egypt. The United States should also acknowledge publicly, after consultations with its ally, the existence of Israel's nuclear arsenal and convene a regional nuclear arms conference with the aim of convincing Israel to offer sharp cuts in its arsenal and international inspections in exchange for pledges from Iran, Saudi Arabia, Egypt, and Turkey not to pursue nuclear weapons and to impose harsh sanctions, including the possibility of joint military action, against any regional country that defies the pledge. An expanded version of the current "Quartet" (US, EU, Russia, and UN) that adds China, Brazil, Turkey, and India would supplant current Israeli-Palestinian diplomacy, proposing a final blueprint as a starting point for negotiations that returns most of the West Bank and Gaza to the Palestinians, allows East Jerusalem to be the Palestinian capital, and sets a reparation payment to the descendants of Palestinian refugees whose lands in Israel proper will remain beyond return. Israel would be recognized by the Arab League member states and invited, along with Turkey and Iran, to join a renamed "League of Middle Eastern Peoples" that would offer observer status to ethnic minorities like Algeria's Berbers, Israeli Arabs, the Druze of the Levant, and Kurds from Iraq, Syria, and Turkey. This expanded "Octet," meanwhile, would jointly guarantee freedom of navigation in the region's vital energy chokepoints, certify compliance with nuclear-free pledges, and should provide logistics and security on a limited basis in the event of unrest, while decreasing proportionately arms sales and military aid doled out to local governments.

- **A remaking of the UN Security Council**. The Security Council remains the most obviously flawed major global institution in the world, reflecting the world of 1945 (or, at best, 1979 when China assumed Taiwan's seat). Efforts to bring the Security Council into sync with the twenty-first century fail largely because of the veto held by five nations—the United States, Britain, France, Russia, and China—that cannot agree on the set of new members that could be permanently at the top table. The solution is obvious: eliminate the veto. The idea that any power should preempt a majority of the planet's most powerful states simply by issuing a veto is the most egregious of all the anachronisms that have survived at the UN. China and Russia recently vetoed sanctions against the vicious regime of Syria's Bashar al-Assad. The United States routinely finds itself backed into a corner on issues involving Israel, which, rather than being resolved through negotiations, wind up unresolved and subject to Washington's imperious "no." This veto power—far more than the theater of the absurd that is the General Assembly—does more to undermine the institution than any other single factor. Once vetoes are gone, the addition of a set of emerging powers and a consolidation of the French and British seats into a single EU vote would be possible. The addition of Japan, Brazil, India, Indonesia, Nigeria, Egypt, and South Africa as permanent members would force real negotiations on the world's most important issues, transforming the UN from a sideshow to the main show. In such a forum, the United States' ability to form coalitions and mediate disputes would be amplified, and while it would lose votes, too, this reform of the Security Council would stand as the ultimate democratizing moment of America's years at the top of the heap.

Such lessons often take generations to fully sink in. But still, with clear decisions by leaders in North America and Europe, the worst can be avoided. The United States, the most resilient and unique society ever founded, may yet find the "middle way" that strikes the right balance between promoting growth and reducing unsustainable promises at home, while carefully turning over some of the world's burdensome security arrangements to its other 6.4 billion inhabitants. If so, it remains a colossus—not *the* colossus, but one entirely in control of its destiny.

Europe's future appears less certain as its leaders continue to pursue policies that deny the depth of the crisis in the euro zone, overreact to its problems with job- and growth-destroying austerity measures there and in Britain, and regard security policy as the responsibility of America and the worry of less-civilized continents. Any or all of these errors could haunt Europe for decades.

American power remains a vital factor in convincing otherwise adventurous despots that attacks on a neighbor or support for terrorism will come with costs too dear to contemplate. But it cannot forever fill that role without the aid of other rising powers. It also cannot enforce the same kinds of blanket guarantees it has issued repeatedly since World War II—think Taiwan, Israel, and minority regions like Tibet or weak states like poor little Georgia, stomped on by Russia in 2008 while the Bush administration wagged its finger. Georgia's brashness before that war suggests that it really did think that the American umbrella protected it—that it could pursue any policy, no matter how it irritated Moscow, without consequences. Moscow taught Georgia a lesson that Taiwan, Israel, Japan, South Korea, and Eastern and Central European countries need to ponder. The United States should remain friends with all of them and should continue to work hard to convince China and Russia, as well as smaller powers like Iran and Venezuela, that coexistence is in the best interests of all nations. But friendship calls for honesty. In its security relations with its close allies, the United States needs to be frank not only about what it can do, but also about what it is actually willing to do in a crisis.

It would be foolish not to be optimistic about America. It would be equally foolish to assume that, by balancing the federal budget, the 1990s will return. That world is gone, and billions are the better for it. Very few nations actually hope that the United States fails—even its most obvious rivals. America can and should play a leading role in the next era, but it needs to recast itself, come down from Mount Olympus, and truly be a leader, not merely insist that it is one. "The United States of America is a country that people around the world admire for its can-do attitude," said Sha Zukang, a Chinese diplomat and his country's top climate change negotiator, during a visit to Washington in 2011. "Here, people believe that no problem is too big for human ingenuity to solve. The world has never needed that ingenuity more than it does today. The world needs your leadership."[8]

ACKNOWLEDGMENTS

A book like this, spanning many disciplines and the entire planet's past, present, and future concerns, demands the humility of someone able to ask the advice of others. To the extent that I am attacked or criticized for anything herein, the fault lies with me. Having said that, I am blessed with friends, former colleagues, and mentors who generously read drafts and provided guidance throughout the process, adding both wisdom and color to the final product.

First, I'd like to thank my agent, Leah Spiro, who helped shape the initial proposal, my editor at Palgrave Macmillan, Emily Carleton, for her enthusiastic support and guidance, her assistant, Laura Lancaster, and my intern, Salil Motianey, who graciously proofread early chapters and helped with footnotes and other thankless tasks.

Among the many experts, practitioners, and simply smart people who offered feedback on various chapters were Frank Barbieri, Emily Field, Jeffrey Godbold, Andrew Nagorski, Jim Baldwin, and Douglas Varga, Kari Huus, my former BBC colleagues Richard Walker, Nick Childs, and Stephen Dalzlel, Asia experts Adam Wolfe and Rachel Ziemba of Roubini Global Economics, Dr. William Turcotte (Emeritus) of the US Naval War College, my former Council on Foreign Relations colleagues Greg Bruno, Steven Cook, and Sebastian Mallaby, and Robert McMahon, with whom I have had the pleasure of working at three different stops along my career: The Associated Press, Radio Free Europe/Radio Liberty, and CFR. For general friendship and advice, no one could have better friends than Suzanne Turcotte, Lynda Hammes, and Amer Nimr.

Nouriel Roubini, founder and chairman of Roubini Global Economics, and Christian Menegatti, his deputy and RGE's head of global research, deserve my special thanks for both friendship and their patience as I pestered them with fundamental questions about the global economy. I also owe a debt to the following people who have guided my career and provided support at key moments that kept my unconventional career on track: Bill Kovach, Stephen Engelberg, and David Binder during my early career at *The New York Times;* Bill McIlwain of the *Sarasota Herald-Tribune;* Merrill Brown, Brian Storm, and Bob Aglow at MSNBC; Richard Haass, Trish Dorff, Jim Lindsay, David Kellogg, and Lisa Shields at CFR; and Gideon Rose of *Foreign Affairs.*

Finally, to my parents—my Irish immigrant, USMC sergeant father, Edward M. Moran, who made all his four children do Saturday morning reports on random chapters of the World Book Encyclopedia, and, my mom, Marie, who uniquely never lost faith in me. I felt you with me every step of the way, mom, and miss you every day.

MICHAEL MORAN

NOTES

INTRODUCTION

1. General Andre Beaufre, interview by the BBC for *The World at War*, Episode 5: "France Falls," produced by Jeremy Isaacs, Thames Television, 1973.
2. Anthony Berry, in conversation with the author, Hamilton, Ontario, 1990.
3. *Meet The Press*, NBC News, March 27, 2011, http://www.msnbc.msn.com/id/42275424/ns/meet_the_press-transcripts/t/meet-press-transcript-march/#.TuyLgnNW6oA.
4. Alexis de Tocqueville, *Democracy in America* (Vintage Books, 1945).

CHAPTER 1: EXCESS BAGGAGE: THE WEST'S STRUGGLE WITH REALITY

1. President Barack Obama, "State of the Union Address" (US Capitol, Washington DC, January 25, 2011), http://www.whitehouse.gov/the-press-office/2011/01/25/remarks-president-state-union-address.
2. The "Super Committee," technically known as the Joint Select Committee on Deficit Reduction, was created after Republicans failed to agree to a routine raising of the borrowing ceiling imposed by previous legislation on the US government. As the government has run a deficit in almost every recent year, this ceiling must be raised in order to avoid a sovereign default and risk panic selling of US Treasuries on global markets. The committee was to recommend a bipartisan plan for deficit reduction, and to incentivize its members to make a deal, draconian "across-the-board" cuts to government spending were added as part of the act that created the super committee that would automatically start in 2013 if the committee failed to produce a plan by November 21, 2011. Predictably, they failed to reach agreement.
3. Typical of this attitude is an article by Fox News contributor and economist John Lott, "Seven Myths about the Looming Debt Ceiling Disaster," Fox News, June 2011, http://www.foxnews.com/opinion/2011/07/15/seven-myths-about-looming-debt-ceiling-disaster/. Lott is the author of such economic standbys as *More Guns, Less Crime* (Chicago: University of Chicago Press, 2010).
4. Ian Bremmer and Nouriel Roubini, "A G-Zero World," *Foreign Affairs*, March/April 2011, http://www.foreignaffairs.com/articles/67339/ian-bremmer-and-nouriel-roubini/a-g-zero-world.
5. Terry L. Zivney and Richard D. Marcus, "The Day the United States Defaulted on Treasury Bills," *The Financial Review* 24 (1989): 475–489, http://econpapers.repec.org/article/blafinrev/v_3a24_3uy_3a1989_3ai_3a3_3ap_3a475-89.htm; http://econpapers.repec.org/article/blafinrev/v_3a24_3ay_3a1989_3ai_3a3_3ap_3a475-89.htm.
6. Mickey Edwards, "How to Turn Republicans and Democrats into Americans," *The Atlantic Monthly*, July/August 2011, http://www.theatlantic.com/magazine/archive/2011/07/how-to-turn-republicans-and-democrats-into-americans/8521/#.

7. This fraught moment in American history makes it all the more disgraceful that the recent debt ceiling negotiations had at least one important faction, the Tea Party, that applied the "inherent bad faith" negotiating model—that is, they had no intention of ever reaching an agreement. This tactic bedeviled US nuclear negotiations with the Soviet Union and has been honed to perfection by North Korea in recent decades. Only ignorance of global financial realities and America's current position in its historical power lifeline can explain its application to the question of America's credit rating.

8. Secretary of Defense Robert M. Gates, "The Security and Defense Agenda (Future of NATO)," Brussels, Belgium, Friday, June 10, 2011, http://www.defense.gov/speeches /speech.aspx?speechid=1581.

9. Anthony Shadid, "A Successful Diplomat Tries His Hand at Politics," *New York Times*, June 10, 2011, http://www.nytimes.com/2011/06/11/world/europe/11davutoglu.html ?pagewanted=all.

10. Niall Ferguson, *Colossus: The Price of America's Empire* (New York: Penguin Press, 2004), 2.

11. G. John Ikenberry, "The Future of the Liberal World Order: Internationalism after America," *Foreign Affairs*, May/June 2011, http://www.foreignaffairs.com/articles/67730 /g-john-ikenberry/the-future-of-the-liberal-world-order.

CHAPTER 2: AS THE WORLD TURNS, GRAVITY BITES

1. For an update on the Thatcherite take on the benefits of radical fiscal austerity, see "Fiscal Stabilizations: When Do They Work and Why," by Ardagna Silvia, *European Economic Review* vol. 48, no. 5 (October 2004): 1047–1074.

2. David Blanchflower, "The Second Great Depression," *The New Statesman and Society*, July 7, 2011, http://www.newstatesman.com/blogs/david-blanchflower/2011/07/growth -niesr-recession.

3. Christian Weller, "Unburdening America's Middle Class," Center for American Progress, November 2011 http://www.americanprogress.org/deleveraging_execsumm.pdf.

4. Bruce Bartlett, "Reagan's Forgotten Tax Record," *Capital Gains and Games*, February 22, 2011, http://www.capitalgainsandgames.com/blog/bruce-bartlett/2154/reagans-forgotten-tax-record.

5. Italy is not the worst in the world, but besides Japan (with debts at nearly 200 percent of its GDP, according to the *CIA World Factbook 2010* it is the absolute champion of debtor nations), Italy tops the G7's profligacy table. The United States looks relatively healthy by this measure, ranked at thirty-seventh in the world and just below the global average computed by the International Monetary Fund (IMF) as being 59.3 percent. Most G7 nations are in worse shape—even Germany ranks worse, weighing in at nineteenth with 83.2 percent debt-to-GDP.

6. Mohamed El-Erian, "Sleepwalking through America's Unemployment Problem," *Project Syndicate*, May 1, 2011, http://www.project-syndicate.org/commentary/elerian4 /English.

7. For a counterpoint to this argument, see Paul Krugman's August 5, 2011, column, "The Wrong Worries," *New York Times*, http://www.nytimes.com/2011/08/05/opinion /the-wrong-worries.html?ref=paulkrugman.

8. Nouriel Roubini and Michael Moran, "Avoid the Double Dip," *Foreign Policy*, November 2010, http://www.foreignpolicy.com/articles/2010/10/11/avoid_the_double _dip?page=0,0.

9. Weller, "Unburdening America's Middle Class."

10. Michael Mandelbaum, "American Power and Profligacy," address to the Council on Foreign Relations, New York, January 18, 2011.

11. Dodd-Frank Wall Street Reform and Consumer Protection Act, Pub. L. No. 111-203, 124 Stat. 1376 (2010).

12. GOP Candidate Tim Pawlenty, New Hampshire Straw Poll Debate, Manchester, N.H., June 13, 2011, http://www.ontheissues.org/governor/Tim_Pawlenty_Budget_+ _Economy.htm

13. Mitt Romney, "How I'll Tackle Spending, Debt," *USA Today*, November 3, 2011, http://www.usatoday.com/news/opinion/forum/story/2011-11-03/mitt-romney-budget -plan/51063454/1.

14. Congressional Budget Office, *The Budget and Economic Outlook: Fiscal Years 2011 to 2021*, Congress of the United States, January 2011, http://www.cbo.gov/ftpdocs/120xx /doc12039/01-26_FY2011Outlook.pdf. Incorrect assertion—see chart in this PDF, pg. xv and full description in chapter 2 (Forecasts).

15. US Office of Management and Budget, *Fiscal Year 2012 Budget of the U.S. Government* (Washington DC: US Government Printing Office, 2010), http://www.whitehouse .gov/omb/budget/Overview/.

16. Budget and Economic Outlook.

17. Representative Paul Ryan, Ranking Member, Committee on the Budget, *A Roadmap for America's Future, Version 2.0*, January 2010, http://www.roadmap.republicans.budget .house.gov/Plan/.

18. Romney, "How I'll Tackle Spending, Debt."

19. "Herman's 9-9-9 Plan for Economic Renewal," Herman Cain Campaign for President website, accessed November 24, 2011, http://www.hermancain.com/999.

20. David Stockman, "Vicious Sell-off in Bond Market Could Force Action on Budget Deficit, Debt," *Distressed Volatility*, May 25, 2011, http://www.distressedvolatility .com/2011/05/david-stockman-vicious-sell-off-in-bond.html.

21. "Kinzinger Statement Against Vote on Raising the Debt Ceiling," Office of Rep. Alan Kinzinger, May 31, 2011, http://kinzinger.house.gov/index.cfm?sectionid=25.2&itemid=96.

22. "America Needs to Accept the Fact that the Good Old Days Are Gone," *Xinhua News*, editorial from Official New China News Agency, via Reuters, August 7, 2011, http:// www.reuters.com/article/2011/08/06/us-china-sp-idUSTRE7750R720110806.

23. Robert J. Gordon, "The Slowest Potential Output Growth in U.S. History: Measurement and Interpretation," address to CSIP Symposium on "The Outlook for Future Productivity Growth," Federal Reserve Bank of San Francisco, November 14, 2008, http://www.frbsf.org/csip/research/200811_Gordon.pdf.

24. Congressional Budget Office, *CBO's 2011 Long-Term Budget Outlook*, June 2011, http:// www.cbo.gov/doc.cfm?index=12212.

25. Henry Paulson, *On the Brink: Inside the Race to Stop the Collapse of the Global Financial System* (New York: Hachette Book Group, 2010), 159.

26. Liaquat Ahamed, *Lords of Finance: The Bankers Who Broke the World* (New York: Penguin Press, 2009), chap. 3.

27. Donald Neff, *Warriors at Suez: Eisenhower Takes America into the Middle East* (New York: MW Books, 1979).

28. A. N. Wilson, *After the Victorians: The Decline of Britain in the World* (London: Hutchinson, 2005).

29. Warren E. Buffett, "Stop Coddling the Super Rich," *New York Times*, August 14, 2011, http://www.nytimes.com/2011/08/15/opinion/stop-coddling-the-super-rich.html.

30. David Kocieniewski, "GE's Strategies Let It Avoid Taxes Altogether," *New York Times*, March 24, 2011, http://www.nytimes.com/2011/03/25/business/economy/25tax .html?pagewanted=all.

CHAPTER 3: A "BOILING FROG" MOMENT FOR AMERICA'S MIDDLE CLASS

1. General Accountability Office, *The Federal Government's Long-Term Fiscal Outlook*, January 2011 update, http://www.gao.gov/new.items/d11451sp.pdf.

2. Ibid.

3. Carmen DeNavas, Bernadette D. Proctor, and Jessica C. Smith, "Income, Poverty and Health Insurance Coverage in the United States," US Census Bureau, September 2011, http://www.census.gov/prod/2011pubs/p60-239.pdf.

4. Avi Feller and Chad Stone, "Top One Percent of Americans Reaped Two-Thirds of Income Gains in Last Economic Expansion," Center for Budget and Policy Priorities, September 9, 2009, http://www.cbpp.org/files/9-9-09pov.pdf.

5. "United States of America Long-Term Rating Lowered to 'AA+' Due to Political Risks, Rising Debt Burden; Outlook Negative," Standard & Poor's, August 5, 2011, http://www.standardandpoors.com/ratings/articles/en/us/?assetID=1245316529563.

6. Paul Krugman, "The Wrong Worries," *New York Times*, August 5, 2011, http://www.nytimes.com/2011/08/05/opinion/the-wrong-worries.html?ref=paulkrugman.

7. *Historical Statistics of the United States, 1789–1945*, Bureau of Census, US Government Printing Office, Washington, DC, 1949, http://www2.census.gov/prod2/statcomp/documents/HistoricalStatisticsoftheUnitedStates1789-1945.pdf.

   It is worth noting that some economists dispute these figures as overly generous because they classify workers in "emergency jobs" created by FDR's New Deal as "employed." Using alternative methods that count such people as unemployed, the numbers are starker: the jobless peak, in this data set occurring in 1933, would be 25 percent, or 37 percent including those who had given up hope. The 1937 figure would be 14 percent, with a jump to 19 percent after the Fed's policy shifts. The numbers track proportionately.

8. Simon Johnson, "Defaulting to Big Government," *Project Syndicate*, July 18, 2011, http://www.project-syndicate.org/commentary/johnson22/English.

9. Roger Altman, speaking at the Council on Foreign Relations, New York, January 18, 2011, http://www.cfr.org/united-states/cfr-90th-anniversary-series-renewing-america-american-power-profligacy/p23828.

10. Includes a $144 billion fiscal year 2012 budget request plus $71 billion for "overseas contingency operations."

11. "GAO Perspectives on Fiscal and Performance Challenges Facing the Federal Government," General Accountability Office Power Point presentation, August 2011, Slide 7, http://www.gao.gov/cghome/d111071cg.pdf.

12. GAO, January 2011 update.

13. John F. Kennedy, Inaugural Address, January 20, 1961, archived by Miller Center for Presidential Politics, University of Virginia, accessed November 24, 2011.

14. Ronald Reagan, speech on behalf of Republican Presidential nominee Barry Goldwater, October 27, 1964, archived by Miller Center for Presidential Politics, University of Virginia, accessed November 24, 2001.

15. Three tremendous and accessible guides to what happened and how both government and the private sector nearly ruined the international economy are: *Crisis Economics: A Crash Course in the Future of Finance* by Nouriel Roubini and Stephen Mihm; *This Time Is Different: Eight Centuries of Financial Folly* by Carmen Reinhart and Kenneth S. Rogoff; and *The Big Short: Inside the Doomsday Machine* by Michael Lewis. For a blow-by-blow account of Wall Street's final acts of venality, Andrew Ross Sorkin's *Too Big to Fail* cannot be beat.

16. Tina Aridas, "Household Saving Rates," *Global Finance Magazine*, accessed November 26, 2011, http://www.gfmag.com/tools/global-database/economic-data/10396-household-saving-rates.html#axzz1Q5LX8KB6.

17. The four original BRICs, Brazil, Russia, India, and China, invited a fifth, South Africa, to join in early 2011—effectively rebranding them BRICS (all caps) and further besotting an already dubious distinction. In fact, Russia, in my view, has no business among the BICs, and South Africa is a midget compared with other potential additions, including Turkey and Indonesia.

18. Mary Curtis, Richard Kersley, and Mujtaba Rana, *Emerging Consumer Survey 2011* (Zurich: Credit Suisse AG, January 2011), https://www.credit-suisse.com/news/doc/media_releases/consumer_survey_0701_small.pdf.

19. Michael Greenstone and Adam Looney, "Have Earnings Actually Declined?" Brookings Institution, March 4, 2011, http://www.brookings.edu/opinions/2011/0304_jobs_greenstone_looney.aspx.

20. William H. Gross, "Off with Our Heads," PIMCO, January 2011, http://www.pimco.com/EN/Insights/Pages/OffWithOurHeads.aspx.
21. Gus Lubin, "Check Out Chris Whalen's Terrifying Presentation on the 2011 Foreclosure Crisis," *Business Insider*, October 8, 2010, http://www.businessinsider.com/chris-whalens-foreclosure-crisis-2010-10.
22. Franklin Delano Roosevelt, address at University of Pennsylvania, September 20, 1040, archived on UPenn website, accessed November 26, 2011, http://www.presidency.ucsb.edu/ws/index.php?pid=15860#axzz1epfEQxJd.
23. He did, though—I hired him as a (poorly) paid intern at Roubini Global Economics in 2010, which led him finally to a job at *Advertising Age*, a trade magazine, six months later. Dylan Byers, as interviewed by author, December 20, 2010.
24. National Center for Education Statistics, "Table 279. Degrees Conferred by Degree-Granting Institutions, by Level of Degree and Sex of Student: Selected Years, 1869-70 through 2019-20," http://nces.ed.gov/programs/digest/d10/tables/dt10_279.asp.
25. Kurt Badenhausen, "Most Lucrative College Majors," *Forbes*, June 18, 2008, http://www.forbes.com/2008/06/18/college-majors-lucrative-lead-cx_kb_0618majors.html.
26. George Orwell, *Down and Out in Paris and London* (London: Penguin Modern Classics, 1933).
27. Anthony Carnevale, Jeff Strohl, and Michelle Melton, *What's It Worth? The Economic Value of College Majors* (Washington DC: Georgetown University, Center on Education and the Workforce, 2011), http://www9.georgetown.edu/grad/gppi/hpi/cew/pdfs/whatsitworth-complete.pdf.
28. McKinsey Global Institute, "An Economy That Works," June 2011, http://www.mckinsey.com/mgi/publications/us_jobs/index.asp.
29. Boston Consulting Group, "Made in the USA, Again: Manufacturing Is Expected to Return to America as China's Rising Labor Costs Erase Most Savings from Offshoring," press release, May 5, 2011, www.bcg.com/media/PressReleaseDetails.aspx?id=tcm:12-75973.

CHAPTER 4: FROM SHORTWAVES TO FLASH MOBS: TECHNOLOGY SPEEDS THE MARCH OF HISTORY

1. Ramy Nagy (Internet entrepreneur), interview with the author, June 14, 2011.
2. Ayah El Said (economist, Roubini Global Economics), telephone exchange with the author, February 3, 2011.
3. Steven A. Cook (Hasib J. Sabbagh Senior Fellow for Middle Eastern Studies, Council on Foreign Relations) and Jared Cohen (director, Google Ideas), conference call attended by the author, January 24, 2011.
4. Shefali Srinivas, "Online Citizen Journalists Respond to South Asian Disaster," *Online Journalism Review*, January 7, 2005, http://www.ojr.org/ojr/stories/050107srinivas/.
5. Steve Outing, "Taking Tsunami Coverage into Their Own Hands," Poynter, January 5, 2006, accessed July 2011, http://www.poynter.org/uncategorized/29330/taking-tsunami-coverage-into-their-own-hands/.
6. Dana Muntean, interview with author, March 2011.
7. Ibid.
8. Kathrin Hille, "China's Microblogs: Confusion, not Crackdown," *Financial Times*, BeyondBRICS blog, October 20, 2011, http://blogs.ft.com/beyond-brics/2011/10/20/china-microblogs-confusion-not-crackdown/#ixzz1f0EXrOGC.
9. Nick Kaltchev (Radio Free Europe/Radio Liberty Bulgarian service presenter), conversation with the author, Munich, May 1995.
10. Pew Research Center, "Arab Spring Fails to Improve U.S. Image," May 17, 2011, http://www.pewglobal.org/2011/05/17/arab-spring-fails-to-improve-us-image/.
11. Kristen Chick, "Clinton, Rebuffed in Egypt, Faces Tough Task on Arab Upheaval," *Christian Science Monitor*, March 15, 2011, http://www.csmonitor.com/World/Middle-East/2011/0315/Clinton-rebuffed-in-Egypt-faces-tough-task-on-Arab-upheaval.

12. A full accounting of deaths caused by US-supported dictators during the period is almost impossible, but some thirty thousand died at the hands of the Argentine military, and about thirty thousand died from 1957 to 1986 in Haiti. Of course, Cold War dynamics also meant that leftists—even those democratically elected, like Chile's president Salvador Allende or Iran's president Mohammed Mossadegh—had to be undermined by the CIA. But that's another story.

13. Human Rights Watch, "Clinton Remarks Undermine Rights Reform in China," February 20, 2009, http://www.hrw.org/news/2009/02/20/us-clinton-remarks-under mine-rights-reform-china.

14. Of course, in some cases of abuse—Iran, North Korea, Myanmar, and Sudan, for instance—American diplomacy has helped put in place economic sanctions. In egregious emergencies, this has even led to military intervention, as in Libya, Bosnia-Herzegovina, Kosovo, and East Timor in the 1990s. But these kinds of actions seem likely to diminish as Western taxpayers balk at their costs and the rising influence changes the stance of emerging powers, which usually go along only reluctantly with such interventions.

15. Ian Bremmer, "Democracy in Cyberspace," *Foreign Affairs*, November/December 2011, http://www.foreignaffairs.com/articles/66803/ian-bremmer/democracy-in-cyberspace.

16. Ellen Nakashima, "Washington Post: Ex-NSA Official Thomas Drake to Plead Guilty to Misdemeanor," Government Accountability Project, June 9, 2011, http://www .whistleblower.org/press/gap-in-the-news/1272-washington-post--ex-nsa-official -thomas-drake-to-plead-guilty-to-misdemeanor-.

17. Jay Rosen, "The Afghanistan War Logs Released by Wikileaks, the World's First Stateless News Organization," *PressThink* (blog), July 26, 2010, http://pressthink.org/2010/07 /the-afghanistan-war-logs-released-by-wikileaks-the-worlds-first-stateless-news -organization/.

18. Hugo J. Black, Concurring Opinion, Supreme Court of the United States, 403 U.S. 713, *New York Times Co. v. United States*, Certiorari to the U.S. Court of Appeals for the Second Circuit, No. 1873, Argued June 26, 1971.

19. Gabriel Schoenfeld, *Necessary Secrets: National Security, the Media and Rule of Law* (New York: W. W. Norton, 2010).

20. Clay Shirky, "Half-Formed Thought on WikiLeaks and Global Action," *Clay Shirky* (blog), December 31, 2010, accessed July 22, 2011, http://www.shirky.com /weblog/2010/12/half-formed-thought-on-wikileaks-global-action/.

21. The original source on msnbc.com, due to the shortsighted company policy on archival material in place until well after the millennium, is no longer online. Luckily, my co-author, Brock Meeks, freelanced this piece based on our work: "India Has Scary Nuke Hack," ZDNet, June 6, 1998, accessed July 23, 2011, http://www.zdnet.com/news/india-has-scary-nuke-hack/99683.

22. "Foreign Spies Stealing US Economic Secrets in Cyberspace," Report to Congress of Foreign Economic Collection and Industrial Espionage, 2009-2011, Office of the National Counterintelligence Executive, October 2011, http://www.ncix.gov /publications/reports/fecie_all/Foreign_Economic_Collection_2011.pdf.

23. Siobhan Gorman, "Electricity Grid in U.S. Penetrated by Spies," *Wall Street Journal*, April 8, 2009, http://online.wsj.com/article/SB123914805204099085.html.

24. Ellen Nakashima and William Wan, "China's Denials About Cyber Attacks Undermined by Video Clip," *Washington Post*, August 24, 2011, http://www.com/world/national-security /state-media-video-candidly-depicts-chinas-developing-cyber-weaponry/2011/08/22 /gIQAqyWkbJ_story.html.

25. Deputy Secretary of Defense William J. Lynn III, remarks on US Department of Defense cyber strategy, National Defense University, Washington DC, Thursday, July 14, 2011.

26. William M. Arkin (expert on US intelligence efforts and digital warfare), telephone interview with the author, November 2010.

27. Author interview with Nagy.

CHAPTER 5: IN THE MIDDLE EAST,
THE WRITING IS ON THE WALL

1. Ernest May, *Imperial Democracy* (New York: Harcourt, Brace and World, 1961), 270.
2. Joseph Nye, "Is America an Empire?," *Project Syndicate*, January 26, 2004, accessed July 2011, http://www.project-syndicate.org/commentary/nye5/English.
3. Ironically, by 2003, the United States had done just that, closing its remaining Saudi bases. See Eric Schmitt, "U.S. Will Move Air Operations to Qatar Base," *New York Times*, April 28, 2003, http://www.nytimes.com/2003/04/28/world/aftereffects-bases -us-will-move-air-operations-to-qatar-base.html?pagewanted=all&src=pm.
4. US Department of Defense, "Active Duty Military Personnel Strengths By Regional Area and By Country (309A)," December 31, 2010, accessed July 2011, http://siadapp. dmdc.osd.mil/personnel/MILITARY/history/hst1012.pdf.
5. International Security and Assistance Force, "Key Facts and Figures," accessed July 2011, http://www.isaf.nato.int/images/stories/File/Placemats/Revised%206%20June%20 2011%20Placemat%20(Full).pdf.
6. Nawal El Saadawi, interviewed by the BBC World Service, November 25, 2011, http:// www.bbc.co.uk/news/entertainment-arts-15892307.
7. George W. Bush, address to joint session of Congress (US Capitol, Washington DC, September 20, 2001), http://georgewbush-whitehouse.archives.gov/news/releases/2001 /09/20010920-8.html.
8. The most consistently reliable polling in the Arab world comes not from local sources but from the Pew Research Center's Global Attitudes Project (http://www.pewglobal .org/2011/05/17/arab-spring-fails-to-improve-us-image/), the Arab-American Institute (http://www.aaiusa.org/reports/arab-attitudes-2011), and the Brookings Institution's Saban Center for Middle East Policy (http://www.brookings.edu/reports/2011/1121 _arab_public_opinion_telhami.aspx).
9. *NewsHour*, PBS Online, transcript of the presidential debate, October 12, 2000, accessed July 2011, http://www.pbs.org/newshour/bb/politics/july-dec00/for-policy_10-12.html.
10. Michael Moran, "Time's Up for the Taliban," msnbc.com, December 22, 1999 (archived at CFR.org), accessed July 2011, http://www.cfr.org/afghanistan/times-up-taliban/p10302.
11. Phil Griffin, in discussion with author, June 27, 2001.
12. This immersion into the culture of the Levant was not all for naught. Copeland's son, Stewart Copeland, would go on to become the rhythmically innovative drummer for the rock band The Police.
13. Daniel Yergin, *The Prize: The Epic Quest for Oil, Money, and Power* (New York: Free Press, 2008), 272–280.
14. Rick Atkinson, *An Army at Dawn: The War in North Africa, 1942–1943* (New York: Random House, 2003), 462.
15. Rachel Bronson (author of *Thicker than Oil: America's Uneasy Partnership with Saudi Arabia*), interview with the author, May 19, 2006, http://www.cfr.org/energy-security /rachel-bronson-thicker-than-oil/p10727.
16. Colonel William A. Eddy, *FDR Meets Ibn Saud* (New York: American Friends of the Middle East, 1954).
17. It is worth noting that some pro-Israeli scholars question Eddy's objectivity in that he had a personal relationship with the king, had spent years as America's proconsul in Arabia, and was born to missionary parents in what is now Lebanon. In effect, the argument is that he had a pro-Arab bias. However, his account is the only detailed narrative by an eyewitness, and doubts about its accuracy may be balanced by the fact that Roosevelt's closest aide, Harry Hopkins, an advocate of an Israeli state, took great pains to limit the distribution of Eddy's post-meeting memoranda, none of which are now known to exist. Accounts of Hopkins's admiration for Judaism can be found in many biographies, including *Harry Hopkins: Sudden Hero, Brash Reformer*, written by June Hopkins (New York: St. Martin's Press, 1999), 40–49.

18. Eddy, *FDR Meets Ibn Saud*.
19. Franklin D. Roosevelt to King Saud, April 5, 1945, Yale University collection, Lillian Goldman Law Library, accessed July 2011, http://avalon.law.yale.edu/20th_century /decad161.asp.
20. Colonel Henry McMahon to Ali Ibn Husain, 1915, Fordham University collection, accessed July 2011, http://www.fordham.edu/halsall/mod/1915mcmahon.html.
21. Franklin D. Roosevelt, "Four Freedoms" speech, January 6, 1941, Marist College collection, accessed July 2011, http://www.fdrlibrary.marist.edu/fourfreedoms.
22. Keith Wheeler, "Egypt's Premier Reveals How He Made Red Arms Deal," *LIFE*, November 14, 1955, 131.
23. Peter Ephross, "Anti-Semitic Diary Entries Dent Jews' Esteem for Truman," Jewish Telegraphic Agency, July 18, 2003, http://www.jweekly.com/article/full/20235/anti -semitic-diary-entries-dent-jews-image-of-truman/.
24. The website of the Harry S. Truman Library and Museum contains the collected documents of this period, many of them accessible from this timeline of the debate over the recognition of Israel. See http://www.trumanlibrary.org/israel/palestin.htm.
25. Alfred Stepan with Graeme B. Robertson, "An 'Arab' More than a 'Muslim' Democracy Gap," *Journal of Democracy* 14, no. 3 (July 2003), http://muse.jhu.edu/login?uri= /journals/journal_of_democracy/v014/14.3stepan.html.
26. Congressional Research Service, *State, Foreign Operations and Related Programs: FY2011 Budget and Appropriations*, April 22, 2011, http://www.fas.org/sgp/crs/row/R41228.pdf.
27. "Panetta Says Israel Is Risking Isolation," Associated Press (via *New York Times*), October 2, 2011, http://www.nytimes.com/2011/10/03/world/middleeast/panetta-says-israel-is -risking-isolation.html.
28. Federal Election Commission filings for 2010 as presented by the watchdog group OpenSecrets.org, accessed July 2011, http://www.opensecrets.org/lobby/top.php?show Year=2010&indexType=s.
29. Michael Moran, "A Road Map to Nowhere?," msnbc.com, May 28, 2003, http:// www.msnbc.msn.com/id/3340058/ns/world_news-brave_new_world/t/road-map -nowhere/.
30. Shilbey Telhami, "2010 Arab Public Opinion Poll," University of Maryland and Zogby International, August 5, 2010, http://www.brookings.edu/~/media/Files/rc /reports/2010/08_arab_opinion_poll_telhami/08_arab_opinion_poll_telhami.pdf.
31. Steven Cook, "Arab Spring, Turkish Fall," *Foreign Policy*, May 5, 2011, accessed July 2011, http://www.foreignpolicy.com/articles/2011/05/05/arab_spring_turkish_fall.
32. Vali Nasr, *The Shia Revival: How Conflicts within Islam Will Shape the Future* (New York: W. W. Norton, 2006).
33. M. Cherif Bassiouni, "The Report of the Bahrain Independent Commission of Inquiry," November 23, 2011, http://www.bici.org.bh/.

CHAPTER 6: CHINA AND AMERICA: THE PERILS OF CODEPENDENCY

1. George Maglione (senior auto economist for IHS Global Insight), interview with the author, July 20, 2011.
2. Robert Greifeld (president of the NASDAQ OMX exchange), in conversation with the author, New York, April 2009.
3. Philip Stephens, "Spasm or Spiral? The West's Choice," *Financial Times*, July 21, 2011, http://www.ft.com/cms/s/0/52ca17f6-b3cb-11e0-855b-00144feabdc0.html#axzz1ce 8ZLwav.
4. Maglione interview.
5. Testimony of Alan Greenspan, Chairman, U.S. Federal Reserve Bank, Senate Committee on Finance, June 23, 2005 http://www.federalreserve.gov/boarddocs /testimony/2005/20050623/default.htm.

6. Yiping Huang, "Krugman's Chinese Renminbi Fallacy," East Asia Forum, March 15, 2010, http://www.eastasiaforum.org/2010/03/15/krugmans-chinese-renminbi-fallacy/.

7. "The Yuan Scapegoat," *Wall Street Journal*, March 18, 2010, http://online.wsj.com/article/SB10001424052748704743404575127511778280940.html.

8. Rachel Ziemba (senior sovereign wealth analyst at Roubini Global Economics), in conversation with the author, New York, July 29, 2011.

9. Richard Fisher, "A Bridge to Fiscal Sanity?" speech, San Antonio, Texas, November 8, 2010, http://dallasfed.org/news/speeches/fisher/2010/fs101108.cfm.

10. Kevin P. Gallagher, interview by Paul Jay, "Emerging Markets Confront QE2: Capital Controls, Reserve Accumulation, or Both?," *Monthly Review*, December 11, 2010, accessed September 2011, http://mrzine.monthlyreview.org/2010/gallagher121110.html.

11. Nouriel Roubini, "How Should Emerging Markets Manage Capital Inflows and Currency Appreciation?," Roubini Global Economics, November 4, 2010, http://www.roubini.com/analysis/137656.php.

12. Office of the US Trade Representative, "China," 2009 figures (latest available), http://www.ustr.gov/countries-regions/china, accessed July 23, 2011. Some analysts suggest that China's FDI in the United States will show increases in 2010 and 2011, but a huge gap remains.

13. Daniel H. Rosen and Thilo Hanemann, *An American Open Door? Maximizing the Benefits of Chinese Foreign Direct Investment*, Asia Society, accessed September 2011, http://asiasociety.org/policy/center-us-china-relations/american-open-door.

14. US Census Bureau, Office of Foreign Trade Data Dissemination, "Trade in Goods with China," accessed September 21, 2011, http://www.census.gov/foreign-trade/balance/c5700.html.

15. Norihiko Shirouzu, "Train Makers Rail against China's High-Speed Designs," *Wall Street Journal*, November 18, 2010, http://online.wsj.com/article/SB20001424052748704814204575507353221141616.html.

16. James Fallows, "China Makes, the World Takes," *Atlantic* (July/August 2007), http://www.theatlantic.com/magazine/archive/2007/07/china-makes-the-world-takes/5987/.

17. World Economic Outlook, International Monetary Fund, July 2011.

18. "Asia's Top 1,000 Brands 2010," TNS Global, July 20, 2010, accessed September 2011, http://www.tnsglobal.com/research/key-insight-reports/FFEF53C4FAC0469DA35356D78872CB6E.aspx.

19. Experts can only estimate the true size of China's sovereign wealth fund holdings since Beijing is under no real obligation to disclose this information. My friend Rachel Ziemba, the sovereign wealth guru at Roubini Global Economics, estimated that China's government had a foreign investment portfolio of about $3.6 trillion in mid-2011, including equities, real estate, and interests in foreign oil companies and other strategic projects. China also has $3.2 trillion in foreign currency reserves, about $400 billion of this held by the CIC (about $140 billion of it in foreign assets, and the balance in foreign assets held by the state banks and other entities).

20. Kate Gordon, Susan Lyon, Ed Paisley, and Sean Pool, *Rising to the Challenge: A Progressive U.S. Approach to China's Innovation and Competitiveness Policies* (Washington DC: Center for American Progress, January 2011), http://www.americanprogress.org/issues/2011/01/china_innovation.html.

21. Ian Bremmer, *The End of the Free Market: Who Wins the War between States and Corporations?* (New York: Portfolio, 2010), 4.

22. Jamil Anderlini, "China's Political Anniversary: A Long Cycle Nears Its End," *Financial Times*, July 1, 2011, http://www.ft.com/intl/cms/s/0/acebc234-a421-11e0-8b4f-00144feabdc0.html#axzz1ce8ZLwav.

23. "China Ranks Fourth in R&D Spending," UPI, December 2, 2010, http://www.upi.com/Science_News/2010/12/02/China-ranks-fourth-in-RD-spending/UPI-89181291310006/.

24. "Illegal Children Will Be Confiscated," *Economist*, July 21, 2011, http://www.economist
    .com/node/18988496.
25. "Medvedev Grants Land Plots to Three-Child Families," *RIA Novosti*, June 16, 2011,
    http://en.rian.ru/russia/20110616/164646607.html.
26. Prabhat Jha, Maya A. Kesler, Rajesh Kumar, Faujdar Ram, Usha Ram, Lukasz Aleksand-
    rowicz, Diego G. Bassani, Shailaja Chandra, and Jayant K. Banthia, "Trends in Selective
    Abortions of Girls in India: Analysis of Nationally Representative Birth Histories from
    1990 to 2005 and Census Data from 1991 to 2011" *Lancet* 377, no. 9781 (May 24, 2011):
    1921–1928, doi:10.1016/S0140-6736(11)60649-1.
27. Congressional Research Service, *Social Security Reform: Current Issues and Legislation*,
    September 10, 2010, http://aging.senate.gov/crs/ss6.pdf
28. Louis Kuijs, "China through 2020—A Macroeconomic Scenario," working paper no. 9,
    World Bank China Office, 2010.
29. William Holstein, interview with author, October 24, 2010.
30. "Made in the USA, Again: Manufacturing Is Expected to Return to America as China's
    Rising Labor Costs Erase Most Savings from Offshoring," Boston Consulting Group,
    May 5, 2011, accessed September 2011, http://www.bcg.com/media/PressRelease
    Details.aspx?id=tcm:12-75973.
31. Arvind Kaushal, Thomas Mayor, Patricia Riedel, "Manufacturing's Wakeup Call,"
    Booz & Company, issue 64, Autumn 2011, http://booz.com/media/file/sb64-11306
    -Manufacturing's-Wake-Up-Call.pdf.
32. Over the past decade, Immelt's company has created jobs overseas and, on balance, has
    shed some of its workforce in America—a pattern typical of the largest American com-
    panies during the first decade of this century. This pattern reversed itself somewhat
    after 2009, but the longer-term trend made Immelt a controversial choice to head Presi-
    dent Obama's Council on Jobs and Competitiveness. Critics, however, blame "offshor-
    ing" for all the job losses when, in fact, a good deal of the problem stems from techno-
    logical advances and the changes in GE's product lines. For more on this, see http://
    philipdelvesbroughton.files.wordpress.com/2011/01/442-graph-employees-region.jpg.
33. Jeffrey R. Immelt, "A Blueprint for Keeping America Competitive," *Washington Post*,
    January 21, 2011, http://www.washingtonpost.com/wp-dyn/content/article/2011/01/20
    /AR2011012007089.html.
34. Interview with Representative Eric Cantor, *Meet the Press*, NBC News, January 23, 2001,
    http://majorityleader.gov/newsroom/2011/01/leader-cantor-defines-cut-and-grow
    -congress-previews-state-of-the-union-on-meet-the-press.html.

CHAPTER 7: THE NOT-SO-PACIFIC RIM

1. Zheng Xiwen, "China's Peaceful Rise Is beyond Doubt," *Guangming Daily*, trans-
   lated by *People's Daily Online*, July 19, 2011, http://english.peopledaily.com.cn
   /90001/90780/91342/7444877.html.
2. Rory Medcalf, "Malcolm Fraser's Baffling China Speech," *Interpreter*, July 27, 2011,
   accessed September 2011, http://www.lowyinterpreter.org/post/2011/07/27/Malcolm
   -Frasers-baffling-China-speech.aspx.
3. Kishore Mahbubani, transcript of remarks at the Council on Foreign Relations, New
   York, October 22, 2010.
4. IMF World Economic Outlook, September 2011, Washington, http://www.imf.org/
   external/pubs/ft/weo/2011/02/index.htm. The IMF rankings by GDP in 2010 (latest
   available) are as follows: United States, 14.6 trillion; China, 5.8 trillion; Japan, 5.4 trillion. These are followed by Germany, France, Britain, Brazil, Italy, Canada, and India.
5. Remarks by Secretary of State Hillary Clinton, Hanoi, July 23, 2010.
6. President Barack Obama, speech to the Australian Parliament, Canberra, November 17,
   2011, http://www.whitehouse.gov/the-press-office/2011/11/17/remarks-president-obama
   -us-and-australian-service-members.

7. World Trade Organization, "Trade Profiles," 2010 figures (latest available), accessed August 2011, http://stat.wto.org/CountryProfile/WSDBCountryPFHome.aspx?Language=E.
8. Commonwealth of Australia, *Defence 2000: Our Future Defence Force* (Canberra: Australian Ministry of Defence, October 2000).
9. Roger Cliff and David A. Shlapak, *U.S.-China Relations after Resolution of Taiwan's Status* (Santa Monica, CA: RAND Corporation for the US Air Force, 2007), http://www.rand.org/pubs/monographs/MG567.html.
10. Fu S. Mei, "Taiwan's Defense Transformation and Challenges under Ma Ying-Jeou," *China Brief* (published by the Jamestown Foundation) 11, no. 7 (April 22, 2011), http://www.jamestown.org/programs/chinabrief/single/?tx_ttnews%5Btt_news%5D=37838&tx_ttnews%5BbackPid%5D=25&cHash=183b175e8af7574c0a1645d6c2912560.
11. Ted Galen Carpenter, "Walking a Tightrope on Arms Sales to Taiwan," CATO Institute, July 26, 2011 http://www.cato.org/pub_display.php?pub_id=13486.
12. Admiral Mike Mullen, "A Step toward Trust with China," *New York Times*, July 25, 2011, http://www.nytimes.com/2011/07/26/opinion/26Mullen.html.
13. "China-Taiwan FTA (ECFA)," 2010," Bilaterals.org, September 21, 2010, accessed September 2011, http://www.bilaterals.org/spip.php?article18166.
14. William Ide, "China Seen Moving Closer to Deployment of 'Carrier Killer' Missile," *Voice of America*, December 29, 2010, http://www.voanews.com/english/news/asia/China-Seen-Moving-Closer-to-Deployment-of--Carrier-Killer-Missile-112629574.html.
15. Bradley Perrett, "China Details Anti-ship Missile Plans," *Aviation Week and Space Technology*, July 19, 2011, http://www.aviationweek.com/aw/generic/story_generic.jsp?channel=awst&id=news/awst/2011/07/18/AW_07_18_2011_p24-347899.xml.
16. Captain Henry J. Hendrix, US Navy, and Lieutenant Colonel J. Noel Williams, US Marine Corps (retired), "Twilight of the $uperfluous Carrier," *Proceedings Magazine* 137, no. 5 (May 2011), http://www.usni.org/magazines/proceedings/2011-05/twilight-uperfluous-carrier.

CHAPTER 8: INDIA, BRAZIL, AND THE NEW AMERICAN DREAM TEAM

1. Chetan Ahya and Tanvee Gupta, *India and China: New Tigers of Asia, Part III* (Morgan Stanley, August, 2010, New York), 6, http://www.scribd.com/doc/36081710/Morgan-Stanley-India-and-China-New-Tigers-of-Asia-Part-III-20100813.
2. Ibid.
3. "World Economic Outlook," Database, September 2011, International Monetary Fund, Washington, D.C., http://www.imf.org/external/pubs/ft/weo/2011/02/index.htm.
4. Independent Task Force of the Council on Foreign Relations, *Global Brazil and U.S.-Brazil Relations*, report no. 66, Council on Foreign Relations Press, New York, July 2011, 14–27, http://www.cfr.org/brazil/global-brazil-us-brazil-relations/p25407.
5. Kishore Mahbubani, "The West Will Use India to Contain China's Rise," *Project Syndicate*, January 16, 2011, http://www.mahbubani.net/articles%20by%20dean/The%20west%20will%20use%20India%20to%20contain%20Chinas%20rise.pdf.
6. Condoleezza Rice, "Campaign 2000: Promoting the National Interest," *Foreign Affairs* 79, no. 1 (January/February 2000), http://www.foreignaffairs.com/articles/55630/condoleezza-rice/campaign-2000-promoting-the-national-interest.
7. "Waiver of Nuclear-Related Sanctions on India and Pakistan," President George W. Bush, Presidential Determination No. 2001-28, Letter to Secretary of State Colin Powell, September 23, 2001, http://usinfo.org/wf-archive/2001/010924/epf103.htm.
8. Stanley McChrystal, remarks in response to author's question, the Council on Foreign Relations, New York, October 6, 2011.
9. My coinage, by the way, in a 2001 column by the same name written for msnbc.com: http://www.msnbc.msn.com/id/3340165.

10. Mark Mazzetti and Eric Schmitt, "Pakistanis Aided Attack in Kabul, U.S. Officials Say," *New York Times*, August 1, 2008, http://www.nytimes.com/2008/08/01/world/asia/01pstan.html.

11. The term took on particular importance after the 1991 Gulf War, when "beyond the horizon" weapons led the British forces to lose more soldiers to American "friendly fire" than to the Iraqis.

12. Jayshree Bajoria and Esther Pan, "The U.S.-India Nuclear Deal," Council on Foreign Relations, November 5, 2010, accessed September 2011, http://www.cfr.org/india/us-india-nuclear-deal/p9663.

13. The F/A-18 was designed by McDonnell Douglas in the late 1970s before Boeing absorbed it.

14. The F-16 was first produced in the 1970s by General Dynamics, which was ultimately absorbed by Lockheed Martin, itself a merger of Lockheed and the old Martin Marietta.

15. Rama Lakshmi, "U.S. Firms Lose Out on India Fighter Jet Contract," *Washington Post*, April 28, 2011, http://www.washingtonpost.com/world/us-companies-bypassed-in-india-fighter-jet-deal/2011/04/28/AFPVwC5E_story.html.

16. Report to Congress on U.S.-India Security Cooperation, U.S. Department of Defense, November 2011, http://www.defense.gov/pubs/pdfs/20111101_NDAA_Report_on_US_India_Security_Cooperation.pdf.

17. US State Department official records.

18. US Foreign Service Officer (not-for-attribution), interview with author, London, May 1996.

19. "Kazakh President Underscores SCO's Great Achievements," Xinhua News Agency, June 9, 2006, http://www.china.org.cn/english/international/170851.htm.

20. Robert Jellenick, "Russia and the Global Meltdown," Carnegie Center for International Peace, March 17, 2009, http://carnegieendowment.org/files/11972Jellinek.pdf.

21. Sreeram Chaulia, "India Inches toward Shanghai," *Asia Times*, June 21, 2011, http://www.atimes.com/atimes/South_Asia/MF21Df04.html.

22. Harish Khare, "From Eisenhower to Clinton to Bush," *Hindu*, March 1, 2006, http://hindu.com/2006/03/01/stories/2006030102961000.htm.

23. Shashank Joshi, "The Cool Peace between China and India," *Lowry Interpreter*, July 28, 2011, http://www.lowyinterpreter.org/post/2011/07/28/A-cool-peace-between-China-and-India.aspx.

24. Matias Spektor, "One Foot in the Region; Eyes on the Global Prize," *Americas Quarterly*, Americas Society (Spring 2011): 55, http://www.americasquarterly.org/node/2424.

25. "Text of the Iran-Brazil-Turkey Deal," *Guardian*, May 17, 2010, accessed September 2011, http://www.guardian.co.uk/world/julian-borger-global-security-blog/2010/may/17/iran-brazil-turkey-nuclear.

26. Obama's Letter to Lula Regarding Turkey-Iran Nuclear Negotiations, Politica Exerna (Brazilian Blog), May 27, 2010 (letter dated April 20, 2010), accessed November 30, 2011, http://www.politicaexterna.com/11023/brazil-iran-turkey-nuclear-negotiations-obamas-letter-to-lula.

27. Alexei Barrioneuevo and Ginger Thompson, "Brazil's Iran Diplomacy Worries U.S. Officials," *New York Times*, May 14, 2010, http://www.nytimes.com/2010/05/15/world/americas/15lula.html.

28. Celso Amorim, "Reflections on Brazil's Global Rise," *Americas Quarterly* (Spring 2011), http://www.americasquarterly.org/node/2420zil's.

29. Mark Weisbrot, as quoted by Franklin Serrano and Ricardo Summa, *Macroeconomic Policy, Growth and Income Distribution in the Brazilian Economy in the 2000s* (Washington DC: Center for Economic and Policy Research, June 2011), http://www.cepr.net/documents/publications/brazil-2011-06.pdf.

30. Paul D. Taylor, "Why Does Brazil Need Nuclear Submarines," United States Naval Institute, *Proceedings Magazine*, vol. 135/6/1,276, June 2009, http://www.usni.org /magazines/proceedings/2009-06/why-does-brazil-need-nuclear-submarines.

31. "Senator McCain Addresses the Hoover Institution," Council on Foreign Relations, May 1, 2007, accessed September 2011, http://www.cfr.org/us-election-2008/senator -mccain-addresses-hoover-institution/p13252.

32. Robert D. Blackwill and Naresh Chandra, chairs, "The United States and India: Shared Strategic Future," Council on Foreign Relations/Aspen Institute India, September 2011, p. 3.

33. Parag Khana, *The Second World: Empires and Influence in the New Global Order* (New York: Random House, 2008).

CHAPTER 9: EUROPE: PIIGS, CANARIES, AND BEARS—OH MY!

1. Nouriel Roubini, "Greece's Best Option Is an Orderly Default," *Financial Times*, June 28, 2010, http://www.ft.com/intl/cms/s/0/a3874c80-82e8-11df-8b15-00144feabdc0 .html#axzz1dAKs3v00.

2. The *pater d'famiglia* of the euro zone doomsday crowd, however, is the British economist Bernard Connolly, a former EU staffer, who saw the flaws in the eurozone's fiscal structure in the run up to the currency's introduction in 2008 and, essentially, lost his job for expressing that view publicly in a book, *The Rotten Heart of Europe*—a book that is, amazingly, out of print as of this writing. See Landon Thomas Jr., "Words of a Euro Doomsayer Have New Resonance," *New York Times*, November 17, 2001, http://www.nytimes.com/2011/11/18/business/global/the-rise-of-a-euro-doomsayer .html?pagewanted=all.

3. Helmut Reisen, "Boom, Bust and Sovereign Ratings: Lessons for the Eurozone from Emerging-Market Ratings," *VoxEU* (blog), May 19, 2010, http://www.voxeu.org/index .php?q=node/.

4. Bank for International Settlements, *BIS Quarterly Review* (Basel, Switzerland: Bank for International Settlements, September 2011), http://www.bis.org/publ/qtrpdf/r_qt1109.pdf.

5. Rowley, "Europe Should Force Greece Out," Charles Rowley's blog, June 15, 2011, http://charlesrowley.wordpress.com/2011/06/15/eurozone-should-force-greece-out/.

6. Daniel Gros, "August 2011: The Euro Crisis Reaches the Core," *VoxEU* (blog), August 11, 2011, accessed September 2011, http://www.voxeu.org/index.php?q=node/6853."

7. Giuseppe Carone and Declan Costello, "Can Europe Afford to Grow Old?," *Finance and Development* 43, no. 3 (September 2006), http://www.imf.org/external/pubs/ft /fandd/2006/09/carone.htm.

8. "Sarkozy Says State to Lead French Industrial Renaissance," France24, April 3, 2010, http://www.france24.com/en/20100304-sarkozy-says-state-lead-french-industrial -renaissance.

9. Export-Import Bank of India, *2009-2010 Annual Report*, New Delhi, August 2009, http://www.eximbankindia.com/ar10/en-us/pdf/EXIM_AR_English.pdf.

10. "Autumn Forecast Statement by the Chancellor of the Exchequer, Rt Hon George Osborne MP", delivered to UK House of Commons, November 29, 2011, accessed November 30, 2011, http://www.hm-treasury.gov.uk/press_136_11.htm.

11. Stephen Fidler and Alistair MacDonald, "Europeans Retreat on Defense Spending," *Wall Street Journal*, August 24, 2011, http://online.wsj.com/article/SB1000142405311190 3461304576524503625829970.html.

12. Steven Erlanger, "Libya's Dark Lesson for NATO," *New York Times*, September 3, 2011, http://www.nytimes.com/2011/09/04/sunday-review/what-libyas-lessons-mean-for -nato.html?pagewanted=all.

13. Constanze Stelzenmueller, "Hands Off Our Shackles, Please," *IP Global*, March 11, 2010, published on *Spiegel Online*, http://www.spiegel.de/international /germany/0,1518,683066,00.html.

14. Kelly Holt, "Tea Partiers Push for Cuts in Defense Spending," *The New American*, January 25, 2011, accessed December 13, 2011, http://thenewamerican.com/usnews/congress/6025-tea-partiers-push-for-cuts-in-defense-spending.

15. "Sen. Hutchinson Urges Cost Savings and GAO Report Reveals Billions in Wasteful and Duplicative Spending," press release from Senator Kay Bailey Hutchison (Republican, Texas), March 2, 2011, http://hutchison.senate.gov/?p=press_release&id=478.

16. Anita Dancs, "The Cost of the Global U.S. Military Presence" (Washington, DC: Foreign Policy in Focus, July 2; 2009), accessed September 2011, http://www.comw.org/qdr/fulltext/0907dancs.pdf; http://www.fpif.org/reports/the_cost_of_the_global_us_military_presence (which recommended the above citation).

17. Stephen Sestanovich (Russia and Eurasia expert at the Council on Foreign Relations), in conversation with the author, New York, April 2009.

18. Nick Childs (defense and security correspondent for the BBC), in conversation with the author, London, January 2011.

19. Heather A. Conley, "Fading Sentimentality: German Assessments of U.S. Power," in *Capacity and Resolve: Foreign Assessments of U.S. Power*, ed. Craig S. Cohen (Washington DC: Center for Strategic and International Studies, June 2011), http://csis.org/publication/capacity-and-resolve.

20. Andrew Osborn and Matthew Day, "Poland Demands US Troops Be Based on Polish Soil," *Telegraph*, November 6, 2009, http://www.telegraph.co.uk/news/worldnews/europe/poland/6515731/Poland-demands-US-troops-be-based-on-Polish-soil.html.

21. Tomas Valasek, "A Race to the Bottom," RealClearWorld, August 25, 2011, accessed September 2011, http://www.realclearworld.com/articles/2011/08/25/us_cuts_leave_europe_defenseless_99640.html.

22. "Putin Deplores Collapse of the USSR," BBC, April 25, 2005, http://news.bbc.co.uk/2/hi/4480745.stm.

23. Ina Ganguli, "Saving Soviet Science: The Impact of Grants When Government R&D Funding Disappears," National Bureau of Economic Research, July 1, 2011, http://www.nber.org/public_html/confer/2011/SI2011/PRIPE/Ganguli.pdf.

24. Nicholas Eberstadt, "The Dying Bear," *Foreign Affairs*, December/November 2011, http://www.foreignaffairs.com/articles/136511/nicholas-eberstadt/the-dying-bear (accessed December 13, 2011).

25. Dmitry Oreskin, "Russia's Sixth Wave" [in Russian], *Novaya gazeta*, January 31, 2011, http://www.novayagazeta.ru/society/7330.html.

26. Mikhail Khodorkovsky, "Mikhail Khodorkovsky: Final Trial Speech," openDemocracy Russia, December 14, 2010, http://www.opendemocracy.net/od-russia/mikhail-khodorkovsky/mikhail-khodorkovsky-final-trial-speech.

CHAPTER 10: IN THE GAME, OR IN DENIAL?

1. "Budget 1991-92 Speech of Shri Manmohan Singh, Minister of Finance," delivered to the Indian Parliament, New Dehli, July 24, 1991, http://indiabudget.nic.in/bspeech/bs199192.pdf.

2. Erika Michele Karp, conversation with author, December 2, 2011, New York.

3. Aaron Sorkin, *A Few Good Men*, Castle Rock Entertainment/Columbia Pictures, 1992.

4. CPS Population and Per Capita Money Income, All Races: 1967 to 2010, US Census Bureau, Table P-1, September 13, 2011, http://www.census.gov/hhes/www/income/data/historical/people/.

5. Josef Joffe, "The Default Power," *Foreign Affairs*, September/October 2009, http://www.foreignaffairs.com/articles/65225/josef-joffe/the-default-power.

6. "The Warning," *Frontline*, PBS Online, October 20, 2009, http://www.pbs.org/wgbh/pages/frontline/warning/view/.

7. Svea Herbst-Bayliss and Katya Wachtel, "Paulson Braces Investors for the Worst," Reuters, October 11, 2011, http://www.reuters.com/article/2011/10/11/us-hedgefunds-paulson-idUSTRE79A67E20111011.
8. Sha Zukang, news conference (National Press Club, Washington DC, June 28, 2011), http://www.un.org/en/development/desa/usg/statements/national-press-club-event.shtml.

INDEX